WRITING TO GOD'S GLORY

A Comprehensive Creative Writing Course from

Crayon TO *Quill*

JILL BOND

Preface by T. Davis Bunn
*Bestselling Author of **The Quilt***

ILLUSTRATIONS BY REED BOND

Homeschool Press

Writing to God's Glory:
A Comprehensive Creative Writing Course from Crayon to Quill

ISBN 1-888306-15-7
Copyright © 1997 by Jill Bond
Illustrations by Reed Bond

Published by
Homeschool Press
229 South Bridge Street
P.O. Box 254
Elkton, MD 21922-0254
Tel. (410) 392-5554
Fax (410) 392-8842
Send requests for information to the above address.

Printed in the United States of America.

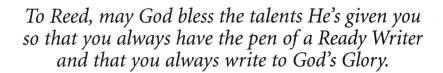

*To Reed, may God bless the talents He's given you
so that you always have the pen of a Ready Writer
and that you always write to God's Glory.*

*"My heart is inditing a good matter: I speak of the things which I have made
touching the king: my tongue is the pen of a ready writer." — Psalms 45:1*

*"That I may publish with the voice of thanksgiving, and tell of all
thy wondrous works."— Psalms 26:7*

"Whatsoever ye do, do all to the glory of God." — 1 Corinthians 10:31b

Table of Contents

Preface

The continued growth of home-schooling is an important development within the Christian community. It brings with it a new need for competent and creative teaching materials in all subjects. Jill Bond helps meet this need with <u>Writing to God's Glory</u>.

In both the Teacher's Pages and the Student's Pages, she blends the basics of sound writing skills with a unique Biblical perspective.

As a Christian author, I am constantly aware that our faith must influence both what we write and how we write it. We must allow God's grace to shine through our work. We must let ourselves be used as His instrument in this most wonderful means of expression, communication, and entertainment: the written word.

T. Davis Bunn

Acknowledgments

Trying to take the credit for the concepts taught here would be treacherous and deceitfiul. Can anyone claim to have invented the theory of long division? No, it simply exists. Yet, the challenge for each developer of mathematics textbooks is to present the facts in a new, interesting, and understandable way.

Like the math professor, I've attempted to take the facts and present them in a fresh light.

For instance, I did not come up with the idea that each story should have a plot or that wasted words make for dull writing. These are some of the universal truths of skilled writing. (Yet, I did "create" bore-bees, et al. — the vehicles to convey the concepts.)

The works of hundreds of other authors have influenced me, as well as the millions of words I've heard from my family, friends, and various media. My sub-goal in this endeavor was to utilize these vast verbal resources into an understandable tool for parents to use to encourage the writer in their children.

Where I have quoted directly from another author's work, I have given him credit. All other presentations were original with me. (Note the section on writer's integrity: Above Reproach, page 76.

In addition to that general acknowledgment, I have to give credit to a special lady:

I love Nancy Trigg. She blessed our lives with her love for the Lord. She poured herself into others' lives with the exuberance of a three-year-old child and the wisdom of an octogenarian. She inspired children to write. She brought out the best in them so they could communicate well. She developed a series of workshops for children and also privately tutored. She made her students feel he had the talent to be the next C.S. Lewis, then she lovingly worked with him to perfect his skill. She began tutoring our son, Reed, when he was six years old, and his path was enhanced by her mentoring. When she died in 1993, I began to feel a nudge from the Lord to continue her work. I know I'm not as qualified as she was; yet, since we have the same Father, I know it is He supplying all the material, inspiration, and creativity. I pray I can impart some of her enthusiasm for children's writing that made her so very much alive. I'm "borrowing" some of the same energy she used — Holy Spirit empowerment.

I am grateful to the hundreds of guinea pigs who were gracious enough to allow me to test this program with them. They helped me figure out what works and what falls flat. They helped me leave in the gold and throw out the dross. The people who have attended my classes have been wonderful. It's their response and encouragement, their drive and enthusiasm, and their improvement in writing which have given me the impetus to complete this workbook. Thank you!

Odd, but a teacher of writing needs her work edited just like every other writer. And my writing needs editing. As we'll cover editing in a section of the book, you'll realize there comes a time when authors are too close to their work to "see" it any more. Editors come in to save the day! Thank you Heather Armstrong, my editor at Great Christian Books. Also, I am grateful to my copy-editors: Donna Conner, Jacqueline J. Howe, Vicki Morrison, Lindsey O'Connor, Sherry Yeaton, and my chief editor and love of my life: my husband, Alan.

I'm very thankful to the many families who gave me their advice, including: a home schooling family in Albany, NY; the Reynolds Family; the Graham Family: Van, Joy, Mason, and Gina; Judy Wayne; Tim, David, Tricia, and Chris Bearly; Gaynelle Brekke, Arroyo Grande, CA; Jamie Prichett; Tina Beckham; the Price Family of Parkton, MD: Cindy, Larry, Larry, Jr., and Barbie Price; and dozens who preferred not to be listed by name. I am thankful to the hundreds of others all across this nation who attended my classes and helped me find out which lessons worked and which ones needed adjustment. Thank you to Barbara and Ryan Doran for allowing me to include their writing story and their story about writing.

Most importantly, I worship my LORD and SAVIOUR and unto HIM be the glory, the honour, and ALL THE PRAISE.
It is to HIM I dedicate this book, my writing, and my very being. For without HIM I can do nothing.

UNTO HIS GLORY ——

Dear Friend

You care about this subject or else you wouldn't be reading this right now. I do, too — that's why I took the time to write this workbook.

I heard so many of you who are frustrated with the task of teaching writing to your students. "My son (or daughter) hates writing!" was the repeated phrase, followed by "HELP!"

Or, "My daughter has talent, but I don't know what I should be doing to harvest that talent," or words to that effect.

I understand. I have children in both categories.

It's impossible to keep Reed from writing. Even as a baby he wanted to "make a book." He has natural talent and a strong desire. My job is to train him in the way he should go.

Stuart, so lovable, approaches writing like I do reptiles: with total disgust. But, even though he'll probably make a living via a hard science (presently he is leaning toward veterinary medicine), he'll still have to write. He can't avoid writing. From letters home to medical reports and school papers, he'll have to write. And I have to teach him.

This system works well for Reed. His talents are nurtured, pruned, and harvested — and they thrive.

This system works well for Stuart. He puts some words down on paper without as much protest as with other systems. At times he even loves it! (If you knew Stuart like I know Stuart, you'd be impressed.)

To give you an idea of what I'm talking about, there is a section in this book that walks you through a writing session with Stuart and with Reed.

I also have two other children (for now) — Trent (he's autistic), and Bethany Kay — so I have included a page on working with the special needs child, and the preschooler. (See *Teaching the Teacher:* "Writing Matters," page 49.)

May I give you some advice about how to tackle this book?

Don't overwhelm yourself by trying to race through this program.

Writing to God's Glory™ is a supplemental program to complement the curriculum you're already using.

The material is arranged into bite-sized lessons. Most lessons are designed to be completed in 15 to 60 minutes.

The book has two major sections: the **Teacher's Pages** and the **Student's Pages**.

The **Teacher's Pages** include: a) general information about teaching writing, called *Teaching the Teacher* and b) information which corresponds to specific lessons in the **Student's Pages**. Read the *Teaching the Teacher* pages as your schedule allows. Read the *Teacher's Guide* sections *with* the **Student's Pages** as you go. I **highly suggest** you present the lesson with the tips in the guides. The activities described in the guides will be the bulk of the lesson. They serve to cement the lesson's concept in your students' minds and give them a visual image to aid retention.

The **Student's Pages** are divided into five major sections. I highly recommend you purchase a three-ring binder for each of your children and in each binder put five dividers: "Writing Well," "Craftsmen," "Outlet Journal," "Ideas," and "Favorites." In this way each of your children can have his own writing notebook to organize and collect his own work.

The *Writing Well* section includes the basics of building a story — the mechanics of writing.

The *Craftsmen* section would match with common grammar lessons, though I tried not to make it anything like a common grammar lesson. In this part of their notebook they should add any additional grammar lessons you give them. Their notebook isn't just for this book but should be a writing notebook in which they compile and collect their work for many years, spanning many writing techniques, exercises, etc. Professional writers keep notebooks (or journals), files, and portfolios, as they track their writing progress and research options. Your students might want to start a page with "Examples of _____," "Commonly Misspelled Words" — whatever helps them grasp English grammar.

The *Outlet Journal* is basically just that — a journal or listing of possible outlets for students' writing. There are only a few student's pages. This is because they need to fill this section with their own research. The *Teacher's Guide* gives you information about getting them started. This section of their writing notebook will change as they mature and their writing encompasses more reader markets.

The *Ideas* section is where they will file their ideas. *Their* ideas. Sometimes it is just a page of words, thoughts, phrasing. That is fine.

The *Favorites* section is for them to keep track of others' works they like. Many times the work of others will spark something in them.

For some children one notebook becomes notebooks and the sections will fill volumes or grow to fill filing cabinets. I know. I'm on my third filing cabinet now. But still I basically stick to those five sections. I keep files of research and favorites (newspaper articles to be used as research someday, etc.)

Do what works for your family. Speed up and slow down as you need to. No one is going to check with you to see how quickly you mastered "Time Travel" or any other unit.

How would I teach the lessons? That all depends on the age and ability of the child.

Primary Children: I would never hand young children the worksheet/lesson and tell them, "Do it." I recommend as you start the lesson that you *first* read the advice in the *Teacher's Guide* for that section and read the corresponding Student's Pages. *Then* present the material. With younger children, I'll paraphrase the lesson in terms they can understand. I'll assign only those exercises I feel the students are capable of grasping. I'll talk through the exercises with them and take dictation for their answers.

Intermediate Children: Depending on their maturity, I'll filter the *Teacher's Guide* material to them and have them read and complete the **Student's Pages** themselves. With some intermediate children, I'll get more involved with the lesson than I would with other students. You know your children and know when to assist and when to release. Of course, you should always be available to answer questions and to clarify.

Advanced Children: With mature children, I'd give them the entire book, tell them to read the *Teacher's Guide* and **Student's Pages** and work through the book. I'd set up a schedule for checking work and answering questions. One tool of teaching I've learned is that "teaching teaches" — I learn more about a subject when I teach it. I like to "hire" my oldest children to teach the younger children. So, if the situation works out, employ your advanced child to teach the lesson to your younger children. He can present the idea from the tips in the *Teacher's Guide*, the lesson from the **Student's Pages**, "grade" his students' work, and input his own answers. You, as Master Teacher, evaluate not only the work but also the tutoring. This will advance his writing skills *and* his ability to educate his own children when you're the grandma.

I "accept" my students' answers depending on the ability they have. For instance, with the "Freds" in the *Craftsmen* section "More Power," on page 205:

Younger Child — "How about if Fred is a German Shepherd dog who works for the police and he goes to work with his policeman partner?" I'd say, "Great! Is there anything else you might want to tell me about him going to work? Does he do anything in particular? Would his partner fasten a special collar to him or something like that?" I like to talk the creativity out of the child and then let go.

Intermediate Child — "Fred licked his partner and wagged his tail because he was ready to start another day of chasing robbers down dark alley ways." I'd say, "Great! Let me guess — is Fred a guard dog? Is he a Doberman pinscher? Is he a dog at all? Or are you going to clue your reader in later on in the story? I like that. It gets my curiosity up so I want to read more."

Advanced Child — "Fred felt the hot pavement on the pads of his paws but he didn't let it bother him as he ran to jump into the squad car to face another day of protecting his human partner from the thugs they would encounter — just another day on the beat." I'd say, "Great! I can just see him; tell me more. This would make a great story. Do you want to develop it some more?"

Just as I try to personalize the lessons for each child, I firmly believe you are the best judge of your child's abilities. If he is too young to understand a lesson, skip it for now and come back to it later. You also know better than anyone what your child's realm of knowledge is. I intersperse the teaching of the lessons with examples I know the child knows. For instance, if his pastor gave an illustration about something, I might refer to it, to a book he just read, or a video he just watched. I try to personalize each lesson for the child. Try to use examples that your child would recognize.

I have testimonies from many families that the ideas here do work. Children enjoy the classes. I've taught ages 5-90 with this workbook. The little ones have dictated adorable stories to their parents, some of the teenagers are working on novels, and parents have had articles published.

When teaching my own children, I use the "little bit each day (or week)" method, with regard to "formal writing lessons." Yet, I teach writing throughout the day also. If we're talking about polar bears, I'll phrase some questions so the answers must be properly worded (just like in writing). I like to think of writing as word processing — anytime my children are pulling words out of their mental dictionaries and pairing them together to make phrases and sentences, they're "writing" or word processing. Their writing is improving. I use the concept of a previous "formal writing lesson" in our daily conversations and while studying other "school subjects." I'll ask for a "Fred" while we're waiting at a traffic sign. If they give me an answer in math, I might encourage them to present the answer in a new format, or answer as if they were an astronaut on the Shuttle informing Mission Control that the Interactive Gyro-navigational Meter is reading "_____(their math answer)."

I realize not every family is going to know all of the literary examples I used in the lessons. That's fine. Don't feel like you've failed your children because they haven't read *Gone with the Wind* or have never seen *Bonanza*. I deliberately chose a wide range of novels and multi-media shows to illustrate the different concepts![1] I'm not endorsing all these programs and books, yet they do serve as memory-joggers. Some of them serve the dual purpose of an allegory and as an opportunity for you to discuss world views with your children. I chose some that are "common body of knowledge" characters from literature and the popular culture. I realize, as Christians, we don't approve of "The Wizard of Oz" — yet, I want my children to be conversant with the expressions: "down the yellow brick road" or "We're not in Kansas anymore." In all these lessons, elaborate the parodies by referencing stories and characters with whom your own children are familiar. Ask them, "Can you think of something we just read that would go with this lesson?" This will reinforce their comprehension and make the lesson more relevant.

Each family will use this program differently. I approve. I have provided a scope and sequence (page 17) to give you ideas of various approaches you could use to go through this program. I want you to use a variety of literary characters to expand the lessons, to teach the lessons in any sequence you like, and to vary presentations to fit your family. God made your family unique. I designed this entire program so you could adapt it to fit your lifestyle. Rejoice that He made you uniquely qualified to teach your children. *There is Joy in the journey!*

The most important thing to remember when teaching writing:

PRAY!

God cares even more than you or I do about your child and his ability to express God's Hand in his life. God will be the real teacher!

---

1. Remember, the apostle Paul quoted from the popular poets of his day during his Mars Hill Sermon. Pythagoras, Heraclitus, and Pindar all wrote to the "spiritual side" of man — of course those poets didn't have their theology correct. Paul, in Acts 17:19-31, tried to relate to his listeners by talking to them in terms to which they could relate. He referred to writings of these three poets and even quoted: "For we are also his offspring."

An Unusual Scope and Sequence

I cringe as I write this section because providing you with a *scope and sequence* for this program is very difficult — on purpose. I designed this program to be highly adaptable and useable for a wide variety of teaching styles and schedules. On the other hand, I realize just as there are thousands of possible routes available to a driver crossing the United States from California to Florida, maps are indeed helpful. With that in mind, I ask you to consider the following only as a suggestion, a map highlighting a few highways. You can "drive" across this program using any route you choose, and most of those won't be on "my" map.

Approach One *(Perhaps for someone who will use this as their sole writing text for a stated period)*: The teacher reads all of *Teaching the Teacher* before she teaches any student's lesson. She thumbs through the lessons and accompanying guides and decides to take two years to work through the program — approximately 70 weeks, 18 months (four-week periods.) She decides to teach one topic or "master lesson" per week. She then spends:

10 weeks on "Action Learning"
25 weeks on *Writing Well* Section
30 weeks on *Craftsmen*
 1 week on *Outlet Journal* (explaining and practicing basics)
 1 week on *Ideas* (explaining and practicing concepts)
 2 weeks on *Favorites* (explaining and practicing concepts)
 1 week for catch-up, review, or testing

She decides to present the lessons in the same order that they appear in the book. She realizes that each master lesson actually contains enough work to give the students a writing assignment each day of the week. (Most lessons have several assignments and can be repeated in a variety of ways.) She remembers to review past lessons and to roll-over the previously mastered concepts into the new assignments.

Approach Two *(Perhaps as a supplement for someone using a full-curriculum program or for someone whose child is enrolled in a public or private school and the parent feels the child needs more writing instruction)*: The teacher decides to approach the program in little chunks and to use parts of the program over a period of years. He reads all the pages himself and then decides to use the program along with the regular curriculum. When the regular curriculum calls for a lesson on capitals, he reinforces that lesson with the *Craftsmen* lesson "Capital Idea" on page 239. He uses the "Action Learning" activities to expound on the full curriculum his children are already involved with. He integrates lessons from both texts to make a composite whole.

Approach Three *(Perhaps for someone who educates for life and integrates text lessons with normal living)*: The teacher reads the entire program and decides to teach it with a "writing-lifestyle" approach. Rather than having a formal writing hour each day, she'll present the writing lessons throughout the day. While she and her children are preparing cookies and cakes for the support group bake sale, she'll take them through "The Batter" lesson on page 173. As they drive around town on errands, she'll have her children conduct "interviews" in "Just One More Question," page 47. As they sit down to write a letter to the editor, she'll present the "garbage collection" example and lesson in "Who's That," page 243. She'll teach them writing skills as they write, work, and learn.

Approach Four *(Perhaps for someone who uses the unit study approach)*: The teacher decides to build a unit study around each writing assignment.

> **For example:** One night my son asked his father, "Where does butter come from?" His father, instead of giving him a quick answer, gave him an assignment: "You find out and write me a 'paper' about your findings." We researched cows, dairies, methods of production, history, sanitation, and cooking. We conducted several science labs in which we made our own butter in a variety of ways. We studied the history of butter making. We talked to dairy farmers and managers of the dairy section at the grocery store. Once we had all the research, we began to tackle the paper. Reed decided to tell the facts in story form: *Betsy's Butter* — butter-making from a cow's point of view. Not only did he write the words, but he drew the illustrations. We published it as a book and he learned more about business — collecting price quotes, researching book production techniques, budgeting his finances, scheduling and meeting deadlines, copyrighting, and distributing the finished book. Out of that one question, we had more than a month's worth of "schooling," including reading, speech, math, health and safety, art, science, history, business, home economics, English, and Bible.

As the teacher tackles different assignments, she teaches the writing lessons from this book. She would teach *the art of the interview* and research techniques as the students prepare to interview the dairy farmer. They would apply the different lessons to this writing work. With this approach, a "paper" becomes a "project."

Approach Five *(Perhaps for someone who has used several other writing programs and whose children are progressing quite well with their writing)*: The teacher reads through her *Guide* and the **Student's Pages** and decides her children know most of the concepts, but that reinforcement and a new approach will improve their writing even more. She has each child start a story (or novel) and write it in tandem with the lessons. She'll teach the lesson "Casting," complete the *Character Sketch,* (page 143), and have each of her students work their *Main Character Development* "worksheet" (page 287). Each of these lessons integrates well with the others — theory, practical application, creative thought, and documentation of ideas. She will continue through "The Process" as they fill in their "Idea Worksheets". (See pages 283-296) As they begin writing drafts, she will present the other lessons to encourage idea formation or to improve their work. At the completion of this program, they should have a "paper" ready to broadcast, submit to a contest, or be published. This would be the "seven-course dinner" assignment they should complete at least once a year (see page 17).

Approach Six *(Perhaps for someone who uses the Bible as the text and supplements with peripheral materials)*: The teacher would assign writing papers to correspond with the Bible study. She might choose the story of Esther and ask her children to tell the Esther story as if it were happening today. She would then work them through various lessons in this book to help them develop their dialogue, phrasing, and pacing. She might choose a Proverb and ask her children to make up a story about a "Fred" who was going to work, learning this Proverb throughout his day. The teacher could integrate these writing lessons with the Bible study. As the teacher explains the story of the woman who touched Jesus' garment and was healed, she might want to teach the "Sub-plot" lesson on page 161. Each lesson was developed out of Bible truths — so they will tie in very well with a systematic Bible study.

Approach Seven *(Perhaps for you)*: The teacher uses a combination of these six approaches and adds her own flair and creativity. She presents the lessons at a pace which doesn't strain her patience or cause stress. She covers the material in a timely manner so her children will be better equipped and motivated to write to God's Glory.

© Jill Bond / Homeschool Press, PO Box 254, Elkton, MD 21922

Writing to God's Glory

Teacher's Pages

Teaching the Teacher

Light, Salt, and Red Marks

Seriously, you can have fun teaching your children writing. Here are three ideas:

1) *Lighten Up!*
2) *Savor the Flavor!*
3) *Nix the Picks!*

What in the world?

May I explain . . .

1) Lighten Up!

Have you ever heard the expressions:

"Cool your jets,"
"Give it a rest,"
"Chill out,"
"You're too tense," or
"Lighten up"?

These colloquialisms are usually hurled at someone who is placing too much emphasis on a trivial matter. What expressions do you think of when someone obviously has their priorities out of whack?

I'm not using the term "Lighten Up!" in the usual sense.
I'm using it in reference to:

Jesus is the Light of the World.

We need to look up to Him and bask in His Sonshine.
Teaching our students is a weighty issue. It deserves heart-felt attention. However, if we try to do it in our own strength, we may become "too tense." We do need to give our efforts "a rest." If we are convicted to teach, then we need to "Lighten Up!" that chore with the idea that it's not a chore, but a blessing. It's a gift that He is giving us.
Satan wants to steal, cheat, and destroy. Don't allow him the mileage. He doesn't want your children to write to God's Glory. If he can worm his way in to malign you with doubts, comparisons, and reminders of past mistakes, this can cloud your attitude. Don't let him.

Lighten Up!

2) Savor the Flavor!

Bland. Boring. Dry. Weak. Wimpy. Insipid. Dull. Vapid. Feeble.
Alive. Vibrant. Vigorous. Powerful. Sparkling. Effervescent. Teeming.

God has challenged us to be salt in this world. Salt adds flavor to things. It doesn't make food bland or boring, now does it?

As your children write, savor the flavor of what they are doing. Appreciate the progress. Delight in their word choices and their imagery. Give them creative room to sparkle so that His Light shines through.

3) Nix the Picks!

Don't dwell on the dreary. This idea is the flip side of Savor the Flavor. Just as we should be looking for the good and encouraging the hearts of our children, we should not dwell on their mistakes. There is a whole section in your guide about how to grade, and it isn't how you might have been graded back when you were in school.

Don't focus on all the room for improvement in your child — pick up on what he's doing right. Nix the pick-i-ness of circling every dot and squiggle that's out of place. Zero in on the one word he *did* spell correctly.

Don't view yourself as the "World's Foremost Literary Critic," but as the "World's Saltiest, most Light-hearted Encourager."

Grading and Other Forms of Torture

I know. It happened to me, too.

You poured your life into a story. The teacher was going to be so impressed with it that she would send it to some contest somewhere without your knowledge. Then a few weeks later the television news crew would pull up in your front yard and want to capture your expression on film as you were awarded the grand prize of $1,000,000 for your brilliant writing. Your big brother was going to be able to go off to college. The phone would ring and the President of the United States would tell you what a tribute to America you were. There would be parades and all the other kids would be so . . .

No bands. No calls. No prize money. No smiling teacher. Nothing but your work of art — filled with red marks. Words circled. Lines drawn at strange angles. Big "X's."

"Your idea had merit, but your execution was pathetic. C-."

You made up your mind that you couldn't write and that it just wasn't worth it. You signed up for basket-weaving the next semester.

Something similar happened to you, right?

I hear stories like this from all over the country as I teach these classes.

Then, why, oh why, do we do the same thing to our kids? Why do we mark their papers up with red — emphasizing their less than perfect words with vivid reminders?

If you want to encourage your child to write to God's Glory, here's a plan that works, and works well.

First draft:

Read it with a smile on your face.

Don't frown and definitely don't groan. Don't yell, "Don't you ever listen to me? I've told you ten thousand times that states are to be capitalized!" Don't grab your red pen and start assailing their words.

Grab your red (pink, purple, green, whatever) pen and circle at least ten to twenty words that are excellent word choices. Write, "Excellent word choice!" Then underline phrases and write comments, like: "I can see your character." "Good thought." "How exciting, I wonder what happens next." "Beautiful." "Descriptive." "Jesus is smiling about your work." "Truth!" "I like it."

Fill the pages with positive comments. I've read thousands of children's works and haven't read one yet that I couldn't come up with a dozen positive remarks. Even if it is, "Congratulations, your handwriting is improving," or "That's the best 'b' you've printed all year!"

Give it back to your child and go over every mark with them. You're a cheerleader and you're rallying your player back onto the field. They just made their first "first down." Now they have to go back out for the next play.

Second draft:

It's getting better, isn't it? Without saying it, you've shown them areas that aren't Pulitzer quality — *yet*. They will fix those areas not highlighted. Continue making positive comments, especially about their concept, their plot, their ideas, and their imagination.

On the second draft you're allowed to make one (1) less-than-positive comment, like: "I've never seen broccoli spelled that way before. Maybe we should look it up in the dictionary together." Or, "I always have trouble with broccoli. I'd better look it up myself to make sure." (Even your author had to look it up when she was typing this manuscript.)

Do I condone the "creative spelling" technique some teachers endorse? I can answer whole-heartily — *no!* I understand those instructors' motives of wanting to develop the creative side of their students' writings. But to allow a child to go through life never having to spell words correctly is an injustice to that child. Yes, their spelling should be corrected, but by *them* — the students. Not the teacher.

I want my students to write with their verbal vocabulary, not just their holographic vocabulary. How many of us can say the word "discombobulate," but may have to double-check the precise spelling? (Does it have two or three "b's"?) The same goes for our children. My son, Reed, could appropriately use the word "facetious" when he was two years old. He did not know how to spell it. I did not restrict his language to only words he could spell correctly. That wouldn't make any sense. Likewise, I'm not going to shortchange his writing by only permitting him to use words he can spell perfectly on the first attempt. I want him to learn and for his holographic vocabulary to grow to the size of this verbal vocabulary.

As they create, your students should use their full vocabulary, including words they don't know how to spell. They should sound them out on the first drafts, *then* pull out the dictionary to correct them (or use a spell-checker system). If they write a few words, stop, grab the dictionary, write the difficult word, then complete the sentence — their work will be choppy and lack cohesion. *After* they have the flow of the words, they should perfect the spelling. Ideally, as they mature, their spelling vocabulary will become extensive. As they write more and more they will have to look up spelling less and less. Though, honestly, I can't imagine a professional writer who doesn't double-check for spelling or definitions — after all, most of us are writers, not typists.

Spelling is a separate subject from writing. It should be taught in tandem with creative writing. I like to use the difficult words from their creative papers as their spelling words for that week. Again, for very young children, take dictation. (Aside: question your students to ascertain that they know the definition of the words they are using. Some children will use a word they have heard, but they don't really know its proper meaning.)

Third through fifth drafts:

It's a process. The work should be tighter and tighter now. The child should be getting a little tired of it and may want to start a whole new story. Great. Set this one down, file it with all the other drafts, and work on a new story. (Many — most — works will not go past this stage.)

Sixth draft:

If it has promise, pull it back out and say, "A few weeks ago, you started a story about a purple kitten who ate string taffy. I thought it was great. Let's pull it back out and see where we left off."

Read it to them out loud. They'll have some fresh ideas, see holes in their logic, and the sixth draft will be so much better.

Ask questions. Don't demand changes.

Here are some ideas:

"Tell me more about Susan. I might have missed it, but how old is she?" (instead of, "You forgot to write how old your main character was.")

"I like the way you're developing the conflict in this scene. Conflict helps a story quite a bit. It keeps the reader reading. Since we're not working with a word limit here, do you want to add some more excitement in this section? You know how you like adventure. What else could be happening in this scene?"

Let the child answer. You can suggest by asking questions. The idea is to get them to think for themselves without you seeming false or phony. Kids can see through you in a minute. As Christians we must have integrity. You can find good aspects about your child's work — after all, you love him.

Draw the words out of them. Prime the pump.

Seventh through Nth drafts:

These drafts should be a continuation of encouragement, more praise, more "atta boys." You should work with the students to correct weak areas.

Next to the last draft:

Type it for them, or have them type it. Send it to grandma to read. Get someone who hasn't read any of the drafts to read it. Ask them for any suggestions or if they see any typos. We'll call this person the proofer.

Final draft (or "tabled"):

I highly recommend you intercept the version edited by others. Most friends know the old method of grading and will cover the sheet with red marks. I like to go through it myself and then present the proofer's corrections to my student. I can accept the comments I like, and delete those comments I don't agree with. Then I encourage the student to make the corrections himself. This isn't just a rote exercise of correcting typos. It is another opportunity to teach a lesson about grammar, syntax, or typing.

Now is the fun part — broadcast it (see page 55).

A few reminders, or restatements:

- Don't write the paper for them.
- Don't put in any (none, zippo, zero, nada) corrections for them.
- Each change must be their idea. They must understand the *why* of the change.
- Please reread "Process vs. Product" on page 59.
- Let it go. If this work is even a smidgen better than the last work, be thrilled. Family, rejoice. Celebrate! Don't make every writing assignment a contest entry.

Dearly Beloved

We are gathered here to unite two concepts into a written form:

Your child's thoughts and your stamp of approval,

For better or worse,

And let the games begin.

Earlier I had suggested that you need to "Lighten Up!" I meant we need to teach in His Light. In the glow of His Light, we need to be careful of any shadows we are casting.

Each writing assignment is not a contest entry. Some are just quick thank you notes to Aunt Bess. The contest entry needs between five and ten rough drafts and months of time spent (hours writing, days praying, and weeks letting it rest). The note to Aunt Bess needs to be written once on scrap paper (and proofed so your child doesn't say anything about her weight) and then copied onto stationery.

Let it go.

Remember your child's age. Don't demand rewrites until your eight-year-old's manuscript is ready to be sent to Frank Peretti's literary agent. Be pleased with her growth. Revel in her attempt. Delight in her spiritual understanding of the plot. Rejoice! She spelled all the words correctly.

Did you polish the silver, sparkle the crystal, wash the china, work in the kitchen for two hours, order a professional flower arrangement, and then adorn yourself in an evening gown for breakfast this morning?

No? Well, why not? Because the situation didn't warrant that much fanfare and preparation.

Keep in mind, just as you prepare different table settings and meals depending on the occasion, you should prepare different levels of writing.

One sure way to kill the writer in your child is to make every writing assignment a "Christmas Dinner" extravaganza. Remember, for some assignments, cold cereal in a plastic bowl while wearing pajamas is all you need (oh, and maybe a clean spoon).

Kevorkian Teaching Techniques

…Or How They Killed the Writer in You

A doctor is trained to promote life. He studies for years to learn his craft. Then he turns on his profession and instead of saving lives, he kills them.

A collegiate falls in love with the English language. He wants to encourage others to love this language — words, phrases, literature. He sincerely desires to draw out the novelists of the future. He studies for years to learn his craft. Then he turns on his first love and instead of producing writers, he kills them.

I'm not sure where along the teacher's path he lost his direction. I'd like to think he is unaware of what he is doing and that his actions aren't intentional.

God plants His story in each person. It is being Christ-like to want to tell that story. We are admonished to be ready to tell others of the hope that is in us. We are equipped from God.

Then where do we lose it?

Why do we allow it to be lost?

Somewhere among dangling modifiers, correct spelling, and penmanship, the creative side of us slowly dies. We are taught to write book reports. We are forced to write My Summer Vacation essays. We are threatened with exposure and classroom ridicule if we don't compose a haiku of world renown.

We turn creative flow into linear thinking. We truncate ideas with average word count techniques. We tune up the car instead of taking a Sunday drive in the country.

Don't mistake writing for penmanship. Writing — creating phrases, themes, characters, and plots — is too often confused with the product of neatly spaced letters on a blue-lined sheet. The words and ideas are what we want.

The typesetting comes after, long after the creative work is done.

Don't hand your child a clean sheet of paper and a pencil, and tell him to write an essay. It will "sever" the right-side of the brain from the left. It will produce stilted writing and a teary-eyed child.

Either hand the child a tape recorder with a sixty-minute blank tape and fully-charged batteries, or take the time yourself, grab the pencil, and write the words that are going to flow out of your child's active mind.

Do you remember a good teacher? Were you fortunate enough to have one? What did she do to inspire you?

I remember a good teacher. She told me I was a writer. I think she told each child that privately, one on one, and we each believed her. She was right. Each one of her students was a writer. Her job was to bring the writer out. She was the only teacher I know who gave double grades. She'd give a grade for the content separated by a hash mark from the grade for the mechanics. I'd get A+'s for content and D's or F's for mechanics. I was a writer! Copy editors can fix mechanics. Spell checkers can remedy spelling errors. But computers can't compose thoughts. Writers can. Miss Barbara Clark, that fabulous teacher, was recently named Teacher of the Year for the state of Florida. She deserved it. I remember her telling me she believed I had the intellect to score high enough to earn credit on the advanced placement English test. I not only earned credits, but scored the highest grading possible. I thank the Lord, I had a great teacher.

© Jill Bond / Homeschool Press, PO Box 254, Elkton, MD 21922

Moms, Dads, teachers, as you work with your children, don't pull the plug on their writing spirit. Plug them into the God-given creativity in them. Don't allow them the easy way out of their writing misery. Kevorkian pulls the plug on those people who want the easy way out of their misery. What Kevorkian does is criminal. He will be judged.

Consider two different ways of handling a typical situation:

Young Bill taps his pencil, fidgets with his chair, adjusts the light, gets a glass of water, writes a word, marks it out, starts again, breaks his pencil lead, and then cries, "Mom, I can't write. I'm not a writer. Why do I have to do this dumb, old assignment anyway? 'What I did on my summer vacation' — ugh!"

#1 Mom, lovingly and with compassion, says, "I'll help you." She sharpens his pencil and goes back to her sewing, "Read that chapter in the manual again, dear. It tells you the way to do the assignment. I'm in here if you need me."

Mom just set up the drip, drip, drip that will course through the child's creativity and leave his writing dead.

#2 Mom, lovingly and with compassion says, "I'll help you." She sharpens his pencil and sits down in his chair. "Bill, let's forget the assignment a minute. Let's do art. I'm going to draw a big beach ball here in the middle of the paper. I remember our first summer at the beach when the beach ball seemed as big as you were. You rolled the ball forward and fell flat on your face. You came up sputtering sand. You were the cutest baby."

"Aww, Mom. Every mom says that."

"Well, it's true. I remember the year we went to the beach and Dad took you out on the boogie board for the first time. I made your Dad put a life jacket on you that was so big you couldn't move your arms. You looked like a neon-orange scarecrow."

"Yeah," Bill says laughing, "I've seen the pictures. You were really uptight, Mom."

"I just loved you so much I couldn't bear the idea that you could be hurt. I was going to do all in my power to protect you."

"Is that why you made me wear the safety strap this year?"

"Well, that new surfboard cost us more than $200 and I didn't want you losing it."

"Right, Mom. You still care. You can't hide it from me."

In the beach ball on the paper, Mom writes the word, "surfing." Then she draws an arrow to another circle and writes, "boogie board." She draws more circles and more arrows all over the paper forming a picture resembling a complex chemical compound right after an explosion. In each circle she fills in words: "protection," "life jackets," "growing," "independence," "photographs," "Dad," "self-confidence," "over-protection" . . . Bill starts blurting out words and phrases. The page fills quickly.

She then takes a new page out and asks him which words "kinda" go together. He grabs her pencil and paper and starts drawing circles and lines and soon has a drawing resembling a techno-toy creation. It looks logical and reasoned.

He is on his way to writing.

We'll talk more about creativity in the course. At this time, I want you, the teacher, to be motivated to teach writing in a fresh way. Forget how you were taught. Most of you were not taught to write — just to produce words on paper. Let go of those two hundred word assignments on George Washington. Let go of worrying about infinitives used as predicate nominatives. Don't go ballistic over "receive" or "recieve." And please store away the hours of penmanship drills and loopy "l's."

Yes, I agree. Penmanship has a place in your curriculum. Spelling should be taught. Correct sentence structure is needed. You must adhere to word-count restrictions when submitting articles.

Those sub-subjects should come after the words flow out of your child's mind. "After-writing" is a valid practice. We'll cover an entire section on "after-writing" called *Craftsmen*. It is for perfecting work, not for creating it.

But for now, let's learn how to get thoughts out of our children's minds and into words, phrases, sentences.

Let's get started. Together.

We don't ever want to be a "Teacher Kevorkian."

© Jill Bond / Homeschool Press, PO Box 254, Elkton, MD 21922

Action Learning

Effective!

Don't we want our teaching to be effective? It isn't that we cover the material that is important, but *that* they *learn*.

Here are some effective learning activities which can be used to reinforce their lessons. They may sound quite unusual for an English class, but trust me, I've used them over and over with adults and children, who not only enjoy the classes, but learn the concepts.

Be creative. Come up with your own activities.

You can do these in any order. I have them listed in the order I use them for my classes. (Some directly correlate with a lesson in the book and are noted.)

Please read this entire section before you get started. Many of the activities have a surprise you need to know about before you involve your children. I don't require written answers from most of the children with whom I work. It's your choice if you want your children to jot down their answers. I like the children (teams) to talk through their answers. Their word processing is so much more vivid when it's oral and not inscriptional. There are a few of you who will want to take notes for them(e.g., I use a write and wipe board for the *Colors* lesson, page 42.).

Listing of Action Learning Activities

1. *Box Top Memory*
2. *Character Sketch*
3. *Director*
4. *Play Tag*
5. *Colors*
6. *Sense–able Writers*
7. *Surprises*
8. *Belt of Truth*
9. *More News at Eleven*
10. *Just One More Question*

1) Box Top Memory

Note: Don't let your children know what you're doing. This exercise works best if it is a complete surprise.

Supplies: (At least one set; best to have one set per child or team)
- Box top (with sides — e.g., shoe box lid, storage box lid) or trays
- Six to ten objects (common objects your children are very familiar with)
  I've used:
  - crayon (same color for all sets)
  - audio cassette
  - folded piece of paper (bright colors are great)
  - plastic comb

- computer diskette
- glue stick
- sea shell
- tag (e.g., garage sale tags)
- Lord's Supper "wine" glass (Our pastor gave each member of our church a cup made of olive wood from his trip to Israel. You could use a plastic one, or a plastic cup.)
- paper cup
- twisty tie (from garbage bags)

The idea on choosing items is to pick things that are easily recognized by *your* children, and also have some characteristics they can notice (shape, color, weight, texture, etc.).

Ideally, you'll set up as many box tops as you have students. (When I have my classes we divide into teams. You'll want each box top to have identical items.)

Before you involve your students, you might not want to tell them you're starting writing class. You can tell them you're doing an experiment. (It's a writing experiment.)

Have the children close their eyes while you explain to them that you are going to set some items before them to study for three minutes (if needed, you can give them five minutes). Then you're going to take the items away and give them a quiz.

Set the box top (or tray) in front of each child (or team). Set a timer for three minutes. Allow them to touch, smell, see, rattle, flip, and shake the items.

Teachers, don't say a word. Don't tell them what to do. (I'm always thrilled with this exercise because the children are so creative as they examine the items.)

After three minutes, take the "tray" to another room. Ask your children to number a sheet one through fifteen. (Yes, of course, you can vary this for your family — I like a parent to take down dictation for the younger students' responses.)

Ask them these questions. Don't hint, but give them mental room to come up with their own answers.

1) What were the items in (or on)?
2) What was the color of the outside of the container?
3) What was the color of the bottom of the container, the surface on which the items were placed?
4) Guess the dimensions of that container. State the answer in words, rather than with precise measurements. (It is okay to give them an example.)
5) What do you estimate the weight of that container to be? (Again, ask them to state it in words, rather then with precise measurements.)
6) What material was the container made of?
7) How many items were in (or on) the container?
8) How many items had a similar shape?
9) For how many minutes did you examine the items?
10) What did you have for dinner last night?
11) Ask a personal question about something they did thirty minutes before this exercise. (In the classes, we ask questions about the introduction of each student.)
12) Ask a personal question about something they did two hours before this exercise. (This could be about morning chores or a previous lesson in another subject.)
13) Which item was the most interesting?

14) Why did you choose that item?

15) Why do you think I asked these questions? (And what do they have to do with writing?)

We have such fun with this exercise in my classes. The children learn that a good writer looks beyond the obvious and sees things others miss. I use this example (especially when I have a room full of teenage boys): "How many editors do you think would print the story entitled: 'Shaq is tall?' None! It's too obvious. Now if you have the inside scoop on what color toe-nail polish Shaquille O'Neill's mother wears to all his games and why (lots of laughter from the kids — they *are* listening), then you have the start of a interesting story."

Anyone can see and state the obvious. But a skilled writer can see beyond that and notice nuances in speech, shades of color, textures of personalities and then weave the story with those elements.

Most of the children will have tried to memorize the items. A few will have even touched the box top. One or two will actually lift the box top. One boy in one of my classes actually memorized all the songs listed on the cassette tape.

Look at how they describe size. Talk them through descriptions that go beyond 2.3 grams. That precise of a measurement would lose many children and have no meaning for them. (Most children write stories for children.) Teach them to describe size, weight, etc., in terms children can understand. For instance, the box I use is about the same size as a video tape. Talk them through comparisons. The box top is bigger then a cassette tape, but smaller than a television. The next time you or your children read a book to a preschooler notice how the author paints the picture in the child's mind with words he can relate to. It would be ludicrous to tell a three-year-old that the man was 27.8 meters tall. A three-year-old can't relate to that, so the writer might say, "The giant was as tall as a building."

Did they remember any of the personal questions? (Questions 10-12) Writers need to notice things and remember them. Now is a good time to lay a major hint to them about journaling.

Lesson

1) Be very observant. Notice things that others miss. Don't state the obvious.
2) Word things so the reader will understand.
3) Remember.

Note: You can repeat this lesson in a variety of ways (well-paced, of course). Next time, ask questions about one of the items. Or, tomorrow ask them about something they saw today. (It can be as simple as, "Describe dinner last night." Some children will describe the plates, the silverware and table cloth, others might describe the food, while another might remember the conversations during the meal.)

You're off to a flying start. Your children should be eager for the next lesson.

2) Character Sketch

Supplies: Paper and pencil.

This exercise can be done in teams or as individuals. I like to pair pre-writers with the older children, who serve as scribes.

The idea is for each child to come up with at least five words or phrases (if your children are really sharp, make it ten) to describe the following ten personalities. If they draw a blank, ask questions like:

- "Are they real? — or fictional?"
- "Any character flaws?"
- "Character growth?"
- "Physical characteristics?"

Change this list to characters you know your children are familiar with. This list is what I use in my classes, and I've been pleased with the children's maturity and understanding in their answers.

1. Sherlock Holmes
2. John the Baptist
3. President or Mrs. Clinton
4. Long John Silver
5. Tom Sawyer
6. Michael Jackson (or someone else who desperately needs Jesus)
7. George Washington
8. Arnold Schwartzenegger (or someone else with distinctive physical characteristics.)
9. Their choice (let them nominate someone, e.g., Charlie Brown, Daniel Boone, Robin Hood, Laura Ingalls Wilder.)
10. Lord Jesus Christ

Create a master list of all the ideas for your children. Add this list to their writing notebook in the *Ideas* section. You can give points for each new idea. The team with the most points wins. (The prize is up to you.) You can stretch this into twenty (or more) lessons. Do a different character each lesson, but place limits on the descriptions — a) only physical characteristics (body suit terms), b) only non-physical descriptors, c) things they might say, phrasing, or dialogue. There are so many variations on this lesson — you can have lots of fun. This is a great "car lesson" during trips around town.

Definitely encourage them to go beyond physical appearances when describing someone. This works into a wonderful gift assignment. I encourage the Moms to work with their children to make Dad a gift of a character sketch. (Or Dads can help make one for Mom.) Have the children make a list of all the ways they describe Daddy. It is priceless. Once they get a handle on this idea, they'll be writing character sketches for grandparents, pastors, and others who would love to receive such a thoughtful gift.

We also play this as a game of **Guess Who.** Each child (or team) works secretly on his (their) list. Ask each group to prioritize their "clues" of descriptive words/phrases. List them in order from the best clue to the "not so great" clue. Ask the child to read his best clue while the other children try to guess the personality. The object is to guess with as few clues as possible. This rewards more precise descriptions and concise writing.

Example For the character Sherlock Holmes, the children might make a list and then number the clues as to the most revealing clue (the order would depend on what you know others might know). This example is very simple. When I work with more advanced children, I would ask them to come up with a listing without referring to any props, visual clues, or any of Holmes' dialogue. You can put as many "constraints" on their list as you feel will challenge them within the limits of their maturity.

⑥ stalker hat
⑩ curved pipe
⑦ cape
⑤ Hound of the Baskervilles
③ British
② sleuth
④ Moriarty
⑨ violin
⑧ deductive reasoning
① "*Elementary, my dear Watson.*" (Not an actual quote from any writings of Arthur Conan Doyle. Yet, most people attribute it to him.)

You could also play this game the opposite way. The object would then be to keep the other children guessing so the student would say his "worst" clue (#10) first and build up to his best clue. The application to writing this "flip-flop" version of the same game is that sometimes an author wants to build the suspense and mystery about a character. He chooses to get his reader interested before he reveals who or what his character is.

I highly recommend that all my students keep a running list of all the words and phrases they can use to describe Jesus. They can add to this and use it for the rest of their lives. Or, in other words, throughout their lives they'll see more and more of Him, and think of more words to describe all He is. It's spiritually healthy to dwell on Him.

Lesson

They learn that people are important and their characters must be multi-faceted.

3) Director

Supplies: None, really, except you might have some fun using movie props. We have a Scene One, Take One clapping board we let the kids use. (One would be very easy to make.) You could also use a megaphone, director's cap, or director's chair.

Have one child be the *director* and another child (or you) be the *actor*. Have the *director* direct the *actor* to say the word "please" so that it has different meanings. Teacher, you might have to hint or help until your students get the hang of it. Here are some ideas for ways to say "please":

1) with no extra directions
2) as a spoiled-brat child
3) as a sweet three-year-old
4) as if it were six syllables long
5) as if you meant anything but please
6) as if you meant the other person was crazy
7) as if your life depended on it
8) as if you didn't care a bit
9) parent saying "please" but meaning "MOVE, or you're grounded for life!"
10) loving spouse to loving spouse
11) sinner pleading with God

As you quickly see, the word "please" can mean many different things depending on the direction. The writer is the *director*.

I like to play a little with the word *said*: "When we say *said* in our writing, like, "'Please' she said," we say nothing because we don't know how she *said* it. Can anyone *say* it, as she *said* it?" This is an example of the "with no extra directions" style (number one in preceding list).

Switch the role playing around and try different words or phrases. Here are some ideas:

• Help
• I don't know
• No, thank you
• I'm sorry

Some children love this game and have fun directing and getting more emotion out of their actor. We encourage the children to ham it up and even to over-dramatize the bit.

Lesson

Children see that directions are important and words can be used in different ways to mean different things.

© Jill Bond / Homeschool Press, PO Box 254, Elkton, MD 21922

4) Play Tag (related to Director)

Supplies: Adventurous minds
Warning: This game is habit-forming.

This isn't like the tag children play when someone is "it." When I present this to the children, I start off by getting their curiosity up.

Teacher: "How do you play tag?"
Students: (Wide range of answers.)
T: "Would you like to learn a new way?"
S: "Sure. Yes, Ma'am."
T: "Have you ever noticed that in books after a speaking part, the author adds a 'tag' like, 'she said'?"
T: "What tags have you read before?"
  Wide range of answers.
T: "She cried, he hollered, she asked, he choked out, and on and on."

Allow them to think for a while. Then ask them how important the tag is.

T: "Remember when we played *director*?"
T: "Do you remember how we gave *directions* about how to say the word, 'please'?"
T: "Let's call those directions the *tag* — the 'she said,' 'she wailed,' 'she exhorted.' " (English majors sometimes refer to this as the *attributive or dialogue attributive*. Don't confuse with the concept of *attributive noun*. I think *tag* is easier to understand and use.)
T: "Now let's play tag ourselves, the teacher suggested." Keep saying things to them and adding in the *tag* until they catch on.

We love to play this in the car. We add the tag onto everyone's sentences.

"Are we there, yet?" "Moaned the children for the zillionth time."
"We just passed McDonald's®." "Stuart hinted."

This is a popular game among our students as they play at the dinner table. Remember to be observant so you can understand *how* the person is using the words they're pronouncing. There is so much more to a sentence than just the printed words. Good dialogue compels the reader to *hear* the words, not just see them.

Extra blessing: When you know your children are playing tag with your verbalizations, you'll be more prone to watch your tone. Nothing like saying something and hearing one of your children play tag, and say, "She yelled," for you to realize you need to practice more self-control.

Lesson

Writing is not just a sight medium, but a hearing medium as well. Your student's writing of dialogue will improve as they practice this process of using tags (or attributives) appropriately.

© Jill Bond / Homeschool Press, PO Box 254, Elkton, MD 21922

5) Colors

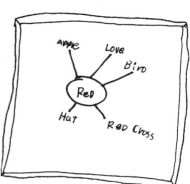

Supplies: Again, all you need are creative minds, paper, and pencils.

Assign each child a color and have him write down every word or phrase he can think of associated with that assigned color. (If you have enough children for teams, group them however you choose and assign the team a color.)

Example: Blue — they might come up with blue skies, blue jeans, blue ribbons, blue mood, azure, navy, aquamarine, royal, powder, robin's egg, blues music, code blue, etc.

Spelling doesn't matter at this point — just words and phrases in this activity. You'll want to take dictation for the younger children.

The idea is to dump as many words onto the paper as possible in five to ten minutes time.

Then play Guess the Color. Have a member of a team read off their list (never using the color itself) and see how quickly the others can guess what color they were writing about.

Have them think about their color for one week and see if they can expand their list. One girl in my class came up with more than 100 phrases/words for the color "white." Example of "Green" in *Favorites* section, page 321.

Use their list later to encourage them to write a short story. Stuart's *Blue* story is in the *Favorites* section, page 309.

Use this lesson for more than colors. Use it to generate ideas for any topic. I use it when I have writer's block. I try to think of everything I know about "xyz" and I may use only one or two words, but it makes my writing more vivid.

Lesson

This exercise is wonderful in helping children observe color in their world, notice how colorful our language is, and to realize the meanings we place on colors. This will help them in setting up scenes, describing characters and settings, and relating mood. (Examples: seeing red, in the pink, down in the blues.)

6) Sense-able Writers

Supplies: Shaving cream (not gel) and whipped topping. (You want to get a brand as similar in appearance as possible to the shaving cream, or vice versa.) Of course, you'll need material to clean up with after the lesson.

This exercise is fun to do when you have a houseful of children. Invite some of your children's friends over to play this game, or get your spouse involved.

Have your children leave the room. While they are out, make two mounds of white foam on a work table — one mound of shaving cream and one mound of whipped topping. Try to make them look as identical as possible.

Meanwhile, blindfold one of the children. He'll be "It." Then assign a "sense" to each of the other children. They should be in this order: One child will be "Its eyes." One will be "Its nose." Do the same for "Its hands," "Its ears," and "Its tongue."

It and *Its Senses* come back into the room with the two surprises on the table. *It* sits as far from the table as possible. *Its Senses* start describing the mounds to *It*. First *Its Eyes* starts and says only a few words or phrases about what he sees. *Its Eyes* can only describe visual input. Then *Its Nose* describes olfactory input. Then *Its Hands, Its Ears*, and lastly *Its Tongue*. (Teacher, be certain to forewarn *Its Tongue* not to taste the shaving cream.)

It tries to "experience" (as opposed to just guessing what the mystery items are).

Extra: When I introduce this lesson, I roll in a "reader" seated on a wheelchair. His eyes are blindfolded, his nose is pinched, there are plugs in his ears, and plastic gloves are nullifying his tactile senses. It is very effective. I push the reader around the room to demonstrate that a reader can only go where I, the writer, take him with my words.

Lesson

The writer is the reader's senses. The reader can only see things the writer sees and tells him about. The reader can only smell things the writer smells and tells him about. The same holds true for the other three senses. As writers, your children must realize that they are the reader's senses. This game impacts the child through his senses. "It" plays the role of the reader and he'll have a new understanding of what the reader must go through to understand the writer. There is more on this in a *Writing Well* lesson. Can you figure out why we used the two different "mystery items?" The sight should have been virtually the same for both. Ah, but the smell, touch, sound, and taste are quite different. Can you already see the writing lesson? You might want to hold off on a full discussion about it now — the next action lesson develops this idea even more.

© Jill Bond / Homeschool Press, PO Box 254, Elkton, MD 21922

7) Surprises

Supplies: Shaving cream (not gel), water-based paint, and clean-up cloths. (I suggest you do this on a day when your children are dressed in old play clothes in case they get any paint on their shirts.)

This lesson is best done after the Sense-able Writers lesson. It will make more sense to your children and it is a great follow-up.

Have your children leave the room. While they are out, spread a protective layer of plastic on your dining room table and make a mound of shaving cream for each of them on your work table. Before the mound is very large, squeeze some drops of a brightly-colored paint in the middle of the foam. Pump out more shaving cream so the paint is not visible. The mounds must look just like a mound of shaving cream, nothing more.

Invite the children to come back and to start calling out words to describe what they see. You, as scribe, write this down. Then invite them to "experience the mound" for themselves. Start gently, then allow them to fully get into it. Children of all ages enjoy this lesson. (I've seen moms up to their elbows in this stuff having a blast!) Have them continue to shout out words of what they are experiencing. You'll hear it when they come to the paint. It'll be a surprise. I usually allow them to play a while and paint the table top. Clean up is very easy.

After cleaning up, we discuss the "why" of this lesson.

Lesson

The answers are difficult but usually follow along these familiar phrases: "Appearances can be deceiving." "There's more than meets the eye." "God sees the heart, not just the outward appearance of a man." Congratulations! Your children have just learned a valuable writing lesson. Writers must have a surprise in their writing. They must go beyond the obvious. They must see beyond appearances. It is a good idea to tie this lesson in with the character sketches they did earlier. — There is so much more to a man than his body. The physical appearance is just a container to hold the real person. Think of King David and King Saul. Get your children to discuss how God sees the real person—how God's touch on us brings the "color" into our lives. There is enough thought-provoking material in this lesson to keep you discussing it for a full week. I like to remind my students as they write to "put the paint in the shaving cream." Ask your students as they hand you a paper, "Where's the paint?" They should be able to point to a particular phrasing or twist of plot.

Note: The next time you want to reinforce this lesson, substitute whipped cream, vanilla, or white chocolate pudding for the shaving cream and use food coloring instead of paint. It'll be a new surprise. You could sneak it to them during dessert.

© Jill Bond / Homeschool Press, PO Box 254, Elkton, MD 21922

8) Belt of Truth

Supplies: Two belts—as identical as possible except for length. I use one of my husband's and a toddler's. Both are black — one is twice as long as the other.

Talk to the children about how important it is to get their facts straight. You might want to tell them how much difficulty there is when sources are misquoted or information is fabricated. I often give the example Rush Limbaugh uses to illustrate how some organizations distort facts or make them up entirely. He has a quote from the National Organization for Women stating that 150,000 people die each year from anorexia. The true official figure from the government is 54. Quite a difference between 150,000 and 54. (Program aired 7/24/94.) Through this "real-life exercise" of completing this learning activity you will be encouraging your students to get their facts straight.

Divide your students into two groups. Separate them into different rooms so each group doesn't know what the other is doing. Don't let them know you have two belts. I'm very careful about handling them and hiding them.

Show the first group Belt #1 and ask them to guess how many "belts" long your porch, driveway, hall, kitchen, or whatever is. Record each person's estimates. (I have them measure my L-shaped porch, guessing each segment and then the total.) Then, just like a science project have them measure the distance and compare their guesses to the actual. Now, take the second group and Belt #2 and repeat the process. (Be careful that groups 1 and 2 don't talk to each other.)

After both groups are finished, have them compare their answers. Watching the children's faces is quite fun. They try to come up with reasons the answers are different. So, I start asking questions. Did you both measure with the belt I gave you? The black belt? The black leather belt? With the silver buckle? Then I pull out the two belts and most of them have instant understanding! We then discuss this exercise and how it pertains to writing.

Lesson

Write from the same frame of reference as your reader. Don't talk in oranges if your reader has only eaten apples all her life. Don't talk in giga-bytes if they don't know what RAM is. Don't talk about double supralapsarianism, if they don't know anything about God's Sovereignty. Do be careful of your facts. Validate them. Don't just accept data without some investigation.

Additional: You might want to tell them the "foot" story of the king who ordered a bed. The carpenter wanted to know what size to make the bed. So the king lay down on the palace floor and a guard walked around the king. He told the carpenter the bed should be three feet wide and six feet long. The carpenter made the bed and delivered it. The king couldn't even sit in it. It was too small. So, the king called the carpenter and the guard. The carpenter stood next to the guard, and his feet weren't even half the size of the guard's. So, a royal decree went out that standards be set up, using the king's footsize, of course. Or, so the fable goes. You can elaborate and embellish this story to make it even more interesting to your children.

9) More News At Eleven

Supplies: None, really, but you can make it more fun by using a toy (or real) microphone. If you have a video camera, use it.

Remind your children of something interesting (the crazier the better) that has happened to them recently. I have no doubt that if you have children, something unusual has happened recently. It could have been the broken grape jelly jar and the subsequent mess. It might be that Billy lost his first tooth. Has anyone been ill? Did anyone get a perfect math paper? Did little Becky try to "flush" her toothbrush? Did George give the puppy a haircut? Did Heidi finish all her vegetables at dinner last night without threat of bodily harm from the chief disciplinarian of the family?

Have the children discuss it, trying to remember every detail.

Now, come up with a teaser. In no more than three sentences (preferably one), write the teaser, the *more-at-eleven* phrase, to interest the viewer to want to know more. This could be: "Family mops up after basement flooded from broken water pipe. News at Eleven."

"Is she, or isn't she? Mother tries to remember_____. News at Eleven."

It can be fun. It can be zany. It can be ridiculous. It can be dramatic. It can be sensational.

But it must be interesting. Enticing. Compelling. You want the viewer to tune in at eleven to know more.

Lesson

By doing this "extreme" example of teasers, your students are starting to learn the importance of beginnings. Stories, articles, and books have to grab the reader early. Your writing must have the idea of "tune in to the next page" for the reader to go beyond the first few sentences. Notably, we don't want to get cheap or tacky with our writing as do many teasers. We don't want to be maudlin or sensational. We just want them to realize that we have to "sell" our writing to our readers to keep them reading. This game is fun to play on and off throughout the year. It will help you to see the humor in trying circumstances. "Mother keeps her patience even after her three-year-old has asked the 13,245th question for the day! How does she do it? News at Eleven!"

10) Just One More Question

Supplies: Notebook, notepad, or audio tape recorder; pencil or pen; and "press pass." (If your students are into play-pretend, or role-playing, then put a man's old fedora hat on their head with a "press pass" note sticking out the hatband.)

Peter Falk, as Lieutenant Columbo, has such a knack for this — the interview. Some people don't. Teach your children how to interview. Allow them to interview you. You role-play as Ruth, Rachel, Florence Nightingale, or whoever, and have them, as the press, interview you.

Assign or allow them to choose who they want to be. Have your students interview each other. My students thoroughly enjoy the interview lesson. I tell them that they, as the interviewer, can be anyone (real or fictional) from any time and the interviewee can also be anyone. We've seen some interesting combinations:

> Miss America interviews Nefertiti
> Troy Aikman interviews *The Four Horsemen of Notre Dame*
> Hillary Clinton interviews Jezebel
> Einstein interviews Isaac Newton
> George Washington interviews King David
> James Michener interviews Margaret Mitchell
> Andy Warhol interviews Leonardo da Vinci
> Apostle Paul interviews Isaac
> Charles Swindoll interviews Peter Marshall

Teach them to make an appointment with the interviewee. Have them research before they interview. Have them show up on time. Then enjoy the interview. Stop precisely when the allotted time is over.

Allow the children to interview each other. But each time, set the "interviewing" parameters. Treat each interview professionally. They can stage a "live broadcast" interview for an imaginary show: "Portraits in Time" or "What You Always Wanted to Ask."

Lesson

Just as it's best to practice table manners at home before going to a four-star restaurant, it is best to practice interviewing manners at home with loved ones, before insulting an interviewee. They'll learn through practice how to phrase questions to draw out interesting answers. They'll learn respect as they show up on time and end the appointment on time, as well. They'll learn the value of research, as they stumble through an interview ill-prepared. They'll learn about note-taking and remembering key elements of the interview. They will have to learn to listen carefully. They will have to learn to be respectful to the interviewee. They will have to learn to "love the sinner and hate the sin" in some instances (especially if you pick questionable characters to interview.)

This "interviewing" can work for two types of media: print (magazines or newspapers) and broadcast (radio or television). They can interview "live" on radio (audio-tape) or television (video-camera), after some rehearsing. They can interview for a print article they are writing. Also, it's fun to stretch the bounds of this assignment to "anything in history or space." You can get fun interviews like the ocean (Mr. Ocean) talking to one of the fish living in it.

Added benefit: As you role-play with fictional, historical, Biblical, and real-life characters, you'll learn quite a bit about the characters.

Note: This lesson could be done on a daily or weekly basis throughout their education. The interviews can last from a few minutes to a few hours, depending on the scope of the interview. These interviews can link with other subjects you're already teaching (e.g., history, science, etc.).

Writing Matters

In this section of the **Teacher's Pages**, I want to discuss some writing matters because *writing matters*. I'm not developing corresponding lessons to these ideas. In most cases, these ideas are over-arching. They are presented here for you to work into your talks and lessons with your children. You might want to read these to yourself and then re-read them to your children or paraphrase them. These concepts are so important, I wanted *you* to present them.

Focus

One of the underlying themes of this book is that our focus is on God. I've attended different writing classes and different "how to get published" presentations, and most of them centered on making a name for yourself. The writer is the focus. The reader is second and God doesn't even receive an honorable mention.

As your children write, their entire focus should be on God and His mighty Works, His Truths, and His Perspective. This skill is developed and can be nourished by you. In the next few sections, I'll give you some specific "tools" to help you and your children keep proper focus.

I recommend that as you teach this lesson, have your students actually focus something: a camera, microscope, or telescope. Let them pretend they are focusing a camcorder. Let them see a tree or couch (whatever) out of focus and then in focus. Let them focus directly on something, so the rest of the picture is blurry.

Their attitude about writing should focus on God and *they* should be blurry. I hope that makes sense. Some children will barely grasp this concept. Be patient. It takes years and years for all of us to beat back the world's banner of "bang your own drum" (I know; I am still learning this lesson). Notoriety, publicity, and applause are intoxicating, but we all need to stay grounded on Who gave us the talent to write, the reason to write, and the hope to write. It is *all* for Him.

His Timing

This is one of the hardest lessons for many writers. It involves the Fruit of the Spirit: *patience.* God knows when He wants His message to be available for His plans. We want to rush His Hand and want our words in print yesterday. His timing is perfect. Trust Him. Frank Peretti waited years for his novel, *This Present Darkness,* to be published. God knew what He was doing. He knew when His body would be ready to receive it and when He wanted to move among us in that way. God's timing is perfect.

A national magazine had contacted me about writing an article about my son, Trent, who is autistic. (More about this in the next section: "Prayer"). I had no control over when the article would run or when it would be mailed. Shortly after I received my copy, a lady wrote me saying that exactly the day before, a similar situation (as mentioned in the article) had happened with her son. The "magical" appearance of my article was as if God had picked her up in His big strong arms and reassured her that He understood and knew what circumstances she was in. She was confirmed by God. I had nothing to do with the timing. God's timing is perfect.

Here's another example:

It was the anniversary of her son's death. A few years before, her son, a fine young man, was home and working on his car. The jack failed and the car crushed him. This anniversary was hitting her hard. She wondered if God still loved her. She was desperate and searching. She had picked up a devotional book and hadn't looked at it, but decided to look up the sentiment for that day. She wept, because for that day's date, she read of another mother who was telling of how she had lost her son and God had sustained her! Some of those devotionals are written months and months ahead. That particular devotional could have been placed on a different day or even month. Yet, God knew what He was doing. He knew when my friend was going to reach out to Him. His timing is perfect.

Rest in His timing. Teach your children to be patient about getting their work published and in print. Rest. He knows what He is doing.

Prayer

I'm often asked how much time I spend writing. I usually answer, "Oh, about ten to one."

What I mean by that is: for every one hour I spend at the keyboard downloading words from my brain to the computer, I've spent ten hours in prayer and Bible study.

For example, the article I mentioned in the section on "His Timing" (above) was one in which I think I invested twenty to one. The editor had asked me to "write about Trent." My friends, Trent is a book! I have dozens and dozens of stories, anecdotes, and illustrations about Trent. Which ones should I use? Prayer, prayer, fasting, and prayer.

Then one day I was released from the prayer and given the gumption to write. I wrote of one of our typical days with Trent when he discovered the joy of throwing raw eggs. He proceeded to decorate the rooms in *Early Henhouse*. I wrote it in a humorous style and tried to show God's love for Trent among the smelly messes. That was the story that touched another mother's heart. The day before she had read my article, her son had had an adventure with eggs. She had felt rejected, stranded, and frustrated. But the next day my article arrived and she knew she wasn't alone.

That wasn't me. That was God. He knew what she was going to go through. So He put it on my heart to write about Trent's "eggstraordinary" day months before her "eggstraordinary" day occurred. He timed the delivery of the magazine. He wanted to love one of His own. And He allowed me to get involved. What a thought — what a humbling experience — what a supreme opportunity.

That's what *Writing to God's Glory* is all about. We, as writers, just serve as His fingertips and mouthpieces to touch one of His own when and how He desires.

I'm *not* equating our Spirit-filled writing with Scripture. Please don't misunderstand what I'm saying. Scripture is God-breathed.

What we're doing is Holy-Spirit-directed. He does want to touch others through us.

Prayer and fasting are integral to our writing and focusing in on Him.

If I have an assignment or idea, I pray, seeking God's thoughts. I ask Him to bring to mind illustrations, verses, and even ideas. I want to present His message in a way that will touch exactly whom He wants to touch, when He wants to touch them.

Prayer, in a way, gets us out of the way so He can develop His message through us. I can't tell you how many times I've had a writer's block and was readmitted into the writing process through prayer. "Miraculously," I'll remember something that happened to me as a child, or something my children did that fits perfectly into what I'm writing. That is exciting. That is when the Holy Spirit Himself guides our thoughts and fingers.

His Mission Field

Not only does God control the timing of our writing and the message of our writing, but He controls the mission field. I don't worry where my work will be published. I don't fret about this magazine or that. I figure God is smart enough to know whom He wants reading what I've written. Sometimes it's for one other person's eyes only (a letter) or it is for thousands (a national magazine or book). I trust God. He knows who subscribes to what magazine. He knows when they are going to pick up that magazine at their dentist's office. He knows and He cares.

The more I walk with the Lord the more I'm convinced He is in the one-person business. I believe Jesus died for each of us individually. He cares for each of us. One person at a time!

That is what writing to His glory is all about. It is one-person writing. As I write, I ask God to show me who my reader is. I write to her (or him). As I write this today, I'm picturing you. Some of you are reading this in a room filled with noise and commotion. Some of you are exhausted after a full day and the kids are all asleep and you finally have a moment to yourselves to prepare your lessons for tomorrow. Some of you have to read this in sentence-sized bites as you supervise your children who are doing math right now. Some of you are reading this for yourself and will start writing as soon as you finish this section. You all love the Lord and want to glorify Him. Writing to you is so easy. It is like writing to my sister or brother.

When I write for a mission field that I know isn't in love with the Lord, I picture them and seek God's direction for them. Can you even imagine what it is like to know something you've written has changed someone's life — has moved him closer to God? It's like that feeling you have when God allows you to be there as He performs His divine miracle of rebirth. What an honor. He didn't "need" us, yet He allowed us to be participants. He wants to work through your writing and your children's writing.

I'm in awe. It is such a remarkable thing, that the God of the Universe would reach down and touch your thoughts and give you words to reach out to others! Writing to God's Glory is such an adventure and growth experience.

As I write this today, I'm praising Him with each stroke of the key. Singers sing. Musicians play. We writers use words to sing our praises. He is so very worthy of that praise.

Just a peek at the lives this book could touch by giving them that little boost of encouragement — you and your children — I'm weeping right now. When I think how God can magnify my words through you to your children and then on to others, I'm overwhelmed with His love. Can you imagine being one of C.S. Lewis's teachers? To think you had even a small part in his writings which have touched and led so many to God's throne! What about Oswald Chambers's mother? Who is one of your favorite authors? Can you imagine what satisfaction their teachers have? That's where you and I are, we're the launchers.

As your children write (and as you write), ask God to reveal your reader to you. Pray for that reader. Write to that reader. God will do the rest.

Bible Study

It seems so obvious — seems silly to even write it down — but Bible study is vital to writing to God's Glory. The more we bathe in His Word, the more our words will be bathed in Him. I like that; I'll re-say it: The more we bathe in His Word the more our words will be bathed in Him.

It's impossible to please God unless we know Him. It's impossible to be Scripturally accurate if we don't know what He says to us in His Word.

I pray I will never write anything which contradicts Scripture. I want every theme, every moral, every point I make to align *perfectly* with God's teaching.

© Jill Bond / Homeschool Press, PO Box 254, Elkton, MD 21922

That comes with Bible study.

I not only study the Bible for life and general personal growth, but for writing. When I'm developing a written piece, I study the Bible for what it says about the topic. I haven't come across a topic yet in which I couldn't find an applicable message in God's Word.

Steer your children so they are always writing out of the abundance of God's Word. Their work may not quote chapter and verse, but the scope should mirror the thoughts and direction of the verses. The book of Esther is a prime example. It is filled with God's Hand, yet God Himself is not mentioned.

Theme

This brings me to discuss theme. It is one of the most difficult subjects to teach. Many children confuse them with plot. If you ask a child what is the theme of a story, he often will start telling you the action of the characters instead of the point of the story. Keep in mind that every work has a theme. Some themes are more difficult to discern than others. Themes should be stated in one sentence preferably in eight words or less:

- Good triumphs over evil.
- Stealing is wrong.
- Fidelity is the best way.
- Lying just causes trouble.

There are two distinct disciplines concerning theme — one relates to the writer (choosing a theme, creating a theme, or using a theme) the other relates to the reader (discerning the theme, evaluating the theme, disregarding or embracing the theme).

Theme and the Writer: As a writer, your child should begin any story (fiction or non-fiction) with a clearly defined theme (the *clarity* will depend on their age and maturity). Children seem to write plots ("and then I did this, and then I did that, and then…"). Help them develop a point — a theme — to frame the purpose of the plot. Coming up with their theme should be step one of their writing assignment.

Even as a child I knew I'd grow up to be a writer, but I thought I'd have to come up with some deep cosmic truth on my own. As I matured I realized that I didn't have to create truth or come up with an original theme on my own. As a matter of fact, I learned that those who *create* their own themes are on shaky spiritual ground. All the Truth we ever need to tell is already printed in our Bibles. Any good story is based on a Biblical Truth. So, choosing a theme to write about can be as simple as opening the Bible to a proverb and developing a story around the concept of that proverb. For example: If you're reading daily proverbs to your children, make one of these proverbs a writing assignment. Proverbs 1:7 is a very popular reoccurring theme in literature and stories — *The Fear of the Lord is the beginning of knowledge: but fools despise wisdom and instruction.* Ask your children to come up with an imaginary situation in which some characters learn this proverb.

Your children should learn to stay with a particular theme throughout their story. Even good novels have one main theme (though some sub-themes are interwoven). It's been my experience that most children should be limited to one theme — it takes a more mature writer to handle sub-themes well.

Here's an activity you might use to help them understand this concept. Get several flashlights (or table lamps). You might have to wait until after dark (or darken a room) to have enough of a

© Jill Bond / Homeschool Press, PO Box 254, Elkton, MD 21922

lighting contrast to cast shadows. Let the children play with casting shadows against a wall. Use a variety of lights and flashlights. Make big shadows and small shadows. Add lots of light to diminish the effect of the shadows. Reduce the light and give the shadows the full impact. Shine several lights from different directions so that there are several shadows going in different directions. After they have had fun and everyone has had a turn, tell them this story in your own words:

> There once was an artist who was very good at what she did. Her paintings looked like photographs. They were that life-like. One of her secrets was to clip a small light on the edge of her canvas so it would shine on the canvas from a particular angle. It was a constant reminder of the light source in the scene. The light in the painting might be coming from a window so all the shadows and shading had to reflect that angle. Once one of her children played a trick on her and moved her light. The pattern was flawed and unnatural. It was visual noise and the artist had to redo it. The finished painting was spooky and unreal.

Then tie that story into writing. When I write, I do the same thing. Instead of attaching a light source to my canvas to make sure my shadows are the right length, I attach the Truth or theme to my computer (a post-it note on my monitor) and make sure all my keystrokes (words) are headed in the same direction. If I try to change the theme in a story, both themes are blurred and the casts are too long. Teach your children to keep their message, their theme, close to their fingertips as they write.

Just as in a room where light is pouring in from a window, there might also be several lamps on or a fire burning. These secondary sources of light cast their own *minor shadows*. This isn't a bad thing. Yes, a good novel will have a central theme, but a skilled author will cover some sub-themes also — but it has to be done well and the themes don't *compete* for attention or contradict each other. In shorter pieces, it is usually best to stay with one theme and cover it well. Even an advanced reader can only absorb so much (beyond word recognition and into heart-reaction). Have you ever noticed how God will reveal deeper and deeper meaning in a Bible verse that you've memorized? You understood it years ago, and yet, today God gave you a new application of it in your life. *That* is perfect writing.

One way you can work with your child about theme is by asking questions. What do you want your reader to feel after reading your essay? Do you want them to change their behavior? Do you want them to think about something they're doing in a whole new light? When they finish reading this, what do you want them to think about their family, children, work, et al.?

Themes touch lives. Themes change lives. Themes affect history. Either for good or evil. If your children have prayed, studied their Bibles, and have been writing to God's Glory then those themes will be Godly and your children will be conduits of the Truth.

Theme and the Reader: As a reader, your child should be discerning themes. I realize this is a writing text and not a literature analysis text, but good readers make better writers. One practice you should start with your children is to hunt for the theme in books, short stories, and articles they read. Likewise, they should be able to summarize the theme of any story they write. *What's the point? What's the message? What's the moral?*

If they are having a hard time grasping this idea, read them some fables in which the moral is spelled out. [A moral is a kind of theme — a theme is a *lesson*.] Start asking them to come up with the moral and test it against the printed one. It's not the plot. The plot is only a device to convince the reader of the validity of the moral and for the reader to remember the moral.

As they start to discern themes in the books they are reading, they should start to appreciate the skill with which the author imparted the theme to his reader. How subtle, how obvious, how clever was the author? What scene convinced them of the author's point? Did a character say the *punch line* or spell out the theme in so many words? Was it just a feeling the reader gets?

To pull this all together, every writer has to deal with theme. Be it a thank you note or a magnum opus, the writer should have a reason for the words being written and he should be trying to communicate some central thought. This anecdote makes the point clear:

A seminary student asked his theology professor, "*How many points should a good sermon have?*" The professor said, "*A least one, or else it is pointless.*"

Our children's writings, and our own for that matter, should have a point — a theme. Every work has a theme and comes packaged in the writer's worldview. Whether writers understand or can classify their worldviews (pantheism, globalism, deism, et al.) their understanding about eternal life, right and wrong, life and death, heaven and hell, the nature of man, will be reflected in their word choices and how they present different aspects of their characters, and in their theme — even in newspaper articles, letters to Mom, and tabloid garbage. It is important that we teach our future writers theme, which leads me to the next topic: Truth Telling.

Truth Telling

This writing matter relates to the "Bible Study" section and the "Theme" section. Everything Christians write must match up with Scripture. Their theme must be a Biblical theme.

This doesn't mean that the scenes are all set in Bible times — what it means is that the theme (the eight-words-or-less moral of the story) is a Truth taught in the Bible.

There are enough lies broadcast now on television. Our job is to present God's truth fully knowing that it is TRUTH. The world has had many philosophers disseminating their own "truth." Some of it has cost people their lives and ruined many others. Think about the lies of Hitler, Marx, and Darwin. Think about the lies of popular authors who depict adultery as okay and actually beneficial. Think about the lies of most TV sit-coms in which the children really are smarter and wiser than their parents and the father is a fool.

Test everything your children write by the real Truth.

Genre

When people find out that I'm an author their first question is usually, "What kind of books do you write?" They want to know if I write for children or adult readers, how-to books or novels, political or satirical themes. They want to know what genre of books I write. Your children should have a working knowledge of what this term *genre* (pronounced zhan' re) means and how it is used in the writing industry. Genre is a category or type of work marked by a distinctive style, form, or content. Examples: Science Fiction, Romance, How-to, Cooking, Historical Fiction.

There are several ways you can teach them this concept:

1) Visit a bookstore where the managers divide their merchandise into topics or sections. Walk your children around and discover the organization. Have them go on a book hunt. Have them make a list of each of the sections of the store.

2) Open a thorough book catalogue. Notice the table of contents and how the books are grouped according to their content or scope. (Examples: Commentaries, Bibles, History, etc.) Notice the sub-sections which give a more refined categorizing.

3) Go on to *Genre Hunt* in your home to *test* their knowledge of what they've learned. Play like it's hide-n-seek. (Notice: you might have to borrow a few books from the library if your private library doesn't have a wide variety of book types.) Ask your child to bring you three books from three completely different genres of writing, then have her describe each type as she presents them to you. Have them find as many different genres as possible from your home library.

4) Go to your public library. Utilize the library's cataloguing system. Yet, acquaint your child with Dewey Decimal System. Though the Dewey system doesn't equate precisely with the recognized genres of literature, it would benefit your child to learn the myriad of styles and types of writing there are in print. You can also do this concept with magazines.

Please recognize that book-sorters file or label at different levels of detail. One librarian might place a book in historical fictional while another might label it as Christian fiction. To give you an example: my own book, Dinner's in the Freezer! is often in different areas of bookstores: Cooking and Christian Devotions. There is not a universal list of *genres* that all English majors would agree on, but here are some of the widely-recognized ones:

Fiction (*general term but might be divided into romantic fiction, Christian fiction, historical fiction, et al.*)
Christian (*general term but could be subdivided into theology, devotional, biography, et al.*)
Romance
Westerns
Science Fiction
Fantasy
Historical
Educational (*math, science, writing et al.*)
How-to (*everything from cook books to photography to removing stains*)
Comedy (*everything from joke books to cartoon strips to humorous fiction*)
Children's
Adventure
Short-story
Sports
Drama (*plays*)
Local (*books about local sights: of local interest only*)
Biography
Business
Political
Legal
Art (*books on artwork [humanities] and artists*)
Technical
Poetry
Horror
Mystery

One other exercise you might want to do with your children is to study the different genres in the art world-from cubists to realists to impressionists to pointillists to surrealists. Or choose several different *sub-genres* within the genre of poetry: Ogden Nash in contrast with Henry Wadsworth Longfellow in contrast with Lewis Carroll in contrast with William Shakespeare.

Some could argue if a *type* is a true genre or just a bookstore marketing tool, but for our purposes we want the children to have a working knowledge of all the ways we can communicate with others. Not everyone has to write a novel. I want your child to learn this so that they can appreciate God's unique calling on individuals. Your child is not like any other child God has ever sculpted. The world likes to place everyone into nice neat little boxes: he's a sanguine, introverted, type A, overweight Aquarian. Keep in mind by teaching genre we're not trying to pigeon-hole their writing style, just the opposite, we're trying to open up their exposure to styles to unbind any prejudices they might have been exposed to. Don't pull limits on what God can do through you and your children.

Me or Thee

This idea ties into the over-all theme of *Writing to God's Glory*. Maybe the best way to explain what I'm trying to say is by example:

If someone compliments me on what a great writer I am, I have failed and just disproved their compliment.

However, if someone writes me and says that as he was reading my work, he was reminded of a time when God did such-and-such in his life, or he was reminded of how worthy God is of praise, or that he appreciated how I shared what God was doing in my life, then I did what I was trying to do.

If someone reads my work and focuses on me, then I failed. But, if he sees God, then I was minimized and He was maximized.

All of us should adopt John the Baptist's words: "He must increase and I must decrease."

This doesn't mean we should only write sentences with "G-O-D" in them. We can write of personal experiences. It's just that the story should be written not to say "Hey, look at me," but rather to say:

HEY, LOOK TO GOD!

Pride or Conduit

Intimately linked with the idea of "Me or Thee" is the idea of pride. Our writing is not something to be prideful about. Either we wrote it by ourselves without His guidance and indwelling and we should be ashamed we were doing something apart from Him; or we were just conduits for Him, in which case we can't claim the praise, or be puffed up because we know that our talent came from Him — our hands came from Him, our memories, our lives, our language, our ability to synthesize words, our IQ, our creativity, our imaginations, our very being — all from Him. We have nothing to be puffed up about except that for some lovely, inexplicable reason He loves us and made us and allows us to serve as a conduit for His work, and then all the pride is in Christ and Him crucified.

Tone

Yelling or whispering. Condescending or apologetic. Emphatic or wishy-washy. Terse or sing-song. Our voices all reflect a particular tone. So does our writing. Teach your children about tone by playing a game similar to *director* (page 40). In that exercise the children learn how important directions are and that a writer must give his characters instructions about how to enunciate a particular word. That exercise excelled in developing dialogue, but we can springboard from that to teach tone. Have them play-act a scene. You can use the same simple scene: getting ready for Sunday worship, fixing breakfast, teaching long division, or some other common scene from your family life. Have them come up with at least two characters and a five-to-ten line script (actual words may vary in each different run through of this scene). Character A is the *authority figure* and Character B is the *follower*. Have them play the scene different ways:

1) melodramatic (A is like Snidely Whiplash and B is like Pauline in those old *Perils of Pauline* plays)
2) menacing (A is a tyrant and ordering B around)
3) milquetoast (A is meek, timid, and unassertive like Casper Milquetoast; and B is a brat)
4) macabre (A is a *Vincent Price* -type character and B is a *Igor*)
5) mischievous (A is a conniver and B is a *Huck Finn*)
6) miserly (A is a *scrooge* and B is his *Tiny Tim*)
7) misconstrued (A is confusing like Abbott (the wiseguy) and B is trying to understand like Costello (the Stooge) — comedy and pratfalls)

This fun exercise will help them to remember how important the tone of their writing is. Two different writers could basically say the exact same thing yet, because their tones are different, one will be well-received and the other ignored. Look in the Bible at the different tones Jesus used. He spoke compassionately yet convictingly with the woman at the well. He was much more demonstrative with the money-changers in the Temple. He was soft and gentle when he wept at Lazarus' tomb. He was very vocal when He called the spirits out of the demoniac. Just as Jesus' tone varied according to different situations, so should your child's from other children's and in different writing assignments. A letter to the editor is going to have quite a different tone than a letter to grandma. Open the newspaper or a magazine and examine with your children the different tones in the articles.

Pacing

Compare readers reactions to two different stories:

Racing to the end of the sentence. Flipping pages. Can't put it down. What's going to happen next?

Gentle. Slow. Digest the flavor and then read on. Savor the sound of the words. Come back to it later.

Writers pace their stories. Good writers spend a fair amount of time developing the pacing of their plots.

Here are some ideas to teach pacing to your children.

1) Play *Mother may I?* Let them have fun with giant steps, baby steps, and scissors steps. Let them run, hop, and race. Let them loiter, saunter, and stop.
2) Watch some sporting events. Notice the difference between the speed of play in golf versus jai-alai.
3) Play chess (good, deliberate, slow). Then play *Hands-down* or some other fast-paced game.
4) Read a fast-action book or article. Then read a slow-paced book or article.
5) Play a video tape on fast forward and then on slow motion.
6) Listen to Tchaikovsky (1812 Overture), then Raffi (some child's song) and then Brahms (gentle lullaby).

Talk about the pacing of these events and activities. Yes, in some of those activities we went to extremes, but that helps clarify the point.

One thing I didn't ask you to do is to watch a soap opera (daytime or prime time), but if you ever have you'll know that they move so slowly. They take several programs to cover one plot-day. They cover minute details of dialogue. They are tortoise shows. (I don't watch them and my *experience* comes from my *working days* trying to schedule my staff's lunches so they could watch their favorite soaps in the break room.)

Contrast soaps with edge-of-your-seat action adventures from Steven Spielburg or George Lucas. Or the staccato pacing of Sesame Street and many of the commercial-blips of images. The pacing is quite different.

What it boils down to is the amount of action compared to time-frame. Do you spend ten pages with your characters strolling down a garden path or do you spend ten pages with your characters strolling down a garden path, being tempted by a serpent, eating the forbidden fruit, sewing together fig leaves and hiding from God?

It's all in the pacing.

His Vessels

One of the exciting aspects of Christian writing is that we are writing the Truth from the *only* Truth-source. Think of all the worldly wisdom out there which is producing *dead writing* — it is not bringing spiritual life to the world. The world is hungry for good advice. They will pay for "wisdom" that tickles their intellect.

I was first appalled, then mystified, then amused, then awed. I was appalled to learn that Barbara De Angelis' infomercial kit, *Making Love Work*, grossed $26 million in 1994. I was mystified because she proposes to be an expert on "making love work" — while she was married to her fifth husband![1] I was amused as I thought of Barnum's showmanship — "There's a sucker born every minute."[2] I was awed as I realized my situation with God Almighty is by Grace and Grace alone. If it weren't for His masterful touch on my life, I could be so duped or such a duper.

I cite this example to encourage you in doing well by your children. As in this example about relationships, the world would consider an expert someone who can't even hold her own relationships together. Her advice is obviously flawed. Yet, think about it: we, as children of God, have the right answers. We know how relationships can hold together. We should be the ones giving the expert advice, because God is *the* Expert.

Encourage your children to be the vessels He uses to get His message out to a needy world.

He's the Editor-in-Chief

In my classes, I present the front page of a newspaper and ask the students, "How different would this page look if someone with a Godly perspective had laid it out?" You can do this project with just about any city's paper. To give you an example, I have a copy of *The Orlando Sentinel* for Monday, July 25, 1994. The main story is about turtle patrols on the beach — "Save those turtles, folks!" It occupied the prime space of the front page. The secondary story is about Israel and Jordan and their peace summit. Barely on the front page was a note about a situation in Zaire — see page A-3. Some situation! More than 10,000 Rwandan refugees were being killed. This front page is just

---

1. One of her ex-husbands is John Gray, author of *Men Are From Mars, Women Are From Venus,* another "expert" on love and relationships. If these people are such experts on relationships, why can't they manage their own? God has a better way: one husband, one wife. The article persisted in collecting more "expert" advice from this hypocrite. Source: USA Weekend, Feb. 5, 1995, pg. 14: "The Love Doctor Is In," by Mary Roach.
2. Although P.T. Barnum doubted he ever said those words, they are ascribed to him. Barnum must have appreciated the added publicity. The saying was supposedly authored by another con man, Joseph Bessimer — nick-named "Paper Collar Joe."

another example of the difference between the world's view of life and what's "news" and God's view. What if God were the Editor-in-Chief of that paper and He was directing one of His children to design the layout? Life is important to Him — the murder of those Rwandans would have been a major story. Israel is important to Him. That would have been the headliner. The turtles might have been in Section G.

Here's an exercise to do with your children. Cut and paste a newspaper so it is the way you think it should be laid out. (A fifty-page newspaper might be cut down to a page and a half!) Keep eternity in view. I love the Bible because it is God's "newspaper." He chose the stories that mattered and should be known. I marvel at the disparity between what man chooses to dignify with print and what God did. Try it with your children. Start analyzing the material that comes into your home, that you see at the dentist's office, or that you avoid at the checkout stand (don't get too close). It's spiritually healthy to look at today's events and try to see them from God's viewpoint. (I know, sometimes you just want to say, "Jesus wept.")

Another helpful exercise is to write *The Israeli Informer* and choose a date to "cover" a Biblical event. A secular paper might have listed Christ's execution on page D-3 under Court Trials and Judgments: "*Three enemies of the state were crucified yesterday outside of Jerusalem. One was a noted troublemaker, Jesus Bar Joseph of Nazareth.*" While an "eternity paper" would have made it the story of the millenniums:

God's Son crucifies death and defeats Satan....

Can you picture all the side-bar stories? Think what the secular paper would write and then the heavenly paper — "*Temple curtain is ripped asunder; police are investigating possible vandalism* 'or' *God has removed the curtain and now allows man to come into His Presence....*"

Process versus Product

God looks on the heart. Isn't that comforting!

I live by Grace. Some days I cling to Grace like a life preserver. I'm drowning in my own failures, yet He lifts me up with Grace.

Let's think for a minute, my friend, about how Grace applies to writing. What do I mean by Process versus Product?

Your child is a child.

Keep that in mind.

If you're like me, most of my schooling was centered around "Products." I had to produce something and then submit it to be graded.

There was very little emphasis put on the process. Most teachers just wanted the product so it could be checked off in the grade book.

As I study the Bible, I see God intimately involved with the process of our lives. He cares about how we do things. The fruit must be good.

If we tithe, but stole to give the tithe, I don't think God would be honored. He cares about where our hearts are, not just the outward show. Jesus rebuked the Pharisees, didn't he? They were product-oriented. Their processes — their hearts — were wretched.

As your children develop their own writing styles, look for the process. Look for how they are improving. The finished product won't be perfect. But are they seeing things more clearly? Are they getting there?

God tells us to train up our children in the way they should go. Think about this with their writing.

Reed is a gifted writer, but he's not going to write the great american novel today. So, I don't want to do anything today that will kill the writer in him tomorrow. Maybe ten years from now he will write a novel that God will use to convert thousands.

I'd better clarify myself before I misrepresent what I'm saying. Children are wonderful. God uses children. We all must be as children as far as faith is concerned. But most children are not the bread-winners of their families. Reed's stories have touched lives and we have dozens of letters to that effect. But I look at this time now as training for the days when he will be writing as an adult.

Few children make much money writing. Those that do, great!

But, what I don't want to be guilty of is forcing Reed, at age eleven, to write the quality of work a thirty-year-old could produce.

I don't want to perfect his writing today so that he hates writing tomorrow.

With your children, give them room to grow.

So, I'm not teaching them so much to write now — but how to think, how to use words, and how to communicate. The novels will come later.

As they grow, concentrate on the process of writing, not the product.

A League of Their Own

If your child shows promise in baseball, are you going to make him pitch at 85 mph with the threat that he can't play anymore? No, you're going to start him in Little League and he'll improve and get better and better. His skills will improve and so will his muscles. He'll grow into it.

Likewise, you wouldn't have your nine-year-old playing ball with the professionals; you'd have him play in his league.

The same goes for their writing. Judge their writing according to their level. Submit their work within their league.

This isn't easy since we are now writing as adults and, of course, can see room for improvement in their work. We want them to excel, but shouldn't make them write the Pulitzer Prize-winning piece *today*. Draw their best out of them and then be satisfied.

Don't defeat them before they make it to the majors. They are only minors.

Broadcasting

This may at first seem a contradiction to the "Me or Thee" idea presented earlier, but it really isn't.

Broadcast their work.

At least once a year, broadcast their writing.

This isn't to shout *"Hey, look at my kid!"* It is to encourage them and give them a taste of what God will do through their writing.

By broadcasting, you take their favorite piece and present it so someone else (besides you) is reading it.

Here are some ideas:

- Contests
- Magazines, newspapers (don't forget letters to the editor)
- Family newsletters
- Christmas cards
- Letters to Grandma
- Church bulletin boards
- Support group newsletters' kids' sections

- Neighborhood gazettes
- Nursing home residents (newsletters, personal letters, et al.)
- Internet posts (Christian or kids' chat rooms or general entries under specific headings)[1]
- Writers' support groups[2]

There isn't one of you who couldn't find a way to encourage your child and evangelize the neighborhood or your family by broadcasting your child's work.

Pray about it. You'll be surprised at the ideas God will give you because you know your child has:

- focused on God
- prayed about it
- searched out Scriptures
- sought God's perfect timing
- heeded God's prompting for His chosen market (God will provide the right readers)

Your work in all this is to be faithful and to guide them through those steps.

Story Detecting

One very important aspect of writing is detecting the stories all around us. Here are three events which could be written into dozens of different stories for a variety of applications:

1) The clock repairman took forever, it seemed, to repair our grandfather clock. Each time Dad called, it wasn't ready yet. Dad decided to go to the shop. As he drove up to the store, he discovered that the man had the clock displayed in the shop window. It was such a rare and beautiful clock, he was attracting customers who wanted to buy it.

2) While visiting the Smithsonian gems collection, one of the Ph.D.-types walked up to me to examine my necklace. I was in a room filled with rare gems: the Hope Diamond, Empress Josephine's necklaces, etc. My necklace was a simple gold cross set on glass from the first century that my husband had bought for me in Israel.

3) Lassie looked beyond Timmy to see her trainer, Rudd Weatherwax, signal her (actually him — Lassie was played by a male collie) to lick Timmy's face.

Situations like this happen in your family. Your children notice things. They see drama, but they just don't know how to recognize the "story" in the event. Our job as parents and teachers is

---

1. For example, I posted one of Reed's book reviews (not a book report) in the Christian Interactive Network Homeschooling Forum in the "Reviews" folder. He received several notes back congratulating his work. This makes the forums not only useful to you (broadcasting) but more informative for others. Your children will also receive almost instant feedback. Of course, you want to choose your web-sites and bulletin boards carefully. There are several good publications available about Christians (and/or homeschooling) on the Internet. I have seen posts about grammar from parents who weren't sure about a phrase on one of their student's papers. They posted their question and within days they had several correct answers.

2. If your area doesn't already have a Christian writers' support group, start one. I did just that in my county by sending flyers to local churches and running announcements in area newspapers. We meet one night a month at my church and any Christian writer is welcome to attend. We have a program (either a guest speaker or one of the members presents a topic of interest) and a critiquing session. Children attend our group and are involved. Occasionally we host a writing workshop. If you'd like more information about starting a group or hosting a writing workshop, contact me through my publisher.

to guide them into realizing the spiritual truths in their world. Spiritual laws are just as "real" as the natural laws God has set up. Our adventure is to run smack dab into them, rejoice in them, and apply them to our lives.

I'm sure you can see several spiritual applications in the three events listed above, but here are the themes I noticed right away:

1) The clock story:
   a) The clock served as a testimony to draw men to the store, so our testimonies must draw men to Jesus.
   b) The deceitful will be found out (Dad discovered the store owner's trick).
   c) Forgiveness is available as Dad dealt with this man very gently.
   d) Our time is not our own.

2) The necklace:
   a) Earthly riches pale in contrast with the cross.
   b) Store your wealth in heaven, not on earth.
   c) Don't cast your pearls before swine.
   d) But honor shall uphold the humble in spirit.

3) Lassie:
   a) Just as Lassie's eyes were on her master to obey him, so our eyes must be on our Master to obey Him.
   b) Lassie ministered to Timmy as her master directed her to — so we must be God's Hands of ministry here to those He chooses.
   c) God is the unseen Master of the servant — though you couldn't see Rudd on camera, his presence was made known through Lassie's behavior.
   d) We must practice obedience so it becomes our main motivation.

There are other applications other than those samples. Have fun with this concept. Look for God's Hand in your life. Guide your children to see the spiritual laws which balance our days. Apply them. Bring the verses and principles of the Bible to life. Then gently lead your children to communicate what they are learning — that's what devotionals and testimonies are all about. Seeing God and telling others what you've seen.

It is exciting work.

Story Opening

Where do we start? How does a writer know where a story begins? With some writers it's instinct, with others it takes practice. Still, it can be learned to some extent.

Do you start the story with the most exciting part (an attempted suicide) and then flashback to what brought the character to this window ledge? Or do you start with the sad girl begging for food?

Some of this will be determined by the genre and tone of the writing. Is it a fast-paced cliffhanger of a story? Or is it more a chick-flick-type of story? Is it obviously *biographical* about the main character? What is the theme? What is going to have the most impact on your reader and catch them, draw them into a story?

© Jill Bond / Homeschool Press, PO Box 254, Elkton, MD 21922

As with some of the other writing matters — developing good reading skills (literature analysis) improves writing skills — the more your children can appreciate the skill with which good writers introduce their story to their readers, the better their own openings will become.

Within the *favorites* section of this book, there is a lesson for recognizing and developing first lines. That lesson could be taught in tandem with this concept. Story opening goes beyond just the first line to encompass the beginning scene, how the story begins and exposition.

Over the span of the next year, ask your children to begin to notice how the books they read begin. Encourage them to keep a log of these beginnings rephrased in their own words. What did they learn about the character, setting, plot, and direction of the author within the first few pages (up to the end of the first chapter)?

A good opening does more than grab the reader into the story. It has to be more than a tacky tabloid headline for the rest of the book. A good opening transports the reader from their bedroom with the familiar posters and bookshelf to the advanced-civilization planet of Zietroc. The reader's landscape will change from their backyard to a green meadow on the Isle of Ireland in the year 485 AD. Instead of smelling the meatloaf you're cooking for dinner, your child, the reader, can smell the horse sweat, hay, and sweet milk of an Amish barn. Instead of being wrapped up cozy in the quilt your grandmother made, as your child enters a new novel, they feel the rough blanket and the hide of a donkey as they travel near a young couple, Mary and Joseph, on the way to pay taxes.

A good writer involves their reader in the lives of the main characters. A reader will begin to care about the hero with the first few pages.

A good writer must begin their story in such a way to minimize all the techniques, skills, and tools presented in this entire book and deliver a powerful opening. Because a good opening sets the mood, reveals the pacing, builds rapport, and entices the reader to read more.

Make your children aware of openings and how they improve what they are reading and writing.

Preparing the Preschooler

"Mommy, I just saw a bird," Bethany Kay says excitedly.

"Oh, how wonderful. What color was the bird?" I ask gently.

She thinks a second and says, "He was blue."

"Where was he?" I continue to prod.

"Over there," she answers and points to the fence.

I am preparing her to be a writer. Anytime you encourage your "pre-writer" to think through words, to observe more, to notice details, to be able to communicate what she sees or feels, you are training her to become a writer.

When Bethany Kay tells a story, I listen. I am interested. It isn't an act. Certainly she has a great many pauses, "and's," "ah's," and half sentences, but I know I'll work with her later about syntax and structure. Right now I want her to know her opinion, her observations, her feelings are important. I want her to feel comfortable communicating. I don't force her to "get to the point." (Unless it really is an emergency — "Just tell me who is bleeding and where they are!") I give her the luxury of rambling and pausing to search her mental lexicon for just the right word. I'm careful not to put my words in her mouth and beat her to the punch line. I ask questions. I want to draw her thoughts out of her and gradually expand her vocabulary.

We include her at read-aloud time. Her vocabulary, appreciation for literature, memory, and taste for story-telling will grow as she does. I'm very careful not to treat her as second-class. Her interest keeps growing.

We take dictation. Verbatim. She knows if I'm typing or editing her words. Here's a sample of a fax we sent daddy:

> "Hi Daddy. I love you Daddy and *supthing* I need to say to you Daddy and Daddy I love you so much Daddy — tonight Daddy! Daddy, and tomorrow we are going to pizza and learn to make it. Daddy how do you spell *Peace-zza* Hut and Daddy I so love you. The end."

She said almost all of that in one breath. I even tried to spell her enunciation so Daddy could "hear" his little girl. I can't think of a single relative who wouldn't love to receive a letter like that personalized for them.

I've even included typing from my preschoolers in letters — from "a;f;jawmaf" to "abc…." It gives them confidence and instills in them that writing is a fun idea. I don't tell them they are bad to want to "play on the 'pooter' (computer)." I just supervise them so they don't damage thousands of dollars worth of equipment.

I work with Bethany Kay on strengthening her vocabulary by asking questions. "You just used the word, 'huge.' Do you know what it means?" I'll ask in a very gentle, curious tone that isn't at all accusatory. You *don't* want to confront or imply: "How dare you use a word for which you don't know the meaning." I'll give her room to try and practice new words. Instead of thinking it is annoying, try to think that it is cute. Bethany Kay went an entire day using the word "exactly" in "exactly" every sentence. I didn't chastise her for redundancy — I encouraged her. She now has the word "exactly" firmly planted in her mental thesaurus, *and* more proper uses of it than I could have imagined possible.

We also accept the input of "pre-writers" in our stories. As we write our "Bond Family Adventures," naturally Bethany Kay wants to help. We listen to her suggestions and plug them in. We seek her out to help us with the "toddler dialogue." In her eyes, she's just as much a "writer" as the rest of us. Because she is.

Anything we do to develop her spirit will improve her outlook and her view of the world, not to mention her eternal life. She sees us pray all day. She prays with us. For her, Jesus is just as much a member of our family as we are. We're pleased when she turns her head to the side and looks at Jesus (where she thinks He's sitting) and says, "Jesus, what do you think about it?" Now if we just could get the rest of us to ask Him what He thinks about each step of our lives.

The Enabled Child

First of all, Trent is not "disabled" — he is enabled by God. He is labeled as autistic. He can do so much, so very much. I think he's the most intelligent member of our family. Our job is to reach him and help him to become everything God sees fit for him.

Basically, we're doing everything with him as we would a toddler or preschooler. I realize we don't get very much feedback, but I'm more interested in input. I'm trying to give him as much to store away as possible. We "do cartwheels" when he says, "lunch," or, "You all right?" Our job is to give him positive examples.

We read to him from a wide variety of quality materials. Also, we make "Trent Books" — books in which he is the main character (this is an excellent writing assignment for his older brothers). We illustrate the books with photographs of Trent and his world.

We show him excellent videos. There are dozens on the market with Christian teachings that will hold his attention. We make "Trent Videos" which are similar to early learning videos except

Trent's world is the focus. "This is Trent's pillow. It is green. It is in the shape of a rectangle." We'll write "p-i-l-l-o-w" on a small board and repeat the word "pillow" and spell it several times. We videotape things and "words" from all over his house and stage the narrative so we are saying his name in almost every sentence.

He must sit in his "position" during our Bible time and read-aloud time. Though he is physically there, it seems he is in another galaxy. He couldn't possibly be getting anything out of it — or so it seems. Then two weeks later he might say something verbatim from what we had read.

I don't say anything around him that I don't want him to hear or remember. I treat him and work with him just as I did with the others. The difference? With Reed and Stuart, I might have to tell them something twice for them to "get it." With Trent, it might take dozens and hundreds of times. He's worth the extra effort.

His body is autistic. His spirit isn't.

Trent's spirit is as healthy as yours or mine — and many times I'm convinced his is healthier. Trent loves Bibles. He has worn out several Bibles by loving them and carrying them around. Other children have "teddy bears;" Trent has Bibles. He finds Bibles in friends' homes. It is almost as if he has a built-in homing device; he can find the Bible. In one home, he went straight to their Bible. It was under a bed!

When a "normal" person writes a novel, it may or may not bring glory to God. Ah, but when Trent can type just one sentence — that will bring so much glory to God. And that is what we should all be about — doing all to the Glory of God.

Through my ministry and friendship with other "enabled families," I am constantly reaffirmed to see how much God loves and works through these children:

- the Down's syndrome child who has a hug for everyone;
- the mentally-challenged boy who has an incredible gift of discernment (he can sense in his spirit falseness and evil and has been proven correct many times);
- the deaf girl who can sign "I love you" and really mean it;
- the boy in his leg braces who limps down the aisle.

They aren't disabled. They are enabled by God.

The Way He Should Go

And hereby, let it be known that all
med students are required to take one hundred hours of law courses,
engineers must attend one hundred hours of music instruction,
every literature major must paint his way through one hundred hours of modern art,
home-makers must enroll in one hundred hours of political science labs, and
all rocket scientists must participate in one hundred hours of phys-ed courses.

That is preposterous! No student would ever graduate from college if he had to become proficient in every other major at a university.

Likewise, realize only some children are called to write as a profession. Other children should have a working knowledge of writing and be able to write well enough to excel in their calling.

© Jill Bond / Homeschool Press, PO Box 254, Elkton, MD 21922

Advantage, Game

We play games at our house. It's fun and very educational.

There are several commercial games we play which definitely help our children with their writing. Obviously, **Scrabble®** helps them with spelling and vocabulary — if it is played well. We've found **Taboo®** to be wonderful in helping them to process words and to think beyond the obvious. **TriBond®** is fun and develops their analytical skills. It helps them to see connections which will make their writing more vivid. *(Note: as I read through the TriBond® "triplets" I just skip the ones that don't fit in with our lifestyle and ones I know my children don't know. For instance, one of the answers was "husbands of Marilyn Monroe." I didn't give them the clues. They wouldn't know it. I just told them a little about the sad, sinful life of Miss Monroe. I'd rather they hear about her from me than from someone who admired her and thought she was beautiful.)* **Pictionary®** is excellent for strengthening their writing skills. Yes, it is a "drawing game," but it makes them handle words and think through situations. **Password®** is also a great game for children to manage their vocabularies. If you can't find a commercial game, make your own with strips of paper.

There might be dozens of other games which will aid your child in word processing skills. These are just the ones we have and do play.

We also make up games. Be creative.

You can make your own board game:
> Roll the dice. Go forward two. Draw a card. "Make-up a 'Fred' in ten seconds." Roll the dice. Go forward five. Draw a card. "Conjugate the word 'swim.'" Instead of "Chutes and Ladders®" call it "**Words and Letters**."

Do a spin-off of television games:
> "**Fix That Sentence**" — a spoof of "Name That Tune®." I can fix that sentence in nine words. Give them a sentence with a grammatical error, redundant words, or bore-bees. See if they can fix it within a certain word count.
> "**Wheel of Knowledge**" — a spoof of "Wheel of Fortune®," except use Bible verses or expressions you want them to know.
> "**What's my Character**" — a spoof of "What's My Line®." Have your children develop a character for a story and the other children try to guess the what, who, and when of that character.

Use card games to develop their writing:
> "**Spelling Rummy**" — like regular rummy, but they have to spell a specific word (you call it out) before they can draw a card. (Or something like that.)
> "**Crazy Mates**" — like regular Crazy Eights, but they have to come up with a synonym for a word you select.
> "**Go Alphabet Fishing**" — like regular Go Fish, but they have to ask for a word that starts with "b" if they want "two's." (c-3, d-4, etc.) (You can make this age-appropriate by requiring two- or three-syllable words, etc.)

These are just to prompt you to think about converting regular games into "Writing Games."

Note: I also think that working jigsaw puzzles is a wonderful writing activity. When you realize the attention to detail your child has to have to be able to finish the puzzle, you'll make the connection to writing. A writer has to be very observant.

A Writer's Mind

In summary, writing goes beyond words on paper. A writer is constantly "tasting words for their flavor." He's adding words to his mental thesaurus. He's collecting characters for future stories. He's listening to dialogue for colloquialisms. He's building plot, suspense, and drama. He's testing plot twists for plausibility.

The Christian writer is doing all that, also. But he should be studying Scripture, humbling himself before God, maturing in the Faith, and obeying His Master. Christian writers should work out all their story ideas with their Father, prove them through the Word, and confirm them with Godly counsel.

Every day a Christian writer's mind should become more and more like the mind of Christ.

Writing
to
God's
Glory

Teacher's Guide for the
Writing Well Section

Teacher's Guide for the Writing Well Section

The Process

This section is self-explanatory. It explains the mechanics of writing. Each student lesson is complete and I can't think of anything else that you as a teacher might need to teach these lessons. You might want to link each of these "Process" lessons to a story your students are writing and have them fill in the *Ideas* worksheets as they go. (*e.g., Fill in Worksheet #3, Main Character Development, page 289) as you work with the "Casting" section on page 143.)*

Note:

I mention right side and left side of the brain in these lessons only to encourage the students to be both logical and creative. Those terms are used in their popular connotations, not in their precise medical definitions. The concept of these two aspects of who we are as human beings is a popular theme in literature — the "battle" between heart and mind — the seeming disparity between the two hemispheres of our cerebral cortex. It is understood by some in this realm of study that the right hemisphere's job is melody, visual patterns, and emotion, while the left side is our verbal and logic center.

In my own family, we have learned by research and personal experiences that the right side of the brain controls the left side of the body and left side of the brain controls the right side of the body. My father had a massive stroke in the right hemisphere and now the left side of his body is paralyzed. Trent, our third son, is autistic as a result of some "brain damage" after a series of vaccinations. Stuart, my second son, had a mixed dominance problem which, once corrected, has helped his learning immeasurably. I'm not referring to that here — not right or left-handedness, brain-damage, or dominance issues — though I speak and write about those topics in other environments.

For this application, I use the terms left and right brain to tap into the idea that a writer must use the logic (reasoning) and the emotional/creative (heart) aspects of who they are. I find this idea that there are different facets of how we act and think referred to in the Bible in several incidents; in *1 Samuel 2:35 — **And I will raise me up a faithful priest, that shall do according to that which is in mine heart and in my mind: and I will build him a sure house; and he shall walk before mine anointed for ever.** And in *Luke 10:27 — **And he answering said, Thou shalt love the Lord thy God with all thy heart, and with all thy soul, and with all thy strength, and with all thy mind; and thy neighbour as thyself.***

Please don't misunderstand that I am putting any limits on how *God* can heal, by-pass, or use us in any way. I've learned enough from my ministry with so-called brain-damaged people, that *God* does "over-ride" any of man's theories about the brain and what man is capable of doing. (Aside: I don't believe in trying to label, classify, or pigeon-hole people into man-defined personality types, learning styles, or so-called disabilities beyond anything specifically taught in the Bible, e.g., that there are two types of humans: wheat and tares, sheep and goats, or redeemed and unredeemed. And with those, I dare not judge who is what.)

Why did I separate this into two parts: "Process" and "Features"? I felt like The "Process" was the nuts and bolts of getting the words down — the foundation, the process. But then there are tricks of the trade which improve writing. I lumped these lessons into this section: "Features." They aren't grammar, but techniques, methods, and styles which your children can master to give their writing that professional touch.

Features

Here are a few comments to help you present the lessons to your child.

Checkmate in 5000 Words or Less (page 153):

If you can, act this one out. I often stage the chess match in my classes for the drama of it. Some children will appreciate this lesson — the ones who love chess. Others can understand the point even if they don't understand chess.

Emotions: Can You Use Them? (page 155):

They'll use this lesson as they fill in their idea worksheets on their major and minor characters (pages 289-292). Talk with them through this. Ask a lot of questions.

Story, She Wrote (page 157):

Before you get into this lesson, read a mystery (or rent a video). As you read (or watch) involve your children. Get them guessing about "who done it." Then introduce this lesson to them. It will have a place to plant. (There are wonderful Christian mystery stories available — I am not telling you to read "blood and guts murders" to your young children.)

> There is one video available which jokes about exposition: *The Great Muppet Caper*. In one of the early scenes, Lady Holliday goes on and on about her brother. Miss Piggy asks, "Why are you telling me all of this?" Lady Holliday states that it is "plot exposition" and it has to go somewhere. *(The Great Muppet Caper, Jim Henson Video™ © 1993)*

You might want to rent that video and show it to your children and talk about exposition. Somehow the reader needs to know most of what the writer knows about a character. It is the writer's challenge to inform the reader without belittling the reader and still allow the story to have some mystery to it.

Conflict (page 159):

Encourage your students to come up with their own answers. When I did this exercise with my own children they had dozens of answers within minutes. Come back and do this exercise again in six months. Also, as you study your Bible with them, ask them about the conflict. See if they are learning and can recognize who is battling whom.

Subplot (page 161):

With this lesson it's best if you and your child are both familiar with the novel they are analyzing. Assign one if you have to. You need to make sure they are getting it.

Shredding (page 163):

There are several ways to introduce this lesson:

1) Link it to actual shredders: watch a shredder in action at a place of business, watch a demonstration at an office supply store, or show a picture of one in an advertisement flyer.
2) Have them cut and paste words from magazines or newspapers to make a few sentences.
3) Have them read newsletter or magazine articles and tell them to cut or mark through words (or sentences) which are superfluous.

"Shredding" is a vital part of writing. Every writer needs to edit his work. Your job is to require it in such a way that it doesn't undermine your child's confidence.

Would this analogy help? Because they have to brush their teeth each day doesn't mean they are filthy people. Brushing is something that has to be done and it isn't reflective on how "clean of an eater one is." Shredding is, in a way, like flossing and brushing. It has to be done for proper "literary hygiene." It isn't something just amateur writers have to do. Just as flossing and brushing have to be done each day, shredding (editing) has to be done on each assignment.

Follow-through (page 165):

Before you get into this lesson, can you attend a ball game, a golf tournament, or go in the front yard and swing a few? Talk through the swing-through — the difference between the bunt and hard hit. The lesson then will have fertile ground in which to grow when you present it. Think about it as momentum.

Angle (page 167):

I have so much fun with this lesson. Pretend you or one of your children is the pilot, the other is the tower, and "radio" each other. This is one I do with groups and the parents even get all involved as they try to think of a new angle for the David story or the football game. You can get a great deal of yardage out of the lesson. I come back to it over and over again and bring it up with many other "situations" which could be stories. When we roll through the football example, I add a new spectator each round and close each "round" by asking, "Is the spoiled daughter seeing the game any differently than the producer, the color guy, the announcer, the fan, the line-backer, the quarterback, the cheerleader, or the boy?" Of course, I'm all out of breath. I let different children "take it for me this time" as we add on a new spectator — like the guy piloting the blimp. The kids love this. It's a game as they try to remember the pattern and series of spectators in the right order and all before they have to take a breath. (We even try to give arm/hand movements for each spectator — it is hard to keep from laughing, so go ahead and laugh with your children.)

The Foreshadow Knows (page 169):

I'm not old enough to remember the old radio show, *The Shadow*, but I know enough to know of it. I understand some of the old radio programs are now available on audiotape and your library might stock them. It might be fun to introduce this lesson to your children via a radio drama. Tell them what you know about the old radio shows. Ask your mother or an older relative or friend to tell them.

In *Love Story*, a best seller thirty years ago — though I thoroughly do NOT recommend the book — you will find an example of foreshadowing. The author, Erich Segal, tells us on the first page that the girl dies. There is no suspense. Just pages of obnoxious characters until the end when you "wish they were all dead." I still don't know why it was so popular, as the characters were all so crude and "unlovable." But he sold millions of books and it was made into a movie. I only refer to it to demonstrate that there is good foreshadowing and bad foreshadowing, and then there is foreshadowing that will sell to a sin-filled world.

The Ingredients — Words (page 171):

Bake a cake. Bake cookies. Use recipes which have basically the same ingredients. As they cook, ask your students questions about the differences in the two batters. Then present the lesson. They'll listen happily as they munch. There are dozens of possible answers — here are a few:

gargantuan	huge	prodigious
bigoted	provincial	discerning
child abuse	reprimand	discipline
starving	hungry	self-controlled
know-it-all	knowledgable	professional
compulsive	involved	sincere
hyper	energetic	vivacious
fanatic	fan	enthusiast
domineering	commanding	charismatic

Word meanings change. Words mean different things to different people in different contexts. The word "discriminating" could be very negative in the text of a civil rights march, but is meant as a compliment in the pages of *Gourmet* magazine. "Caring" now has the connotation of false piety and *wimpy emotion* as in the context of election campaigns. As always, teach your children to keep in mind who their readers are and what a word will mean to that particular reader.

The Batter — Sentences and Paragraphs (page 173):

This lesson may be a little too advanced for some children. But even for your younger ones you can introduce them to the concept. Older children can test others' writings. Have them check out Mark Twain or Arthur Conan Doyle or Dr. Seuss and compare results from their own word count study.

Expanding Universes (page 177):
Here is the answer to the nine-dot problem:

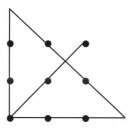

There are dozens of possibilities for the "Pair Exercise." Interestingly, the first pair (sandpaper, light bulbs) was presented to a group of developers and they came up with the laser. Here are some possible "links."

Pair 2:	Jesse carefully braided the soft stems of his infant avocado plant. One day it would be a beautiful trunk of an avocado tree.
	Maria, with her neatly plaited black braids, sold avocados from a basket in the open-air market in Puerto Vallarta.
Pair 3:	Becky had a pet bird named Bubbles and loved to stroke his brightly-colored-feathers.
	The children all laughed as the clown jumped out of the cake amid a flurry of feathers, balloons, and bubbles.
Pair 4:	We saw a beautiful quilt on our vacation in the mountains. It was made using the "wedding ring" pattern.
	Carved on her wedding ring was an interesting design. The pattern looked like a setting sun coming over a range of mountains.
Pair 5:	The garage was a mess! Billy had tried to make his dad a Father's Day gift, but had only badly sawed wood and broken glass to show for his efforts.
	Louis Comfort Tiffany fingered the broken glass and wood. He had an idea and reached for his soldering iron.
Pair 6:	"Here comes trouble," the teacher laughed as Billy walked into the room.
	"I'm having stomach trouble and it hurts when I laugh," he told his doctor.

Adjectives and Preservatives (page 179):
I was most sincere when I wrote this lesson. Even if your children don't ever enter a contest, they must start writing down their experiences. At the very least they should keep a Praise Log listing the mighty works God is doing in their lives and answers to prayer. Just do it!

Above Reproach (page 183):

This lesson grew out of some observations of mine. I've been very discouraged to hear Christian moms at book fairs say, "I'll buy the book and then we'll copy it for you." They must know they are doing something illegal and beneath reproach or why would they be whispering and talking over to the side? They are stealing. Take away the smock-dress and white shoes and they might as well be planning a major "job" in a shack along the water front. They are planning a heist. In this caper, they are heisting the "goods" of the writer, the publisher, and the bookstore employees/owners.

When you buy a book you're not just buying ink on paper — or else all books would be sold by weight and size. No, you're buying the words; the hundreds of hours the author and editors put into it; the years (lifetimes) of expertise which the author poured into the book; the risk, capital, legalities, overhead, printing, layout, design, equipment, discounts of the publisher; the overhead, labor, location, and advice of the bookstore. To copy (beyond what is allowed in the copyright statement) is stealing. Please teach your children this.

They may see another woman from your church or support group copy a page. They may see their friends working from copied pages. Please rear your children above reproach. They might be confused, "But Mrs. Smith is a nice lady and she says it saves her money to copy books rather than buy them." Here's an answer, "It would save me money to steal groceries, but I'm not going to do it."

I was recently among a group of ladies, whom I love. They were talking about a great curriculum out now — but it was rather expensive. So, they were going to have the public library order a copy, then they each could photocopy it and save about twenty dollars a book. No one thought it was wrong. They thought it was clever and "being a good steward of God's provision for their family." As lovingly as I could, I explained the copyright laws of our land. They didn't know. Most of them thanked me for telling them.

Your children also must give credit where credit is due. It is wrong to claim something as your own work when it isn't.

This happened to me. I started getting calls from people asking me how "XYZ" magazine could use my material. So, I got a copy of the magazine. Yes, it had some material from one of my books with no notation that it was not the writer's (of the article) own work. I wrote the publisher and the writer asking them to print a clarifying statement in another issue since our testimonies are important. I had several independent evaluators check the correspondence. They all agreed I approached this publisher in love and with a calm, sweet spirit. The writer called me immediately with such a lovely spirit. She was sorry. I forgave her. It was a positive experience. The publisher of the magazine turned into a viper. I was appalled. The writer did print a correcting paragraph so our testimonies were vindicated. The publisher has since been revealed as a phony and a fraud. She had stolen others' works, removing their copyrights and putting in her own. To my knowledge, the writer is no longer associated in any way with that publisher. (Don't ask me who it was, I won't tell. And please don't try to guess. You probably never heard of the magazine, anyway.)

Kathy Henderson cites an eye-opening example of the damage plagiarism can cause. As she was judging a contest, all the judges were impressed with the quality of entries. She came across an entry which was merely two chapters from a published novel by Dorothy Haas. The judging atmosphere changed to suspicion. All the entrants suffered. The whole story is printed on page 86 of Mrs. Henderson's book, *Market Guide for Young Writers,* published by Writer's Digest Books. I'd highly recommend you get a copy for yourself and request your public library to carry a copy also.

© Jill Bond / Homeschool Press, PO Box 254, Elkton, MD 21922

Why? (page 185):

Writers must be deliberate. There aren't enough spare pages and resources to waste text on unnecessary words. Every part of this book has a purpose. I can give an answer for "why?" for each sentence. Many times I wrote in such a way as to make the point by the style, phrasing, and juxtaposition of ideas (example: I deliberately had fun varying the word count and sentence count in the lesson "Words"). Not that I'm the example, but I didn't want to give your children cause to say, "Why are we doing this?" As a student and a teacher I suffered through many different writing texts and I'm sure the answer to that question for those texts would have been: "To keep busy, of course!"

Obviously, I love children's writings. I'll allow some unjustifiable sentences in a young child's work. It makes it cute and very believable (that a child wrote it). But as children mature, his writing should also. While I allowed Stuart to keep the clown in his *Blue* Story, it should be cut in any final or polished version. The clown distracts. It is not needed for the flow of the story, or else he'd have to give the clown more of a link to the story-line. He'd have to justify the clown's existence in his story. Doesn't that sound mercenary? I am so happy we don't have to justify our existence in the real world. But then God created each of us. He knows the "Why." That's good enough for me.

SAM — Simile, Allegory, Metaphor (page 187):

One of the best all-time allegories is *The Pilgrim's Progress*. If you haven't read it with your child, do. Have them go on SAM hunts. One humorous line I remember related to SAM is from Catherine Marshall's book, *A Man Called Peter*. She wrote that her husband went overboard once with his metaphoric prayers as he prayed among some large casement windows:

"Oh, Lord, open the casement windows of our souls, so that the fresh winds of Galilee may blow in and recharge the batteries of our souls. AMEN."
[McGraw-Hill Book Company, Inc. © MCMLI Catherine Marshall]

But misuse for him was rare, usually he developed pictures to create understanding in his listeners' minds: "He has a gift for word pictures, for little dramas and folksy incidents." It's a wonderful book to read with your children. Recently we heard it dramatized on Christian radio. I'd like to buy those tapes if I could ever track them down. For as many years as you have your children to teach, look with them for SAM and point them out. Their writing and reading will improve. Jesus was the Master at this. He used SAM repeatedly. He knows how our minds work. He wants us to learn, to understand, and to respond. We should strive to be like Him, don't you think?

Fact or Fiction (page 189):

"Locinda" lived in a dorm room a few doors down the hall from me. She was in danger of being kicked out of school — she *had* to get her grades up. I started tutoring her. Her freshman English professor gave her the assignment of writing her autobiography. She was mortified. I started asking her questions. "Who you want to be tells us a great deal about you. Where do you want to be in ten years?" She started telling me that she wanted to be a comedienne. I reviewed the parameters of the assignment and started drawing out of her an A- plus paper. I didn't write the paper, all I did was ask questions and encourage her. She had the talent — she hadn't been given the opportunity to use it. She wrote the paper as if it were ten years in the future — she was the celebrity she wanted to be and was a guest on the *Tonight Show*. She answered every aspect of the assignment, but she did it from the perspective of who she was on the inside:

> Television Host: "Locinda, your humor is so refreshing. Have you been like this since you were a child?"
> Locinda: "Why, yes, Johnny. I was always the class clown…."

The professor loved the paper and told her she had the freshest approach to that assignment he'd seen. Most of the other students wrote, "I was born on — "

Your children can write their autobiographies and give so much glory to God. As Christians we are writing our testimony and His story in our lives. Encourage them to write the story from a variety of angles. The family dog might write it in first person narrative. It might be a future look back at now. It might be a "dream" of where they want to be. Do your children have a vision of where God is directing them, of what their lives could become if they surrender to His loving Guidance?

Additional Assignment:
Document that vision with a "future time 'autobiography.'"

Reminder:
Encourage your children to pour as much energy into their non-fiction as they would their fiction stories.

Oink, Oink, Purr, Purr (page 191):

Before you start this lesson with your children, find a child's picture book in which the author uses some onomatopoeia. Read it out to them just like "story-time" when they were little. Ask them to imagine they are three years old and are hearing the story for the first time. What effect do the sounds of the words have on them?

Before you explain alliteration, find some examples in the books, articles, and tapes around your house. "Ponderosa Participles" is an example. Advertisers use alliteration to make their slogan easier to identify. Do you have any book titles which are alliterative?

Likewise, have a few real life examples of parallelism on hand as you teach this concept.

There are examples of parallelism throughout this book, including some in the **Student's Pages:**

Page 145	The Process, Section C, Setting — Drifting
Page 193	Features, Section S, Style — several lists at beginning of lesson
Page 197	Features, Section U, Thick Skin and Open Heart — There are hours…
Page 317	Favorites, Section 6, Words — For example…

Style (page 193):

I designed this lesson to ease your and your children's minds of the pressure of "developing a writing style." Their style will develop. If you keep drawing them closer and closer to the Throne of God, He will work through their distinct personality to reflect His touch on their lives.

© Jill Bond / Homeschool Press, PO Box 254, Elkton, MD 21922

Please be careful how you present this lesson, that they don't interpret the comparison of styles as any form of judgment. This is not a "I like this and I think that is *gross*" exercise. This lesson should be taught so that they can learn to appreciate the wide range of styles that please Him. One Godly woman might like Queen Anne furniture and write poetry. Another Godly woman might like contemporary furniture and write humor. God loves both and can bless both.

Additional: This lesson may give you an opportunity to discuss the world's concept of "diversity" (meaning anything goes and sin is acceptable) versus the Christian idea of *love the sinner and hate the sin.* One person's preference for a four-wheel drive vehicle in lieu of a station wagon is not the same thing as one person's preference for buddha in lieu of Jesus Christ.

Don't Feed the Flesh (page 195):

"Don't we all want to live Ozzie and Harriet-type lives?" I'd heard "paradise" described in terms of the Nelson family so often, I tuned in when some of their television shows were re-aired. I was appalled. Every show I watched (about five) glamorized lying and deceitfulness. Ricky had lied to a girl and had two dates for the same night. Instead of being honest, he fooled them all — ha, ha. I wasn't laughing. The shows, though light and airy, free of profanity, and showing an intact family, fed to the flesh of their viewers. They made lying humorous and cute.

That is one example of feeding to the flesh which is subtle. Teach your children to be aware of ever making light of sin or of making a good person the schmuck of the story-line.

Also, be watchful and pray about your children's writing. Is there a repeated theme in their stories? Perhaps they are dealing with some besetting sin or judgmental spirit they have about this recurring idea. By studying your children's writing you might have a better idea of how to best pray for them. It might give you opportunities to help them figure out in their own minds the right way to view a situation.

Guide them away from enjoying developing the unsaved character's dialogue or actions. Just as we don't want our children playing with demon dolls, we don't want them reveling in the sin of their characters. In the Bible, the sin of David and Bathsheba is not given in detail. We know just enough to know it was sin and God dealt with David about it. An ill-grounded writer would be tempted to wallow in the sin and develop it for paragraphs. A grounded writer would communicate the sin as briefly as possible and concentrate on the rebukes, recovery, and repentance.

We, at the Bonding Place, receive a great deal of mail because of our ministries. Once in a while we receive a "doozy" of a letter. One of those came in an envelope with no return address. It was three pages long. It requested prayer for a wayward Christian sister. The prayer request could have been communicated in two sentences. It seemed the person requesting the prayer was enjoying the retelling of this sister's sin. I never finished reading it. It was that explicit. It was a prayer request which was feeding the flesh of the writer and some of the readers.

Guide your children away from feeding the flesh of others and themselves with their writing.

Thick Skin and Open Heart (page 197):

Because I'm often asked about writing as a profession, I decided to add this section to answer some of the most repeated questions. A different writer would have given different answers. I have several friends who are also authors. If I were to mention their names, you'd recognize them immediately. Many of them have been on *Focus on the Family, 700 Club,* and some of the secular talk shows like *Oprah* and *Donahue.* Also, I am friends with quite a few editors of magazines.

When we talk, I ask questions — some of the same ones I answer here. Though my answers are phrased with my own words and experiences, the thoughts behind them encompass many of my friends' experiences, also.

I alluded to Mr. Newt Gingrich's famous book deal not to tempt your children with greed for money, but to stress that deals like that might happen once a century. Just as we think giving children false expectations of multi-million dollar pro-sports contracts — how many little boys aspire to be the next Michael Jordan because of the big bucks? — it would be equally wrong to flaunt dollar signs at potential writers. My friends and I are writing in obedience to God, not for greed. Yes, some writers might write out of their greed, but then they aren't writing for God's Glory. (Note: I'm not saying writers have to take a vow of poverty; after all a *workman is worthy of his hire* and God can bless his faithful children in many ways.)

A friend recently told me that the average published book sells only 1200 copies. When you figure in all the books that sell hundreds of thousands of copies, that means some book sales are in the hundreds. So, even if a book makes it to print (which is about 1:100 — one book published for every 100 submitted)[1] the odds are against it being a best-seller. That is why I tried to stress that our rewards are greater than sales volumes and royalty checks because our reward is serving Him who is worthy of praise. (Though those royalty checks are nice when they happen, we recognize The Source of those sales.)

I think my writing friends would want your children to know that writing is writing: hundreds of solitary hours at a keyboard. But it is our calling and we "don't have a choice." In the same way, God has called some people to sing — and sing they must. Some of your children may have a *Writer's Call*. Their motivation shouldn't be the parameters of the writing profession, it's God's touch on their lives. I want them to realize that sometimes (most of the time) the earthly rewards are minimal — they have to do it for the True rewards — out of a loving and thankful heart to their Creator.

---

1.   Jeff Quinn, *In the Beginning Was the Word, and the Word Was Published*, Fort Worth Star – Telegram, Final AM, December 3, 1995, Page 1 — Life Section.

Writing to God's Glory / Teacher's Pages

© Jill Bond / Homeschool Press, PO Box 254, Elkton, MD 21922

Writing to God's Glory

to

God's

Glory

Teacher's Guide for the Craftsmen Exercises

Teacher's Guide for the Craftsmen Exercises

Craftsmen exercises are designed to help fine-tune writing.

Remember, the emphasis is on the writing, not the grammar.

Use these exercises to improve the work, not to create it.

You might want to tackle a *Craftsmen* exercise once a week or whatever fits your schedule.

I'd recommend you go ahead and look through them so you'll be familiar with each lesson. The lessons are not in any particular order. In other words, they don't have to complete "Ponderosa Participles" before they are ready to start "Inventive Writers". Each lesson stands on its own. You should teach the lessons according to your child's needs.

Why are the lessons "cute"?

Because grammar is boring enough. I've seen many writing programs in which grammar is taught in such a *Pit and the Pendulum* approach that it is a wonder anyone knows how to handle an antecedent properly.

The object is for the children to know how to write properly, not necessarily to be able to quote the "chapter and number" from a style book. I have numerous "style" books and some of those authors disagree about what is proper.

Purpose

Each *Craftsmen* serves several purposes:

1) To involve the student in the exercise
2) To teach a grammar concept
3) To make the rule easy to remember
4) To demonstrate the "why" of the principle
5) To show the students, by example, how creative and fun writing can be
6) To relate Biblical ideas to each lesson

1) **To involve the student in the exercise** — Have you ever read a book on writing which was a monument to bad writing? It's as if a writer must ostracize all rules of creative writing to teach grammar. Forget about writing excellent openings, memorable characters, and caring about the reader — or so it seems.

Each *Craftsmen* exercise was styled to involve the student. They may seem "corny." That was planned. As each student reads the exercises, he can get into the lesson.

2) **To teach a grammar concept** — Eventually, without teaching the concept, there wouldn't be a lesson. Each *Craftsmen* does teach the student a rule or an idiom of our English language.

3) **To make the rule easy to remember** — How many rules of English do you remember from your school days? That many! Mmm!

One trick to memorization, according to memory experts, is to form a mental picture of what you are trying to memorize. Supposedly, the more bizarre the image, the easier it is to memorize.

Okay, some of the *Craftsmen* are a stretch — on purpose. The children will remember "Bore-bees", "Nitro-Commas", and "Which Hunt" because the lessons have ties to something. Each lesson is designed to help the child remember the concept.

4) **To demonstrate the "why" of the principle** — If you know why you are doing something, somehow the pain doesn't seem so bad. If you can understand the reason, you are more apt to comply. Do you floss your teeth each day for the fun of it, or because it is a most excellent way of protecting your smile? Admittedly, some rules of grammar are about as much fun as flossing your teeth — the students can get through the lesson if they can see the point.

5) **To show the students, by example, how creative and fun writing can be** — Example: Remember "Purpose One"(a few paragraphs back), and the boring writer? Those writers not only lose their audience to, "Mom, I'd rather take out the trash than diagram another sentence," but they propagate the myth: "Do as I say, not as I do." I try to instill the idea of "alive" writing by taking one of the most boring topics on earth and making it fun, interesting, and meaningful — as an example.

   Your student can memorize a long list of rules of capitalization or he can become a secret agent for the CIA and hunt out Red defectors who want to become Capitalists deploying his Operatives. If we can make capitalization more enjoyable by word play and imagination, just think what your child can do with writing a story about your last family reunion!

6) **To relate Biblical ideas to each lesson** — Most importantly, *of course*, is the *big why* of what we're doing. Each *Craftsmen* exercise teaches an important lesson which goes far beyond moving a pencil across a page. The Lord touches everything we do, say, feel, and are. Don't we want our children to see the *Lord's* side of it? Can they understand how much *He* loves us and shows us this love every day through His involvement in our lives?

   It is very important for the Christian writer to be able to understand and convey Biblical truth in his writing. Sometimes it may be subtle as in the book of Esther in which God is not mentioned by word, but the entire book speaks of Him. Or it may be spelled out as in the Gospel of John.

   So, my goal was to not only tie the lessons into a Biblical truth for the sake of the learning, but to subtly lead by example. Biblical truth is happening all around us. We just have to see it — see the relevance to our lives and communicate it to others.

Reminder

Please teach these *Craftsmen* lessons as tools to improve your children's writing, to make it more understandable, and to make it work.

Don't teach these *Craftsmen* exercises as if they were *the* writing itself.

Just as parsley, a color-coordinated napkin, and spices add to a meal but aren't the food — so *Craftsmen* exercises aren't the writing. They're the spices — the techniques.

Specifics on Each Lesson

1) More Power

"Fred" is fun. Adults and children have been having so much fun coming up with "Freds." Many families come up with a "Fred" each week. There are hundreds of dozens of "Freds" — as many as your child's imagination can create.

Here are some "Freds" others have created:

- A knight in King Arthur's court
- A police dog sniffing for narcotics
- A goldfish swimming in a bowl
- A baby crawling

- An astronaut on a space lab, year 2056
- A movie actor on a set
- A baker of wedding cakes

There are a few more examples in the *Favorites* section. *Example*

At first, just have your students create "Freds" sentence-free. In other words, don't place a big emphasis on the sentence structure. Place the emphasis on their coming up with a distinct "Fred" with a particular job. Ask questions to encourage them to make "Fred" as specific as possible.

Once they've created a "Fred," they'll want to make more. We play "Give me a Fred." I ask my children to "Give me a Fred" and they come up with a bumbling nerdish character headed to audition for a he-man role in a movie — or…. (Of course, don't forget "Fredericas.")

2) Beware the Bore-bees

This is an important concept of good writing. When you present this lesson, use your best Peter Lorre voice to talk about bore-bees — those insipid little creatures who sneak into your writing and render it boring.

Encourage your children to hunt for those little bore-bees and to rid the world of them — as much as possible.

Remember, some "to be" verbs are necessary. They just aren't necessary in every sentence. When a professional editor picks up a written article and starts seeing "to be" verbs, he'll stop reading, realizing he's dealing with a very amateur writer.

Find examples of good writing and show your children the lack of bore-bees. As you read aloud to them, point out the way in which the author packs a punch in his sentences by using power verbs instead of "to be" verbs.

After they have written their work — on the second or third draft — help them to hunt for bore-bees and have them rewrite the sentences.

Examples for some of the sentences are in the *Favorites* section. If your student can't think of a way to reword the sentence, skip it and go to another. Come up *Example* with your own sentence which they can rewrite. Use real examples from their writing.

On the flip side — don't become a bore-bee snob. Be patient with others who are still learning about bore-bees.

3) Less is More

This exercise should be mandatory for every government bureaucrat — don't you think? Why not say something easily?

This exercise is needed by children, as I haven't read a paper yet which couldn't be cut — for the better.

There is balance, though. Don't turn their work into sterile "Just the facts, Ma'am" articles. Just don't allow them to use three words when one well-placed word would better serve their readers.

 Each of the exercises has several possible answers. Ask them to explain the "why" for the word cut. You'll like this exercise.

After you finish these (and only do those appropriate to your student's ability) try editing published material. Pick up your newspaper and you'll find several articles which could be improved.

4) Railroad Crossing

The object of this lesson is "that" your students learn the proper use of the word "that."

Not only should the student slash out the extra "thats," they may want to rewrite the entire sentence.

The exercise is absurd. Purposely so. We want the children to "hear" how ridiculous "that" can become.

After this exercise, they'll be slashing "thats" everywhere. As with many of these exercises, follow-up is important.

Encourage them to edit their old written work and to look for extra "thats" in published articles. Lesson 22 — "Which Hunt" — is related, as it also deals with "that."

5) Time Travel

Students enjoy this lesson. Start off by asking them to think about time travel. Ask them to list stories, movies, shows, and books which "play" with time travel. Here are some titles students in our classes have come up with: *Flying House, Superbook, Superman, Quantum Leap, Hardy Boys, A Wrinkle in Time, Time Bandits, Darien Lambert, A Connecticut Yankee in King Arthur's Court, A Spaceman in King Arthur's Court*, and, of course, *The Bible*.

If rewriting the exercise story is too difficult, then have them rewrite any paragraphs from another book or article.

On page 309, I've included an example of my own children's rewrite of an article which was published as well as some other examples of ways to rewrite the exercise story.

This exercise is excellent to do at least once a month with your children. Stop during your read-aloud time and have them rewrite a paragraph into a different tense. It will improve their writing skills. Give it a try, you'll be pleased.

Look for time travel in the Bible. This is a wonderful opportunity to talk about time and God. He is timeless. He created time. He transcends time. He gave some of his prophets a peek at the future. You'll enjoy this part of the lesson as your children begin to grasp the magnificence of God.

© Jill Bond / Homeschool Press, PO Box 254, Elkton, MD 21922

6) The Boy Who Cried "!"

This lesson is pretty much self-explanatory. This is another common error I see in newsletters tabloids, and children's writing. They need to learn to use "!" when it is appropriate. Give them the encouragement to use the words to build the excitement, not just the punctuation.

Too many writers make up for weak writing by trying to use "!" to make the point. Teach your children to do better than that.

There are no right answers for these exercises. The writer decides on the emphasis. Remember in most cases, the surrounding sentences determine the emphasis. For instance the "Help!" could use the "!," but if four other sentences in the same paragraph have the "!," then it might defeat the emphasis.

7) Auntie Cindy

Please note that by using *The Wizard of Oz* for this parody, I am not endorsing the movie or book. I chose it because: 1) many children are very familiar with the story, and 2) analysis of the convoluted brilliance of L. Frank Baum can help you teach your children about theme and how important it is for Christians to write. (Think of all the people whom Baum influenced with his warped view of reality.)

This lesson might serve you well to reintroduce the concept of themes. The book (or movie), *The Wizard of Oz,* serves as a prime example with which to talk through the idea of themes or meanings of stories. A young child might only see the "non-theme" or obvious, planted theme of "There's no place like home." The more advanced child will "see" how "water" defeated the evil witch and could make the analogy to the Water of Life — Christ — defeating death and satan. The astute child will recognize the theme of the *Wizard* series as the author entwined it into the plots — one which meshes perfectly with New Age philosophy — the "godhead," the "power" was in us all along — we just have to become self-actualized and call upon the innate power within each of us, and by the way, "God is a fraud."

I don't recommend you force the term "antecedent" on your children. If they are studying for a standardized test, then, yes, they need to know the term. Otherwise, just present this lesson as a *Craftsmen* to enable them to help their reader better understand what they are trying to say. ("They" in the last sentence refers to your students; confusing wasn't it? It would have been better if I had written "…what the writer is trying to say." Ah, now YOU are getting the hang of it.)

There are several ways your children can rewrite the three paragraphs and still make the meaning clear to the reader. Your job is to verify their work so each "Dorothy" gets back to her "Auntie Cindy."

It is a good idea to show them how easily the meaning of the paragraphs could be misconstrued:

1) Who ate the lunch? Was it Susan and Billy? Or, was it the whales and dolphins?
2) Who finished 33-1/2 hours later — the museum tour guide or Lindbergh?
3) Whose chest heaved — the intern's or the patient's. Was this a medical examination test on the intern to see if he knew his cardiac procedures, or was it a cardiac test on a patient?

The way the paragraphs are written, any of those meanings are valid. As you point out the absurdity of the writings, your students will begin to appreciate the importance of linking pronouns to their antecedents.

8) Peace Talks

This is a basic lesson. You've probably heard it taught as verb agreement. How boring. Role-play with your children as if they are ambassadors to a Department of State summit meeting and they are seeking agreements. Picture a round table with miniature flags, translators, country name-place cards, and many protocol specialists flittering around to make everyone feel important. If *you* make it a game, they will enjoy this exercise and learn the lesson for life. They will remember the reason verbs and nouns must agree: to avoid global thermal nuclear war — right?!?

1) Billy rides in
   his father's new car.
2) They play on the
   computer game.
3) You write well.
4) Susan and Jane go
   to church together.
5) The Harris Family
   has seven children.
   (Family is singular.)

The bracketed words on the following chart are only one way of wording the answer. Encourage your child to use a variety of articles and pronouns.

Plural Noun	Plural Verb	Singular Noun	Singular Verb
They	write	[He]	writes
[The] boys	sang	The boy	sang
Horses	whinny	[My] horse	whinnies
Bunnies	hop	[His] bunny	hops
Politicians	gloat	The politician	gloats
Preachers	laugh	The preacher	laughs
Doctors	operate	[My] doctor	operates
Girls	play	[A] girl	plays
Parents	sing	A parent	sings

9) Article Attractions

The first part of this lesson — regarding the articles "a" and "an" — is so very basic. Your children must master this grammar rule. Drill them until it becomes automatic.

The second half of this lesson is considered more of a fine-tuning lesson than a basic lesson. If your student can master this lesson, his writing will be even more polished.

In addition to this lesson, examine with your children several published articles, e.g., look in today's newspaper, your favorite magazines, and several short stories or books. Find examples where the writer polished his work correctly, and ones you could improve by using this lesson of placing the adjective closer to the noun.

© Jill Bond / Homeschool Press, PO Box 254, Elkton, MD 21922

When in doubt, read the sentence out loud. Hear how the words fit together. You'll be amazed at how much easier understanding their sentences will become. When you get a feel for this, you'll be on the watch everywhere for these writing blunders. Sometimes they are quite silly. Once in one of my rough drafts, I had the cook crawling in the pot with the rice. When an editor pointed it out, I roared with laughter. I know what I meant to say, but I didn't say it. When you reread drafts, look out for such wording. We don't want to make our reader do mental calisthenics to catch our meaning. Let's make it easy for them so they'll want to read your children's work.

Here are some answers for you to use as a guide as you review your children's work:

1) a pair of purple shoes
2) a cup of steaming hot tea (the cup wasn't hot, the tea was)
3) a plate of delicious food (the food was delicious, the plate was china and not delicious)
4) did she rip off the wrappings to open the box, or did she rip off the box? Was the box filled with wrappings? Or was the box wrapped in pretty paper? Was the box pretty, or was the wrapping paper pretty? We all know what the writer meant, or so we think, but when you stop and examine the sentence, you can see how silly it really is. There are a number of ways your children can rewrite this sentence to convey the message properly. Here is just one: "Robin ripped off the pretty wrapping paper as she opened the box to find her present."
5) rows of green plants (The plants were green, or was it the dirt?)

10) Alkaline Adjectives

As with all these lessons, the skill of the teacher can help the student to internalize the data. Reinforce these lessons and other lessons throughout the week. Don't wait until your child is sitting properly at his desk to work on this lesson. One of the best ways to introduce this lesson is to physically work with your children at a park or by pulling weeds in your flower bed. Talk to them about gardening and the need to weed out the unnecessary plants. Then throughout the week, weed your sentences — the sentences you speak, read, and write.

Children quite naturally want to show off their vocabulary. They want to impress their reader that they know fourteen different words that mean lovely. Teach your children to show restraint and to conserve their adjectives.

Teach your children to give their readers some credit. "Show the readers, don't tell them." That writing axiom should be drilled into your kids. Their writing will improve. I like to show my children real examples. Jesus Himself chose to show us spiritual truths via parables. He could have said, "Lost people are important to God." But no, He showed us a shepherd leaving the 99 sheep and going in search of the lost one.

Help your children to use verbs, situations, dialogue, contrast, and setting in place of the easy adjective.

On the other hand, don't teach your children that adjectives are bad. They serve their purpose. Use them sparingly — as if they were expensive and not to be wasted.

A good rule of thumb (for a beginning writer) is not to exceed a 1:2 ratio — one adjective for every two sentences of writing. As your child's writing skills improve, that ratio will become 1:3, then 1:4 and….the goal *isn't* to reduce it to 1:10. The goal is to show the reader, not to tell him. Depending on the style of the writing, a 1:2 might be excellent (dialogue, or a children's story), 1:3 (narrative), 1:4 (fiction), 1:200 (governmental manuals — just joking). These ratios are not laws, they are just a tool to help your children focus on ways to improve their writing.

There are many, many answers to the exercises. As you work with your children, encourage them to paint the beautiful sunset with words so the reader concludes that the sunset is beautiful. One alternative to this is for one of the characters to say, "The sunset was beautiful," in the dialogue.

Tip:

Link this sunset exercise with the words list for your children's *Ideas* section. As they brain-storm for all the words they could use to describe a sunset, get them to include this list in their *Ideas* section. And ADD TO IT. Encourage your children to keep lists. It will aid them with their writing for the rest of their lives.

Here's just one example of how to rewrite sentence #5 (page 227) — to get your mind thinking. (Yes, please expand the sentences into vignettes, if you want.)

Bill strained, groaned, and lifted the box. A smaller man wouldn't be able to grasp its girth. The muscles on his back rippled as he endured the weight. As he coped with the pain, he had to admit he was thankful. At least he had a job. He would learn to shift the work from his back to his legs. His legs were in great shape. He would make first string in the fall. "This summer job isn't so bad after all," he thought as he headed for the next mammoth carton.

11) Ponderosa Participles

Just as with the other lessons, reinforce this lesson away from the school room. As you drive around town, talk "COWBOY LINGO" and make up sentences in your head for your children to fix.

This lesson and the lesson "Article Attractions" are similar. Once mastered, your children's writing will be less confusing.

At first reading, some of the exercise sentences seem fine. Then, when the mistake is pointed out, you "get it."

1. "My mother drew a graph showing the history of the kings of Judah" makes more sense, doesn't it?
2. Some television sets can do homework, but I think the writer meant: "After June finished all her homework, she turned on the television."
3. "Oh, were we ever exhausted running at full speed, when we saw him win the race" sounds pretty silly, but that is basically what the sentence says. Really, the racer was running at full speed: he was running at full speed when we saw him win the race.
4. Ah, a self-calculating deposit — wouldn't that be nice? How about: "When she calculated her bank balance, she noticed the deposit was for the wrong amount"?

Are you getting the knack for this? It's *kinda* fun. Now you try a few before you work with your children:

5. _____
(Who was wanting to drink the blood?)

6. _____
(Walt Disney has salt shakers that shake themselves, but most people don't. Who is salting the food?)

7. "Yuck, Mom! Do you always have to be so gushy?" the lanky teenager smirked as he wiped off his mother's kiss.

8. With all these new-fangled kitchen appliances, some burners might be able to check the temperature of the candy, but I think it makes more sense to say: "Once Susy Homemaker checked the temperature of the candy, she turned the burner to simmer."

12) Whoot-n-nanny

Now is a good time to discourage your children from ever gossiping. This lesson is predicated on gossip. Sometimes a good story can teach a point very well.

Many good writers have to stop and think of the whose/who's rule when typing.

It is very logical — when to use who, whom, who's, and whose.

Here are answers to the exercises in your children's workbook:

1) who	7) who
2) who	8) Who
3) who	9) whom
4) Who	10) Whose
5) Who's	11) whose
6) who	12) who, who

This lesson also gives you the opportunity to talk about dialect and the fun a writer can have in conveying the accent of a character.

13) And of Green Gables

I love to hear children write. They automatically connect their sentences with the word "and." It's their way of linking thoughts together. It's cute for the preschoolers, but as children mature, so should their writing.

There are many possible ways to construct the sample exercise. Talk through the "why" of their choices with them. They'll start to see the difference the proper use of "and" can make in their writing.

Don't forget to include the spiritual truth with each lesson. They are not afterthoughts. They are "the horse in front of the cart."

14) Moreover

Rarely does a day go by that I don't see this basic rule of the English language misused. In fact, it is so often misused, many people don't even know it's wrong.

One useful game to play with your children is to find all the improper grammar in advertising. Advertisers use a great deal of license when constructing their slogans. They purposely misspell words such as "Drive-Thru," "Vu-Graph," and "nite-lite." In certain cases, they butcher the English language — on purpose. Go on a grammar hunt with your children and spot all the acceptable misuses of our language in billboards, ad copy, slogans, and commercials.

Over should be used to mean physically over as in above, located directly over, or over a span of time. It has to do with physical location. **More than** should be used when writing about numbers or quantity. The same rules apply to **under** and **less than**.

Yes, your children will show you examples in the newspaper of **over** used incorrectly. Advertisers use this for a very simple reason — they save four letters and one space in the display. "Over one million sold" takes up less space than "More than one million sold." And in some cases it costs less (some advertising fees are charged on a per word basis or on a space basis.)

In addition to writing the five sentences using **more** and **over** properly in the exercise, a few weeks from now go through the whole exercise again, but use **under** and **less than**.

15) The Then Man

Just as small children use "and" incessantly, they also throw **thens** around needlessly. My sons love their Lego® blocks. They politely ask to play with them. I'm reluctant, unless I know they have enough time not only to pull the blocks out and build something, but also to pick back up all the little pieces. I know what their rooms become. Carpet covered in colored plastic — like land mines to a parent rushing to aid a child in the middle of the night. "Yes, you can, but you have to clean every one of them up before you go to bed."

That's how some children's writing looks — a bunch of **thens** randomly strewn across their paragraphs. Let's encourage our children to police up those extra **thens**, like the Lego® pieces which weren't needed to build the Freedom-Fighter-Retro-Grade Battle Cruiser, and store them away.

The three vignettes, if I did my writing well, should keep your child interested. I tried not only to present the rule, but a vehicle for the rule to ride in. As your children work over their rough drafts, let them role-play as Sherlock Holmes, Colombo, or the Hardy Boys. Then they can hunt down those villain **thens**.

As you complete these three exercises, talk about each **then**. If you both agree it is needed for the story to make sense, leave it in. If the story makes sense with the **then** out of there, strike it. Teach your children to double-check each **then** in their writing.

16) Capital Idea

Why not make grammar rules fun? I remember learning the rules of capitalization in the most dreary way possible — from a list, from a boring textbook, with a pointless set of drills to reinforce the exercise.

But what if your children could work for the CIA (Capital Investigation Agency) and use operatives in the field to discern the "nationality" of the agents? Or something like that.

You can have a great deal of fun with this *Craftsmen*.

With this exercise, not only should your children capitalize correctly, but they should be able to state the reason (operative) they used.

We regularly do exercises like this with our children. For instance, when they dictate a story, I don't capitalize anything. We go back over the rough draft to search for those letters we should capitalize.

17) Who's That

This lesson is very simple. It emphasizes the difference between man and other creations.

This rule is developed in our current language. You'll notice as you read the King James Version that several times "that" is used instead of who (several in John 1, for example). I wanted you to know in case your children point to it and say, "See, the Bible uses…." I believe the Bible is the perfect Word of God. I explain it to my children that our current language is different from Elizabethan English. We don't use "thou" and "sayest" either.

As you work through these exercises, talk to your children about letters to the editor (see section on "Broadcasting," page 55-56). Work through each sentence highlighting the words "that" and "who," and decide if it is correct or needs to be changed. (Sentence #4 does not have "that" or "who" in it, but it does have a problem with "Auntie Cindy." See if your children find it and how they could correct it.) As we work through these *Craftsmen*, the children need to remember their past lessons. Many of the sentences/exercises could be greatly improved by using all the *Craftsmen*'s rules. The samples/exercises are purposely written in a rough form — so your children can improve them.

As your schedule permits, have your students rewrite the entire "letter to the editor" exercise, or write their own version about a problem they see in your neighborhood.

18) It's Us or Them

This is a basic grammar concept, deciding between nominative (subjective) or accusative (objective) case of pronouns. If you want, you can teach your child the words nominative, accusative, objective, and subjective, or just teach them the "why" of the choices.

To remind you of your fifth grade English class: If a noun or pronoun is the subject, it is in the subjective case (popularly called nominative). If it is the object of the sentence, it is in the objective case (popularly called accusative).

"I" is nominative, while "me" is accusative. As the children work these sentences, they could diagram the sentence to discover if the "missing word" is for the subject or object of the sentence, then fill in the correct pronoun. That is much more difficult than using the "ear" method described in their exercise. I've taught English for a state university and every time I have to decide which form of the word to use, I use the "ear" method. It gives the children the why, not the law.

It also teaches a parallel to Spiritual truth. We live under Grace, not law. Our actions should be an outpouring of our love and caring, not a list of rules. I'm always looking for times to teach my children Spiritual truth. So, I teach them the why of rules in grammar (for that matter, in math and other subjects) so it isn't just another set of rules with no logic or reasoning behind it. It makes sense. This way I'm teaching my children for life, not just so they can pass the next test.

Here are the answers to their exercises:

1. me
2. I
3. her
4. he

5. We
6. him
7. us

19) The Three MUSTketeers

Your children should enjoy playing as a MUSTketeer and learning the rules of comparison. Remember, anything you can do to reinforce the lesson will help them to internalize it.

For these exercises, your children could either go up or down (more or less).

Rule #	Positive	Comparative	Superlative
1	red	redder	reddest
2	precious	less precious	least precious
3	much	more	most
1	high	higher	highest
1	long	longer	longest
1	little	littler	littlest
3	bad[ly]	worse	worst
2	concise	more concise	most concise
1	happy	happier	happiest
1	free	freer	freest
2	elated	more elated	most elated
1	brave	braver	bravest
2	precise	more precise	most precise
2	conspicuous	less conspicuous	least conspicuous
1	great	greater	greatest

Special note:

Did you catch it as you were working? "Bad" could be bad, *an adjective; or* badly, *the adverb. Also, littler and littlest could be used for "little" depending on the use (see chart below). Most adverbs which end in "ly," and ones with two or more syllables are compared according to rule 2 (using less and least, more and most).*

Here are a few of the most commonly used irregular adverbs (please note that in the same form, four of them can be used as adjectives):

Positive	Comparative	Superlative
far	farther	farthest
much	more	most
little	less	least
badly	worse	worst
well	better	best

20) Racing to the Finish Line

Though this vignette of racing is fiction, it was inspired by a friend of ours who is an evangelist. Reverend David Cobb goes to football games, races, and other events where he reaches the lost for Christ.

The answers to the exercises will be as varied as the children doing them.

You'll notice that sometimes negative writing can be very effective. It must be purposeful and intended. It is a developed skill and rarely done well by beginning writers. (Sentences #6-10 are provided to show you examples of negative writing to make a strong contrast between *what isn't* and *what is*. The sign wasn't the usual advertisement — it was a proclamation of Christ.)

I'd advise you at this early stage of your children's writing to encourage them to write in a positive mode.

To help teach them this concept, you might want to use a photograph and its negative. Have them compare the two. Which one would they rather look at? Which one is a more accurate representation of the image? Tie in the concept with their writing.

A positive style of writing would be represented by the photograph — it gives a true picture.

If these sentences are too difficult for your child, simply substitute your own sentences.

This lesson can be expanded to your conversation around the house. Practice stating things in the positive — as they are — not as they are not.

To give you a better handle on this concept, here's an example:

Stated in the negative: The shirt *isn't* clean. Stated in the positive. The shirt *is* dirty.

Sometimes it stretches your child's vocabulary to think of a word which can translate the same meaning, but in the positive form.

I admit, this lesson isn't a clear-cut, dot your "i's" type of lesson. It is a matter of style. As your children's command of the English language increases, they'll be able to discern the difference between positive and negative writing and the advantages of employing both styles.

As a Christian, I encourage my children to go beyond the positive style of writing to the positive way of thinking. My mother summed it up this way: "If you can't say anything nice, don't say anything at all." It's good practice to look on those things which are pure, lovely….

21) Splitting Infinitives

There are several approaches to this lesson you can take. You might want to prepare your children ahead by using some split infinitives in your conversation at the dinner table and see if they register as odd to your children's ears (e.g., to ravenously eat). One of our goals in teaching your child proper English is for them to be able to hear the errors.

We've all heard someone hit the wrong note on a piano. You wince. It's a musical hiccup. It doesn't sound right.

The same can happen with your children's speech and writing. Expose them to good writing. Teach them the rules and they'll develop an ear for proper phrasing. Their writing will automatically improve and they'll need less and less grammatical editing.

One of the best ways to develop this sense is to read aloud their work and others' works.

Identifying split infinitives is rather easy. Each time you see a "to" in their writing, check the placement of the adverb. In almost every case, the adverb should be placed <u>after</u> the verb.

There are a few exceptions (more from repetition than from love of grammar) like the one cited in your child's workbook pages — "to boldly go." You'll notice some professional writers will adopt this *misuse* of the English language on purpose: to make their writing more reader-friendly, to relate to a more basic reader, or to add realism to dialogue.

After you finish the exercises with your children, come up with your own. Have them hunt in their own books and writing for examples of infinitives.

22) Which Hunt

It's up to you if you want to get into a lesson about witches with your children. This may give you the opportunity to teach them what the Word of God has to say about the television show *Bewitched* and other attempts by the world to popularize evil. I've seen several witchcraft bumper stickers. The one that shocked me the most was on a minivan: "Have you hugged your witch today?" I looked at the woman driving it and she was dressed like us. She would have fit right in at any home education book fair I've been to. Externals only. Spiritual discernment would have singled her out. How much she looked like a good mother. Satan deceives.

I discuss things with my children according to their level of understanding.

I used the vehicle of the Salem Witch Trials to link the lesson in their minds as a mnemonic device and to impart a historical perspective on the trials. Do with it as you wish.

Your children need to learn to tame down their uses of the words which and who. They should learn the difference between which and that.

Here's another example of the differences:

1) "Please, hand me my stapler — the one that is black." [Distinguished between that stapler and any other staplers.]
2) "Ah, here is the stapler, which I bought last week."[Gives more information about the stapler.]

Here is one way of correcting the sentences:

1) Don't need the "who is." The sentence makes perfect sense written as: "Nathaniel Hawthorne, an author, wrote *The House of Seven Gables*." Or for those children who are retaining their past lessons, the sentence could be written: Nathaniel Hawthorne wrote the book *The House of Seven Gables*. If he wrote a book, obviously, he is an author. Your children could rewrite the sentence in a number of different ways, as long as they understand that "who is" is superfluous in the exercise.
2) The "who was" can be omitted. [Salem Witch Trails could be capitalized to emphasize — the same way you would capitalize the Great Chicago Fire.]
3) The "who" is needed in this sentence as it is constructed. Your children could totally rewrite it.
4) Do your children understand what the sentence is saying: the gavel was made of oak (added information) — rather than the gavel, that was made of oak to distinguish it from his gavel made of mahogany?
5) The "who" is part of a parenthetical statement. Either the whole parenthetical should be removed or remain as is. Of course, the whole sentence could be reconstructed.
6) The "which" is properly used.
7) The "who was" is superfluous and should be "stricken from the record."
8) How would the meaning of the sentence be changed if "which" was replaced by "that"? Are your children grasping the meaning of these words?
9) Ditto as in #8.

23) Gone With the "Than"

As with several of our other lessons, misuses of this concept can present some hilarious results.

Essentially, your children must compare at least two things. They must communicate precisely to their reader what is being compared to what.

Sometimes it seems so obvious in their minds what they mean that they can't see how anyone could misinterpret it.

Do you have a copy of the picture which could be a young lady or an old hag? If you look at it one way, she's a beautiful girl with a feathery hat. Another way she's an old lady with a scarf.

Or have you seen the picture which can be either a vase or two people talking?

Just as artists can draw optical illusions, writers can mistakenly do the same with their writing. Two different people can see two different things among the letters.

1) "Dagny looked more like a Labrador than an Airedale looks like a Labrador" OR "Dagny looked more like a Labrador than she looked like an Airedale." (Two totally different meanings!)
2) "Miss Melanie is more ladylike than Aunt Pittypat is ladylike" OR "Miss Melanie is more ladylike than Aunt Pittypat is silly." (Are we comparing ladylike with ladylike OR ladylike with something else?)
3) "Scarlett was closer to Stuart than Brent Tarleton was close to Stuart" OR "Scarlett was closer to Stuart than she was to Brent Tarleton." (Two different meanings.)

24) Choosy Writers Choose...

This lesson is just a springboard for your children to start to learn to use words properly. Always! When in doubt, double-check in a dictionary.

We blundered royally: my husband wrote a brief article and used the word "penultimate." I didn't check it. We had several alert readers tell us how badly we had misused the word. It means *next to the last*, not the *ultimate-ultimate* as he had used it. How embarrassing! We printed a correction in the next issue of our magazine.

May I preach a minute? Okay, how about a sister-to-sister suggestion. I don't want to become an *English* snob and I don't want my children to put on grammatical airs.

It is one thing to correct your own work; it is another to belittle someone else. Do you remember how you stumbled and were so precise with each word as you spoke to Miss Feathershall, the literacy matriarch in school? She even corrected the principal on his English. It's difficult to feel comfortable around someone if you know she is listening not to what you're saying but to how you're saying it.

Don't get so bogged down with commas, split infinitives, and precise definitions that you squelch your children's words. Please don't teach them to think more highly of themselves because they know the difference between "among" and "between."

I'll jump off my soapbox now. I've been around some real jerks who almost worship grammar, syntax, and enunciation, and each one seemed very empty and out of whack.

Do encourage your children to keep a word journal to log differences in words, so they won't mix up:

- anticipate with expect
- amass with accumulate
- authentic with genuine
- capacity with ability
- compare with contrast
- concise with brief
- decisive with decided
- compliment with complemen
- difficult with hard
- interpolate with extrapolate
- i.e. with e.g.
- adroit with dexterous
- happiness with joy

- puritanical with sanctimonious
- punishment with discipline
- manipulate with maneuver

The list could go on for hundreds of pages.

25) Inventive Writers

There is a big difference between creative word play — using words not in a dictionary for effect — and using the language improperly out of ignorance.

Throughout this workbook, I've used words which my spell-checker kicks back: flittering, sayeth, horn-swoggled, thats and thens, "kinda," new-fangled, and MUSTketeer. Of course, it has a hard time with proper names also.

Each override serves a purpose: either it is correct usage of a word, just uncommon — as when I refer to "Freds" — or it is put in for comic relief or mood-setting — as in "horn-swoggled" and "kinda."

Your children will quite naturally want to make up words in their stories. That is great if it's a new name, a new "substance," a new planet or country, or some new creation of their imaginations. C.S. Lewis invented words such as *Narnia* and *Cair Paravel*. Gene Roddenberry came up with *dilithium* and *transporter*. Walt Disney gave us *Imagineers* and *Mousketeers*. Your children will come up with character names, new animals, and imaginary lands. Inventing words can be fun.

But, there is a difference between the purposeful use of words which aren't in *Webster's* and unintentional misspellings and word manipulation.

If you have a spell-checker program, just test each anomaly for deliberacy. (Deliberacy isn't a word, but it is just the type of "word" a young child might try to use. The correct word to use would be deliberateness. Or even better — reconstruct the sentence entirely to avoid the awkward phrasing.)

Of course, there are exceptions, but again they are intentional. There is a comedian who has made a living by butchering words. It would work in the dialogue for the character of a kid who is always trying to impress others with his big vocabulary.

Yet, if a non-word is used for no effect, reason, or purpose, it should be fixed either by using a proper word or by restructuring the sentence.

In the exercises, the incorrect words can either be replaced or the sentences can be reworded.

1) **tiredly** is debatable, though the proper texts say no, not a word; because of usage some editors accept it. I think it best to change it.

2) **agitatedly** fits the same category as tiredly. It's too much of a stretch for my editing tastes. English is a growing language. While slang is acceptable to some editors, others won't tolerate it. Know your audience — your readers. When in doubt, go with the sure word. If you can't find it in your dictionary, change it.

3) **exhaustedly** wasn't considered a word until very recently. It became acceptable between the writing and the printing of this book. American English is constantly changing. In my original manuscript I had written that "exhaustedly" isn't a word, "exhaustibly" is — but it has a different meaning. My most recent edition of a dictionary now includes "exhaustedly." I still think it sounds awkward. My computer's spell-checker program still spits out "exhaustedly" as improper.

4) **frustratedly** is not a word

5) **incredulously** is a word, but don't confuse it with incredible (The sentence would flow better if rewritten. It is in the same "newness" status as exhaustedly.)

6) **pompously** is a word

7) **meekly** is a word

8) all okay

9) **discompassionately** (not a word)

10) **sophomorically** is a word (It is in the same "newness" status as exhaustedly.)

11) **soporificly** is not a word, soporifically is

26) Gotcha

Got is not the past tense of *have*, though many of us use it as if it is. Got implies action. It is the past tense of GET. The subject must actively get something through his own desire and work, then he has got it. Many of the gots which I read are incorrectly used and an editor must cut them or replace them with another word.

Listen to this sentence: *"Have you got the time?"* Got is not used correctly. The sentence should read, *"Have you the time?"*

"What has love got to do with it?" should be *"What has love to do with it?"* or *"What does love have to do with it?"*

If the writer could write the same sentence in present tense and use the word get, then got is correct. If not, reword. Also, gotten is the past participle form of got.

Parents, please teach that sometimes proper grammar is not the *right way* to write. A street gang member-type character isn't going to go up to a dude and ask, *"Pardon me, but have you the time?"* Often in dialogue good writers will intentionally use improper grammar, slang, and common usage to make their characters believable. Some writers will even use common, though technically incorrect, expressions and speech patterns to make their message understandable and more user-friendly. There is a fine line between *"not being legalistic about the language"* and *"compromising and dumbing down the language."* If a writer intentionally uses improper syntax he should have a *justification* for doing so. That justification should be obvious. It shouldn't appear as ignorance on the writer's part — that the writer just didn't know better. A good example of intentional improper grammar is an Eliza Doolittle-type character saying *ain't* to reinforce the idea that she is not well educated. Or a computer dweeb dumbing down the technical terms (not precise semantics) to a level where someone who is web-challenged can understand.

Remember we thrive on Grace and reel with pain from Pharisees. Be gentle with your children on some of these grammar dogmas. Re-read "Kevorkian Teaching Techniques" and "Grading and Other Forms of Torture." Dwell on whatsoever things are true, whatsoever things are honest, whatsoever things are just, whatsoever things are pure, whatsoever things are lovely, whatsoever things are of good report; if there be any virtue, and if there be any praise, think on these things—Phillipians 4:8. We do *have a Life* beyond commas, unrhymed lambic pentameter, and squinting modifiers.

1. It should read "I've gotten a lovely bunch of coconuts." or "I have a lovely bunch of coconuts." *I've got* is incorrect. Remember, if your child could rewrite the sentence in present tense and use the word **get**, then **got** or **gotten** would be appropriate. Also keep in mind that they might convey more meaning to their reader by substituting with a more powerful word.

2. What time have you, Mate?

3. Billy did do it and I have gotten the proof (I am the one who got the proof). Or, Billy did do it and I have the proof in my possession.
4. The sentence is correct **if** we actively get the fish or don't get the fish.
5. Got is used correctly **if** the writer means to imply there was action on her part. It wasn't passive.
6. Have you heard this expression before? What do you think? Is it correct, or incorrect? Test it according to the "rules." Much depends on the "it." Are we talking about the weather, the situation, the dog? Is the "dog" getting himself better? Good, you're getting the hang of it. Just question the sentence to see if it really says what you want it to say.
7. If Jennifer "got" more — it was fair. If Jennifer received more — it may not be fair. If Jennifer took more than her share — it isn't fair. Talk it through with your children so they can see what is really being said.
8. Though we see and sometimes talk like this, it isn't proper. Unless he "got" himself caught. Isn't the writer really trying to say, "Dad caught John …"?

27) Love is Lovely

C.S. Lewis wrote about the neutering of words in *Mere Christianity*. He wrote of how the word "gentleman" used to have a definite meaning, but because of misuse and overuse, has lost its strictest definition. He goes on to state that the word "Christianity" has been watered-down also.

Likewise, many other words seem to have become meaningless.

Love is one of those words. It is a special word and should be used as such. In English we don't have four words for love (*storge, philos [or philio], eros, and agape*) as the Greeks do. But we do have other words to use: fondness, affection, like, attachment, enthusiasm, passion, or zealousness. There are dozens of possible synonyms your children could use to describe correctly the emotion they are feeling.

There are other words which are losing their true meaning. Some of the changes are deliberate and part of "political correctness." Do you want your children's vocabulary to reflect your core beliefs or someone else's?

Examine your children's language to see if they are using redefined words in a way which is pleasing to God.

Satan isn't a creator. He can only distort, deceive, and warp what is good.

For instance, "gay" was a good word at one time. Now it is banished to the nomenclature of the homosexual activitists.

Here are some words:

- Sale (Going out of business, etc., are just ploys which mean nothing in some cases.)
- Healthy
- Lady
- Organic
- Natural
- Hate
- Born-again (I was horrified to see a writer make up the term "born-again atheist!")
- Devout
- Awesome
- Cool
- Really
- Peace

There are many other words which are being so misused that the true meanings have lost their punch. Think up a list of your own.

28) Nitro-Commas

My mother remembers an illustration her teacher taught her back in 1942 — I've used it in this lesson: "The teacher wrote this…."

A writer uses anecdotes from all over. As I write I pray for the Lord to bring to mind ideas and memories to make my writing easier to understand. This is one of those examples. My mother had taught me this lesson about commas when I was young. I remembered it as I was trying to think of what to say for this unit. I double-checked with her to make sure I had it correct. I mention all this to encourage you and your child.

We're building writers for tomorrow. Very few of our children will be the "great writers of today." But, a decade from now, when they are adults, they'll benefit from the time you're investing today in preparing their minds for writing. Some events that are happening in their lives now might appear in a short story they write twenty years from now. Isn't that encouraging!

Commas are misused and abused. Commas can change the meaning of sentences. There are several sentences in this *Teacher's Guide* that Alan and I "argued" about. The removal of the commas changed the meaning entirely. Most of the time, I went with Alan's suggestion, but one I didn't change, because I did mean to say it that way. Reading it out loud helps a great deal.

Your children should have a reason for every comma they place in their work. If they can't justify it, then they should remove it. This doesn't mean they have to know the proper rule that one should "use commas to set off appositives unless the appositive is a close appositive." (Whew! That was exhausting just typing it. Can you imagine speaking like that! That is a direct quote from a dreary book on grammar I had to use when I taught English: *You Can Learn English Grammar* by W. Loys May ©1963, reprinted in 1980; published by F.E. Braswell Company, Raleigh, NC.)

They should be able to, in their own words, explain the "why" of the commas. You probably have several books on your shelves right now which give the rules for commas. I don't want to take up space now to go over the litany of them, but *briefly* (just in case you're in a comfortable chair and you don't want to go digging through a box of books) here are ten of the most agreed upon rules:

1) to separate lists — *Trent likes to eat apples, steak, and ham.* (Placing the comma before the "and" is optional. Be consistent throughout a written work. I prefer the last comma for clarity. It is absolutely necessary in some sentences for the reader to comprehend the writer's intent. Consider: *They ate beans and franks, corned-beef and cabbage, and potatoes and gravy.* Without the commas after "cabbage," the sentence would not be as easy to understand. If a writer has to add the last comma in any sentence for clarity then all their sentences need the last comma — the consistency rule.)

2) to separate names (nominative of address) from the rest of the sentence — *"Bill, can you get that?"*

3) to separate items of addresses — *He lives at 3434 N West Street, Gartherton, Ohio 77665.* (Don't use a comma to separate state and zip.)

4) to separate opening phrases, introductory expressions, and long prepositional phrases from the rest of the sentence — *No, but I would like some more sweet potato* — *Seeing the effect the speech had on the audience, I wanted to learn more.*

5) to separate days from the year — *Bethany was born September 10, 1990.*

6) *My husband Alan is the love of my life* (close appositive, no comma); or *Alan, my husband, is the love of my life* (commas used for appositive).

7) In the salutation of a friendly letter and at the complimentary closing of all letters — *Dear Aunt Janet,* — *Sincerely yours,*

8) In numbers, except if those numbers are addresses. We don't write *1,600 Philadelphia Ave.* We do write *23,456,789.*
9) to separate clauses in a compound sentence — *Green apples are tasty, but they cause indigestion.*
10) to separate parenthetical expressions and non-restrictive clauses from the rest of the sentence — *Tuesday, the day after Monday, is when Reed has his orthodontic appointment.*

Please don't depend solely on this list. I have several style manuals and they go on and on about rules for the proper placement of commas. I just synthesized the different lists into those ten most common rules. Remember on some of the obscure rules, even professionals disagree.

One of my professional writing friends told me how upset she was when she learned what a school teacher had taught her son. Nancy, checking her son's composition, found an inappropriate amount of commas. He placed thrice as many commas as the sentences needed. Carefully, Nancy approached her son because obviously he didn't know his comma rules. He told his mother that his teacher taught him there was one quick rule for using commas — "Whenever you take a breath, put in a comma." This poor boy was asthmatic so he had placed commas every three words! What insanity for a teacher to teach. I've told this story several times and each time I've told it, someone in the audience tells me they were taught the same thing! Can you imagine? I guess a long distance swimmer could go pages before needing another breath and thus using a comma! If some teacher taught you that, forgive them and get on with your life.

29) The Incredible Shrinking Intellect

This lesson works like a brake. Some writers think the bigger the words they use, the better their writing.

Teach your children that using the correct word is better than using the big or small words.

If an "expert" really understands his topic, then he can explain it to anyone in terms she can understand. Ronald Reagan is considered one of America's best communicators. He talked with people. He didn't try to make them feel stupid; rather, he helped people realize their God-given potential.

Keep in mind that character development and narrative are two different things. A character might use bombastic phrasing, but the narrative should communicate at the readers' level of comprehension.

FYI—

Funambulist: a tightrope walker

Fossarian: a gravedigger

Sierodromophobia: the fear of riding on trains

Allochtonous: not native to a particular region

Pyknic: having a body type that is short and stocky

Cacozelia: very affected diction, with particular use of Latinate words

Parepithymia: morbid longings or carvings

Source: Vocabulary Building at the College Level by Elton F. Henley, Kendall/Hunt Publishing Company, Dubuque, Iowa, ©1975; ISBN 0-8403-1088-9

This incident was told to me by a graduate student in a professor's class. She told me it was true. I can't verify it, but whether it is or not, it does get the message across quite well.

> The students entered the classroom filled with anxiety. The professor had a reputation of being hard, cold, and extremely intelligent. It was an honor to study under him, but it would be work. They were afraid to open their mouths as they might give him cause to belittle their use of the English language in front of their peers. This was a class open only to graduate students getting their Master's degree in English.
>
> The professor, full of his own importance, eyed the new students. He puffed himself up and made the same offer he had done for years, which no one had ever been able to cash in on:
>
> "If any one of you can bring me a list of ten words for which I don't know the meaning, you will get an A in the class and need not attend the rest of the semester."
>
> Hundreds of students had tried it during the years. But try as they would to dig up some word he wouldn't know, no one could. He just flipped through his mind and retrieved the definition almost instantly. Had the professor memorized the Oxford dictionary? No, some thought, he wrote it!
>
> As the story goes, one heroic student came up with a list. He handed it to the professor and said, "You don't know the meaning of these words." The professor looked at the list, which began: *Humility, Charity, Compassion*....

I feel ignorant at the orthodontist's office. They speak a foreign language to me there. I can understand the gist of what they're saying, but I don't know precisely the difference between the various *bonding techniques*, *arches*, and *bilingual cuspids*.

Alan, my husband, is a "rocket scientist" and at work he uses phrases like: *acoustic impedance, phase analysis, flux density, piezoelectric effect, mode conversion, magnetic coupling,* and *anomalous indications*. While I know the meaning of *phase* and *analysis*, I don't know the precise meaning of *phase analysis* as it is used in his world.

We, as writers and teachers of writers, need to make our writing understandable. We need to communicate, not the opposite.

Occasionally I'll test my writing to see if I'm meeting my readers. For instance, after running these 26 pages through the computer, I find that according to the Coleman-Liau Grade Level scale I'm writing at a **13.7** grade level. But according to the Bormuth Grade Level determinant, it's at **10.2**. And for laughs, if I consider the Flesch-Kincaid scale, it's at a remarkably low **3.8**. Don't you find that helpful? Normally, I'll try to write at a ninth grade level because it's highly readable. Even though the concepts might be a bit lofty, the presentation of those concepts isn't.

One of my friends in my Toastmasters Club, Yonel Valme, gave me this advice: "Speak to express, not impress." It's good advice for writers also —

"Write to express, not impress."

30) The Name Above All Names

This section comes from my heart. Capitalizing words referencing God is (albeit small) one way of worshipping Him. It helps your reader understand the difference between spirit (human spirit, team spirit, and mineral spirits) and Spirit (*the* Holy Ghost). The unit is self-explanatory.

Overview of Craftsmen Exercises

These exercises do not cover all the rules of English grammar. I chose to emphasize those areas in which I see the most errors. I narrowed down the most common mistakes I read as I review works submitted to me, works of other authors, and, yes, even published works in print. To restate the concept:

- Don't teach these *Craftsmen* lessons as writing, but more as polishing the writing. The writing is the "coming up with words." Polishing (or editing) is how we make our writing more enjoyable, comprehensible, and uniform.

- Keep in mind that these are different occupations:
  Writer   Copy Editor   Typesetter

- All three jobs are very important and all three must work together to produce a readable book, story, or script. You, as the parent, must help your children become what they should become.

- A writer must have a workable command of grammar. A rough draft will not "get the time of day" from an editor. It should be polished to the best state the writer can produce. It is still going to go by editors and proof-texters.

- Enjoy these *Craftsmen* exercises. I designed them so your children will learn and enjoy learning.

Writing to God's Glory

Teacher's Guide for the Outlet Journal

Teacher's Guide for the Outlet Journal

The **Student's Pages** for this section are few. Here's why:
They will be collecting and inserting their own work into this section of their notebooks.

Master List:

Keep a master list of possible outlets for their writing. I'd recommend they start listing ideas on a sheet of notebook paper: names of magazines, newsletters, and contests, as they find out about them.

They should begin with magazines your family already subscribes to or knows about. Go to the library. Start evaluating different outlets. If they have only an address, they can write the editor for sample copies (often there is a charge), writer's guidelines, and any upcoming themes. As they collect these sample issues, they can start working on the evaluations.

Evaluations:

For the ones they want to seriously consider, they should start a notebook page. Or use the magazine evaluation form provided and start writing down addresses, editors' names, etc.

Date: The date they started the evaluation

Magazine: The official title of the magazine (nickname of the magazine to the side if they wish); if they contact the magazine they should only refer to it with its official name.

Copies evaluated: How many copies did they look through? ("3," if you have three sample issues)

How often published: Dates and frequency, e.g., four times a year (March, June, September, December)

Lead time: The advance on submittal deadlines (**example:** editors want submissions six months in advance)

Publisher: Who publishes it and the correct address

POC (Points of Contact): Do you know anyone who knows anyone at the magazine, anyone you could reference in your query letter — so you don't have to address the letter to "Dear Editor"? Call the magazine's headquarters and ask the receptionist for the name (be sure to double-check for correct spelling) and title of the editor to whom you would submit your work.

Referrals: Who told you about the magazine; any references?

Circulation: How many magazines do they print or ship out?

Subscription rate: How much do they charge for a subscription?

Types of articles: What do they publish?

Fillers: Do they use fillers? What kind? How long?

Titles: Are their titles short, involved, or dramatic? What kind of titles do they use?

Style: What is the magazine's style — old-fashioned, modern, futuristic, user-friendly, snobby?

Quotes: How do they handle quotes? Do they use them at all?

Mission Statement: Do they print a mission statement; can you agree with it?

Lead: Can you think of any leads for a story?

Remember to use one sheet per outlet. On the back of the sheet, the writer should keep track of the history of contacts with that source. For instance, he might only have a title and address on one sheet and on the back a note that he wrote them on 5/5/97 for a copy of their guidelines and sample issues. A sample form is provided on page 275.

Note:

Teach your children to be considerate — if they are requesting information or want a reply, send an appropriately-sized self-addressed, stamped envelope. You'll see this referred to as SASE (self-addressed, stamped envelope). The smallest envelope you should ever use for an SASE is a standard business-sized envelope (9" x 4 1/4"). In some cases you'll need to send a "full-page" envelope (9"x12" or larger). Always, if you expect to have anything returned back to you, send an SASE large enough to hold the material and enough stamps to cover the costs of postage. I know of several smaller publishing houses who do not have a budget to answer any mail that doesn't include SASEs. I'm one of them.

Query Letter

Once they've evaluated a magazine, you're ready to teach them how to write a query letter. This will save you and your child hours of unnecessary work. Write the editor (the head of the department where their idea will fit) a simple letter explaining your idea to see if there is any interest. (Sample on page 277)

The letter should be one page. It should demonstrate your child's writing ability. It introduces not only the idea to the editor, but the writer. The editor might like the idea, but may not consider your child talented enough to handle it.

Your child should not only include his idea but some background of how and why he's qualified to write the piece. Cite any other published works or contest awards.

Note:

Many family-published magazines and children's editors don't require a query letter. However, your children should get in the habit of writing query letters, because in the adult world, query letters are standard operating procedure.

I didn't see any point in reinventing the wheel by spending pages on query letters. There are several good books at your library which cover this topic. My favorite is *Market Guide for Young Writers* by Kathy Henderson, published by Writer's Digest Books. If your library doesn't carry it, insist that they do. Mrs. Henderson's book covers getting published. She is a personal friend and a lovely Christian lady. Not only does she give you the ins and outs of how to prepare a manuscript, query letter, etc., but she lists more than 156 outlets including contests, magazines, and newsletters. Because there are entire books about article submissions, I haven't spent a great deal of time in this book writing about the subject.

Tracking and Record Keeping

Keep track of where and when a manuscript was sent. Simple. Keep track of replies, rejections, re-submit requests, and returns (no longer in print). Log dates and response.

Keep a list of published works. Include the name of the publication and the date published. This list will grow and become a writing resume.

Manuscripts

I'd like to think students will expand this part of their notebook so it fills several notebooks — their manuscripts. These are copies of the finished, typed, manuscripts sent to magazines and other outlets.

FYI

Cross & Quill, The Christian Writers Newsletter, "Encouraging and Equipping Writers Since 1976": official publication of Christian Writers Fellowship International; Rt 3, Box 1635 Jefferson Davis Road, Clinton, SC 29325; POC: Sandy Brooks, director. CWFI can be reached on-line at the following:

http://www.gocin.com/cwfi/writer~1.htm

or

http://members.aol.com/cwfi/writers.htm

The Christian Communicator, "For Christian Writers and Speakers;" Joy Publishing, PO Box 827, San Juan Capistrano, CA 92675

Writing
to
God's
Glory

Teacher's Guide for the
Ideas Section

Teacher's Guide for the Ideas Section

Ah, now your students are writing their own material. Put it in the *Ideas* section of their writing notebooks. Some of the entries will be a few words, phrases, or full paragraphs. This is the place to jot down ideas for stories, as well as the stories themselves.

As their writing gets more involved and they want to write full stories, they'll appreciate the time they take to lay the groundwork. I recommend the forms I use; however, any sheet of paper will do. The forms serve to get their minds going, to put those ideas on paper. We want them to write down these details here, so they won't forget their ideas and also so the characters will stay consistent.

I'm including the planning sheets for a story Reed wrote on one of our plane trips. He was accompanying me to a speaking engagement. We were trapped on the plane so he made up his own "In-Flight Movie." Reed never did anything else with it, but one day he might, and then all the groundwork will be there. I've given these worksheets to you to demonstrate the quick noting style I use when I take down my students' ideas. I want you to know that they are for your children's work. They don't have to be beautifully typeset or in perfect grammatical form. These are for ideas.

The forms are self-explanatory. The children just fill in their ideas. They might not use even half of their ideas, but the work will be evident in their writing.

Have fun with this part of writing. It is the easy part.

If you find it helpful, I've drafted a "Writer's Checklist," for you to use yourself or with your children as you work them through the various drafts. With some children, you'll want to use the checklist privately, and then filter the results to them. Remember, you don't want to devastate them with negatives. You could work any kind of a merit system out for them using positive reinforcements for each box checked. It's up to you.

Your children are at different levels of ability. Either make a custom checklist including the items your child is learning, or use the "req'd" column on the form provided. If you want to pick and choose which of the items you want to require, simply check them off in the "req'd" column.

You'll start to notice trends in your children's writing (e.g., perhaps overuse of the word "just," or misspelling "original"). Add that to the blanks and start congratulating them when they master those personal areas.

Writer's Checklist: The items correspond with various lessons or are general in their focus. Specific items on page 299 of the checklist correspond with "Action Learning" and *Writing Well.* Page 300 encompasses the *Craftsmen* lessons.

Worksheet 1: The Master Plan

Working Title: Jungle King or The Epic Adventure

Date: 8-4-94   **Name:** Reed Bond

Bible References: (log actual verses and references on separate paper)

John 3:1-21 and Proverbs 16:18 and more, look up later

Theme: (best to use 2-3 words, but no more than 10-15) You must be born again to come into the Kingdom of God

Main Characters: (separate worksheet) Hero: Groupa (wolf cub) & Bad guy: Viper (Snake)

Minor Characters: (separate worksheet) Jadeedee (Groupa's sister), a rhino, and Groupa's mother and father and a variety of Jungle folk

Time Frame: Start time long before the Africans controlled the jungle

End time months after start

Setting: Describe the settings and props needed for your story. (*separate worksheet*)
(*25-50 words for each setting, can be in list fashion*)

Jungle

Research: What do you need to do for research? (*separate worksheet*)

Read up on jungles, wolves, snakes, and know the Gospel inside and out

Plot line: How are you going to develop your story? (*separate worksheet*)

Jungle version of Pilgrim's Progress, Viper comes to Lord

© Jill Bond / Homeschool Press, PO Box 254, Elkton, MD 21922

Worksheet 2: Bible References

Working Title: Jungle King or The Epic Adventure

Date: 8-4-94   **Name:** Reed Bond

Log actual verses you are using as your basis for this story:

John 3: 1-21 — There was a man of the Pharisees, named Nicodemus, a ruler of the Jews: The same came to Jesus by night, and said unto him, Rabbi, we know that thou art a teacher come from God: for no man can do these miracles that thou doest, except God be with him. Jesus answered and said unto him, Verily, verily, I say unto thee, Except a man be born again, he cannot see the kingdom of God. Nicodemus saith unto him, How can a man be born when he is old? can he enter the second time into his mother's womb, and be born? Jesus answered, Verily, verily, I say unto thee, Except a man be born of water and of the Spirit, he cannot enter into the kingdom of God. That which is born of the flesh is flesh; and that which is born of the Spirit is spirit. Marvel not that I said unto thee, Ye must be born again. The wind bloweth where it listeth, and thou hearest the sound thereof, but canst not tell whence it cometh, and whither it goeth: so is every one that is born of the Spirit. Nicodemus answered and said unto him, How can these things be? Jesus answered and said unto him, Art thou a master of Israel, and knowest not these things? Verily, verily, I say unto thee, We speak that we do know, and testify that we have seen; and ye receive not our witness. If I have told you earthly things, and ye believe not, how shall ye believe, if I tell you of heavenly things? And no man hath ascended up to heaven, but he that came down from heaven, even the Son of man which is in heaven.

    And as Moses lifted up the serpent in the wilderness, even so must the Son of man be lifted up: That whosoever believeth in him should not perish, but have eternal life.

    For God so loved the world, that he gave his only begotten Son, that whosoever believeth in him should not perish, but have everlasting life. For God sent not his Son into the world to condemn the world; but that the world through him might be saved.

    He that believeth on him is not condemned: but he that believeth not is condemned already, because he hath not believed in the name of the only begotten Son of God. And this is the condemnation, that light is come into the world, and men loved darkness rather than light, because their deeds were evil. For every one that doeth evil hateth the light, neither cometh to the light, lest his deeds should be reproved. But he that doeth truth cometh to the light, that his deeds may be made manifest, that they are wrought in God.

2) Proverbs 16:18 — Pride goeth before destruction, and an haughty spirit before a fall.

Worksheet 3: Main Character Development

Working Title: Jungle King or The Epic Adventure

Date: 8-4-94   **Name:** Reed Bond

Main Characters: (*make up separate worksheets for each main character*)

Name: Arthur McViper III   **(Nickname):** THE Viper

Is character saved or unsaved? unsaved

Age? adult   **Sex?** M   **Race?** snake

Physical characteristics? Big snake

Social and educational background? Smart and yet, stupid because he doesn't realize the Joy in loving God

Religious experiences? never within a mile of anywhere near a church

Besetting sin? sorcery, witch doctor, Prideful

Strengths, talents, gifts (*if saved, list at least one Spiritual gift*): born leader, army-type person, manipulates people

Growth? Yes — he becomes a good guy and serves in King's army

© Jill Bond / Homeschool Press, PO Box 254, Elkton, MD 21922

List at least ten other details about this character. (For ideas review: "Casting," page 143) Write what another character could say about this character. How else could you reveal this character to your readers? Are you going to show this character to us slowly, or will we know him immediately? How are you going to get us to care about this character?

1) He's an evil sorcerer and says horrible things like: "A pinch of salt and the rind of coconut, the slime of a slug and the juice of banana and give it a wicky-whacky shake in the wicky-whacker. Add in the eyes of two bubble fish and the heart of a toad that has been sorely missed — stir it around for an hour of time. Set it out in a rainstorm to get shocked by lightning. Take the mystery fumes from the pot you have now to give your spell some more consistency so it will work better."

2) "Don't even trust him — he's the meanest of the mean." What someone else says about Viper.

Worksheet 5: Setting

Working Title: Jungle King or The Epic Adventure

Date: 8-4-94   **Name:** Reed Bond

Opening Setting: (*key words, phrases; use all the senses to describe*)

Big Jungle

trees moving in wind

hear many sounds of the jungle

palm tree leaves near ground

little red caterpillar quickly squirms behind the security of a larger leaf

Other settings: desert near jungle

very cold mountain top

beautiful palace full of jungle treasures

nice big house for servants on estate

inside castle huge table where King and servants eat together

very big kitchen near dining room (big as a plane)

you could smell dinner being cooked

deep dark cave—where the bad guys are

Worksheet 6: Research Plan

Working Title: Jungle King or The Epic Adventure

Date: 8-4-94   **Name:** Reed Bond

In addition to the Bible, what is your plan for research? (check box, once completed)

What do you need to research? *(copied from Master Plan)*

jungles, wolves, snakes, and know the Gospel inside and out

Research Strategies:

Start in encyclopedia and library computer

Primary Research:

☐ memories of Panama's jungle

☐ watch the "real person" Jungle Book video and take notes about settings
(Ed: This could be considered secondary research, but since he'll be doing his own "investigation," and I'm the teacher, I'll count it as primary.)

☐ _____

☐ _____

☐ _____

☐ _____

☐ _____

☐ _____

☐ _____

Secondary research:

☐ Re-read Pilgrim's Progress

☐ Library books
  (Ed: after library trip, we'd list the exact titles, etc.)

☐ Re-read "Just So Stories" by Kipling

☐ _____

☐ _____

☐ _____

Interviews: *(calls, face-to-face, letters)*

☐ interview Dad for details of Panamanian Jungle and for proper wording of plan of salvation

☐ Interview Mr. Hall, my Sunday School teacher to learn about any of his witnessing experiences

☐ _____

☐ _____

Quotes: *(to be added as research develops)*

☐ _____

☐ _____

☐ _____

Statistics: *(to be added as research develops)*

☐ _____

☐ _____

☐ _____

© Jill Bond / Homeschool Press, PO Box 254, Elkton, MD 21922

Worksheet 7: Plotline

Working Title: Jungle King or The Epic Adventure

Date: 8-4-94   **Name:** Reed Bond

Plot line: Kid goes on an adventure — born again experience

Action to introduce characters: a baby playing with sister starts to ask questions

Main plot: (*be brief*) Groupa leaves home—he needs to do it — they allow — goes to wise

Rhino — goes places and learns Truth

Sub-Plot(s): Little Sister conquers fear

She has to cope without big brother

Conflict: He tries to overcome all the obstacles to the King's Palace

Bad guy is Arthur McViper III and he tries to trip hero up

Surprises:

Resolutions: _____

_____

_____

Divine Connections: (*obvious or subtle*) _____

_____

_____

_____

Climax: _____

_____

Denouement: _____

_____

Epilogue: _____

_____

Outline: (*Use additional sheets, as needed*) _____

_____

_____

_____

_____

_____

_____

_____

_____

Bible confirmation?	General; does it confirm Biblical teachings?	Reader's Language?	Action Learning #4, Play Tag, page 41, & #8, Belt of Truth, page 45
Prayer?	Did they invest in sufficient prayer for the assignment?	Characters?	The Process B, Casting, page 143
		Setting?	The Process, C, Setting, page 145
Theme?	Can they define the theme?	Timing?	The Process, D, Timing, page 147
Word limit requirements?	Are they within their word limit?	Conflict?	Features D, page 159
		Sub-plot?	Features E, page 161
Above reproach?	Have they given others proper credit? Footnotes?	Follow-through?	Features G, page 165
		Foreshadowing?	Features I, page 169
		Sentence count?	Features K, page 173
Where's the paint?	Action Learning #7, Surprises, page 44	Justifiable?	Features O, page 185
		Any SAM's?	Features P, page 187
Sense-able?	Action Learning #6, Sense-able writers, page 43	Results given to God?	General & Features Q, page 189
		Blank	your choice

Power Words?	#1–More Power, page 205	Capitals hunky-dory?	#16–Capital Idea, page 239
Bore Bee check?	#2–Beware of the Bore-Bees, page 207	Who or that?	#17–Who's That, page 243
Fewest words possible?	#3–Less is More, page 209	Pronouns correct?	#18–It's Us or Them, page 245
That check?	#4–Railroad Crossing, page 213	Comparatives correct?	#19–The Three MUSTketeers, page 247
Tense agreement?	#5–Time Travel, page 215	Positive wording?	#20–Racing to the Finish Line, page 249
"!" under control?	#6–The Boy who cried "!", page 217	Any split infinitives?	#21–Splitting Infinitives, page 251
Antecedents linked?	#7–Auntie Cindy, page 219	Whiches hunted?	#22–Which Hunt, page 253
Noun/verb agreement?	#8–Peace Talks, page 221	Full comparisons?	#23–Gone With the "Than", page 255
Articles?	#9–Article Attractions, page 223	Double-check meanings?	#24–Choosy Writers Choose, page 257
Judicial use of adjectives?	#10–Alkaline Adjectives, page 225	Any new words?	#25–Inventive Writers, page 259
Participles okay?	#11–Ponderosa Participles, page 229	Gotcha	#26–Gotcha, page 261
Who's proper?	#12–Whoot-n-nanny, page 231	Full meaning?	#27–Love is Lovely, page 265
Too many ands?	#13–And of Green Gables, page 233	Commas cared for?	#28–Nitro-Commas, page 267
Over/under?	#14–Moreover, page 235	Pompous at all?	#29–The Incredible Shrinking Intellect, Page 269
Then?	#15–The Then Man, page 237	Glory to God?	#30–The Name Above All Names, page 271

© Jill Bond / Homeschool Press, PO Box 254, Elkton, MD 21922

Writing
to
God's
Glory

Teacher's Guide for the
Favorites Section

Teacher's Guide for the Favorites Section

This section of the book is fun. It is *some* work, but not the mind-bending work of creating words from scratch.

Here is where your children will appreciate the work done by others and really start the groundwork for the writing they'll be doing in the years and decades to come.

The thing to remember about this part of the book is that it is for the work of others. Not their own creative work — that goes under *Ideas*.

Section 1: Welcome to Favorites

Section 1 is an introduction to your children about what they can expect. This is the time to encourage them to keep a writing notebook. Encourage them to write down anything they want to. There are no "wrong" journal entries. I collect things I like and things I don't like and briefly note the "why" of the entry.

Some children will naturally keep a log that is a work of art. Others will have notebooks that look like a disorganized mess. Both have potential to be great writers. I personally flip back and forth and have a very eclectic approach — depending on how much time I have to keep it up. Some of my notes are literally written on napkins. I keep a set of paper protectors as pockets to stuff all those loose ideas that I'll organize some day.

Just encourage them to start noticing words and why they like a particular book. Those who are natural-born writers have already been collecting on their own. This section of the book helps them think through options and gives just one way of organizing their collection.

Section 2: Shorts

This will bring out the reporter in your child. Shorts are just little snippets of sentences, phrasing, ideas, or couplings of words that suit your child's fancy. They may be colloquialisms. For instance, if your child ever wants to write a story about a Texan, he might start collecting phrases like: *sidewinder, sunnier than a skyscraper in Dallas, prettier than my horse*, etc. Listening to conversations is a wonderful way to pick up these "shorts." Another example? Okay. One day I'm going to develop a character who talks about *thing-a-ma-bobs*, and *flang-dangles*, so I'm making a list of fun words that people use that have meaning but aren't in the dictionary, like *do-fliggie* and *patootie*. (This corresponds with the "Words" list in the *Favorites* section.) You might not want them to distinguish between single words and phrases. My "Words" list is really a combination of "shorts" and "words."

Section 3: Stu's Blue

It's up to you how to approach this section. I put this in to encourage those children who really struggle with their writing. Even I was amazed that the ideas in the book worked and Stuart went from "I like blue" to a cute story about a jet with the Midas touch. Try it with your children. Choose a color and let them come up with as many words as they can that relate to it. Then invent a story, using just some of the words. (Their own work would go under *Ideas*.)

Please notice on "Stu's Blue" what I actually wrote down as I took dictation. I wrote down every word and tried to do some of the sound effects. As your children mature they will do more and more editing, and you'll do less and less teaching.

• Remember to ask them questions.
• Don't give them the answers.
• Re-teach that sentences start with capitals without pointing out specific words.

You might want to read the story to them and make definite pauses for the sentence breaks. We're teaching writing, we're not writing for them.

For the editing section of "Stu's Blue," have fun. Stop when your children appear bored. Have them debate about alternative ways to say things. Each person will have his own style and there are hundreds of right answers. Teach them to use the proper editing symbols.

This sample serves only as an example to encourage you with what you can do with your children, when you get involved and let them write.

Section 4: Vignettes

Vignettes are not short stories, really. They are short descriptions or character sketches. They could be several paragraphs long or just a few sentences.

The two I chose for examples are from my own children, so they were handy and I knew I owned them. Also, I think they are good examples of what even small children can do when they are given the room to come up with thoughts on their own. I also liked the idea that they reinforce a *Craftsmen* lesson about tense.

Your children will want to keep their own vignettes or slice-of-life paragraphs in their *Ideas* section and others' works here in the *Favorites* section. Sometimes they will copy something over in their own pen, or just cut and paste from a magazine. Just be sure to document where the piece came from and who wrote it.

Section 5: First Lines

Sometimes that's all a writer has — the first line.

Sometimes that's one of the last things a writer has — the first line.

Every piece of writing has to have a first line. Don't let your children fall for the misconception that writers start on page one and end on page 278 as they write. Some will write chapters 2, 8, and 11 and then 5, 12, and 4. The first page might be one of the last things they actually write.

Have them start noticing first lines, because it is the first line (as well as the title, about which sometimes a writer has no input) that will sell the article or book to the reader.

Here are the answers to the "First Lines" exercise: (The first lines may differ from the copies you have. After hours of research at various libraries, I found different versions of the classics and several different first lines. I used the one which, according to the copyright page, was closest to the original — when I could find it.)

Answer Key to "First Lines" exercise on page 313

"'?' was not beautiful, but men seldom realized it when caught by her charm…"	*Gone With the Wind* by Margaret Mitchell
"My name is Ishmael…"	*Moby Dick* by Herman Melville
"When I look back, my first memories are of a large rolling meadow…"	*Black Beauty* by Anna Sewell
"Squire Trelawney, Dr. Livesey, and the rest of these gentlemen having asked me to write down the whole particulars about '?', from the beginning to the end…."	*Treasure Island* by Robert Louis Stevenson
"When '?' was sent to Misselthwaite Manor to live with her uncle everybody said she was the most disagreeable-looking child ever seen…"	*The Secret Garden* by Frances Hodgson Burnett
"It was seven o'clock on a warm spring evening in the Seeonee Hills of India when Father Wolf woke…"	*Jungle Book* by Rudyard Kipling
"On the morning of January 6, 1842, the people of Paris were awakened by the deafening peals…."	*The Hunchback of Notre Dame* by Victor Hugo
"In the year 1192, the people of England feared for the life of their beloved king…"	*Ivanhoe* by Sir Walter Scott
"The eyes of the starving wolfpack gleamed like hot coals in the blackness of the frozen arctic forest…."	*White Fang* by Jack London
"True!–nervous–very, very dreadfully nervous I had been and am; but why will you say that I am mad?"	*The Tell-Tale Heart* by Edgar Allan Poe
"Christmas won't be Christmas without any presents…"	*Little Women* by Louisa May Alcott
"Mr. '?' , who was usually very late in the mornings, save upon those infrequent occasions when he was up all night, was seated at the breakfast table…"	*The Hound of the Baskervilles* by Arthur Conan Doyle
"Looking back to all that has occurred to me since that eventful day, I am scarcely able to believe in the reality of my adventures…"	*A Journey to the Centre of the Earth* by Jules Verne
"'?' was dead, to begin with."	*A Christmas Carol* by Charles Dickens
"If you want to find Cherry-Tree Lane all you have to do is ask the Policeman at the crossroad…"	*Mary Poppins* by P. L. Travers

Play this game with other books. If that exercise is too difficult for your children, give them clues or make it a matching exercise (which first line from column 1 matches which book from column 2 and matches which author from column 3). That exercise is typed for you on page 137.

Section 6: Words

This exercise is mostly self-explanatory. Adapt the lesson to your children's abilities. Take dictation for the younger ones. They may only come up with ten words for a category.

I get ideas and words from everywhere. I remember listening to(the television was on while I was doing something else and I listened for the word-play) a re-run of the old "McCloud" television series from the seventies (starring Dennis Weaver) about a Western policeman transferred to New York City. It was a wealth of colloquialisms.

Your children's vocabulary will grow, but not randomly like some vocabulary-building programs. "Now I know 'chagrin' — but what do I do with it?" Now, as they learn a new word, they can "put it away properly" along with other words — similar words — for later use.

Don't forget to review their lists and to add to them.

Remember that their own lists should be placed in their *Ideas* section. If they want to share their lists with other children (swapping, perhaps in their writing club) then those other children's lists should be placed in *Favorites*.

Section 7: Quotes

How do "Quotes" differ from "Shorts"? That's a good question. I use "Quotes" as exactly that: quotes — words I'd use verbatim, giving credit to the author. This is for those "facts" that should be recorded precisely and most definitely documented with the source.

Also, here is where students might want to keep their "writings" scrapbook of articles clipped from magazines and newspapers. It might just grow into filing cabinets. Be forewarned!

Section 8: Reed's Dictation and Review

Do what you want with this lesson. Some children will get bogged down by its length, others will find it a perfect challenge to edit.

(FYI: Reed dictated this story years before Disney's *Toy Story* came out. So it isn't a case of *personalizing* a story he had already seen. Sometimes that might get your child to start thinking creatively — to tell the story of *Pinocchio* in his own words.)

I purposely included it so you, the teacher, could get a feel for this Questioning Technique of teaching. Printed for you is the straight dictation with no editing whatsoever. If you are in the habit of using a typewriter or have done much writing, this manner of dictation does take some getting used to — unlearning the habit of automatically capitalizing and punctuating as we type or write.

[Note: I have to disengage the "auto-correction" tool on my word processor. For instance, it will automatically capitalize the pronoun "I" and the first letter of each sentence. If my student has a firm grasp on a particular grammar rule, I might opt to adjust my computer program accordingly, to allow for those automatic corrections as a time-saving device.]

Sometime after the original dictating (depends totally on your schedule and your child's ability), you'll start reading his dictation back to him:

© Jill Bond / Homeschool Press, PO Box 254, Elkton, MD 21922

T: "Signal me when we get the end of the first sentence. it was an early spring day in April just about lunch time when the little girl put her doll and new toys in her basket a specially made basket — "

S: "there."

T: "Great. Now let's punctuate that sentence correctly. Do you need to capitalize any of the words? (Remind them of any rules, but have them apply the rules.)

S: "The first letter in every sentence should be capped, so, up the 'I.'"

T: "Good. What next?"

S: "April."

T: (Continue on once all caps are "discovered" and corrected.) "What about commas, periods, and other punctuation?"

S: "I think a comma should go between April and just. Then, after lunch time — "

We continue through for a few sentences just like that.

T: "What about paragraph breaks?"

We set off paragraphs. Once a paragraph is complete, I'll reread it to them and then ask questions about other changes.

T: "Do you like how you've informed your reader so far? Any changes you want to make? I notice you've kept the reader in suspense about what your character's name is. Was that intentional? Do you want to tell your reader more about this character (e.g., size, coloring, etc.)?"

I continue asking questions, working with each student at his own skill level. For example, "You used the word 'said' here. Remember 'said' doesn't really say very much. Can you think of a way you can reword this 'tag' to tell the reader HOW she 'said' it?"

> **Aside**: I have found that the more I teach and work with students (*and I teach children from all over the nation through my seminars, workshops, and private tutoring lessons*) the fewer and fewer questions I ask. Also, I ask more and more advanced questions (e.g., foreshadowing, plot exposition, etc.). The students start making changes as soon as they hear a "glitch" in the word flow. I do like to read it out loud — so they can hear the cadence, the sound, the flow of the words.

Notice, I don't tell him to change something. I don't put in any corrections myself. I'll continue asking questions and teaching concepts until he makes the corrections himself or until I sense I "maxed" out his ability and creativity. I try to keep in mind that yes, I could improve the writing dramatically myself if I were writing it — just like you can write better than your child. Yet, I'm not writing the work. My students are. So, I "let it go." I'm pleased if they are improving and re-membering more of the concepts of *Writing to God's Glory* than they did during the last lesson.

Are your children as different as mine are? All four of mine have such distinct personalities and so, different writing styles. Reed writes a story like this a week (sometimes a day). It's a full time job just keeping up with and listening to his stories, much less getting them to paper and edited and finished. "I wonder where he gets it from?" We laugh because as I write this, I have twenty novels rolling around in my brain and about as many non-fiction books. All those words crammed into such a little living space. Reed is the same way. Do you have a child like this — the natural- born writer? Your job with such a child would seem so easy: just get out of the way and let him at it. But no, in a way, they are far more difficult because they will be held to a higher accounting. Where God gives a talent, He expects it to be used and used beautifully.

My goal for Reed is to help him go in the way he should go and when he is older he'll write and love writing and write to God's Glory. I encourage you with your children. Do you have a Reed (natural-born writer), a Stuart (allergic to writing), a Trent (learning difficulty) or a Bethany (a beautiful butterfly, flittering through her pre-school days and into everything)? Your children are each as special and wonderful. Do your best with them. They are gifts and we'll be held to a higher accounting for the talents He's given us in our children. My friend, I salute you.

Section 9: Hero in the Skies

This story provides a great example of how your children can touch others' lives through their writing. It also reflects how Ryan worked out in his own mind a situation he had with his father.

[Note: This story is mythological and corresponded with his course of study.]

Section 10: Sample Answers to Craftsmen Exercises

These answers are only examples! They are written by students who range in age from "pre-writer" to adult.

© Jill Bond / Homeschool Press, PO Box 254, Elkton, MD 21922

Matching Exercise (see page 142)

"'?' was not beautiful, but men seldom realized it when caught by her charm…"	A. *Jungle Book*	1. Edgar Allan Poe
"My name is Ishmael…"	B. *The Hound of the Baskervilles*	2. Jules Verne
"When I look back, my first memories are of a large rolling meadow…"	C. *The Tell-Tale Heart*	3. Robert Louis Stevenson
"Squire Trelawney, Dr. Livesey, and the rest of these gentlemen having asked me to write down the whole particulars about '?', from the beginning to the end…."	D. *A Journey to the Centre of the Earth*	4. Rudyard Kipling
"When '?' was sent to Misselthwaite Manor to live with her uncle everybody said she was the most disagreeable-looking child ever seen…"	E. *Black Beauty*	5. Charles Dickens
"It was seven o'clock on a warm spring evening in the Seeonee Hills of India when Father Wolf woke…"	F. *White Fang*	6. Anna Sewell
"On the morning of January 6, 1842, the people of Paris were awakened by the deafening peals…."	G. *Gone With the Wind*	7. Jack London
"In the year 1192, the people of England feared for the life of their beloved king…"	H. *Little Women*	8. P. L. Travers
"The eyes of the starving wolfpack gleamed like hot coals in the blackness of the frozen arctic forest…"	I. *Mary Poppins*	9. Frances Hodgson Burnett
"True!–nervous–very, very dreadfully nervous I had been and am; but why will you say that I am mad?"	J. *Moby Dick*	10. Arthur Conan Doyle
"Christmas won't be Christmas without any presents . . ."	K. *The Hunchback of Notre Dame*	11. Louisa May Alcott
"Mr. '?', who was usually very late in the mornings, save upon those infrequent occasions when he was up all night, was seated at the breakfast table…"	L. *Treasure Island*	12. Victor Hugo
"Looking back to all that has occurred to me since that eventful day, I am scarcely able to believe in the reality of my adventures…"	M. *The Secret Garden*	13. Herman Melville
"'?' was dead, to begin with."	N. *Ivanhoe*	14. Margaret Mitchell
"If you want to find Cherry-Tree Lane all you have to do is ask the Policeman at the crossroad…."	O. *A Christmas Carol*	15. Sir Walter Scott

Writing
to
God's
Glory

Student's Pages

Writing Well: The Process

Pre-Writing
(The Process of Writing)

How many hours do you invest in a writing challenge before you ever allow your fingers to touch a keyboard?

If you begin to write first, your words and thoughts will be random, unstructured, and very difficult to follow. Your illustrations will be contrived. Your prose will be formulated, your conclusions unproven, your characters flat, and worst of all, your theology shaky.

Think first. Better yet, *pray* first.

For starters, develop a two-for-one ratio in your pre-writing skills: for every hour you will spend putting words onto paper, spend two hours pre-writing. As your talent is blessed, you'll want to raise the ratio.

Pre-Writing Stage One: Idea Generation

You have an idea. Great! Allow it room to grow.

Nurture it with prayer. Where does the Lord want it to go? What does the Lord want it to become? How can He use it for His purpose?

Pray for words. Pray for concepts. Pray for linking ideas. Pray for characters. Pray for prose.

Pray.

Pre-Writing Stage Two: Research

Study. Study His Word.

Research His Word to match your concept with His Truth. Don't be flippant about your theme. Don't be cavalier about the plot. Don't promote satan's agenda.

© Jill Bond / Homeschool Press, PO Box 254, Elkton, MD 21922

Pre-Writing Stage Three: Right Brain Work

Talk it through. Bounce it off your family and friends. Make yourself accountable.

Jotting down ideas, notes, research, or phrasing is all part of pre-writing. Don't lose those gems.

Don't bury that inspiration.

Pre-Writing Stage Four: Pre-production

Formulate your story. Formulate it so it won't appear to be formula writing.

See separate sections on casting (page 143), setting (page 145), and timing (page 147).

Pre-Writing Stage Five: Blocking

No flats are painted yet. The music might not be completely scored. The costumes are still being fitted. Yet, the director assembles the cast for a "blocking party." He has the characters walk through the script.

In the same way, you, as director of your story, need to block your characters through your story-line. Some might refer to this as outlining.

You might jot down bits and pieces of ideas. Fine. Just prepare in your mind, with notes for reference, the framework for the plot.

At this stage, don't worry about detail. As you begin to write, details will fit together and develop as you go.

As you write, you'll be so glad you invested the mental energy in pre-writing. Your story will have depth. It will have emotion. It will be professional. It won't have the style of an amateur who hates writing. It will sing with the glory of God.

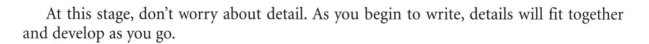

Cast thy burden upon the LORD, and he shall sustain thee: he shall never suffer the righteous to be moved.—Psalms 55:22

© Jill Bond / Homeschool Press, PO Box 254, Elkton, MD 21922

Casting
(Character Development)

Develop three-dimensional characters. Imagine their life stories. Know more about them than you'll ever tell the reader. Go beyond the standard demographics of age, race, height, weight, and head-of-household statistics. Develop them into human beings:

☆ What do they look like?
☆ Where did they go to school?
☆ What early childhood memories affected their attitudes about adulthood?
☆ What are their favorite movies?
☆ What have they named their pets?
☆ Why don't they have any pets?
☆ What do they read?
☆ What are their salvation testimonies?
☆ When they are alone, what do they do?
☆ What are their besetting sins?
☆ What were their dreams when they were ten years old?
☆ Why haven't they reached them?
☆ What are their styles in clothes, cars, dwellings?
☆ What will they NOT eat under any circumstances?
☆ What would they kill for?
☆ What will get them off the couch and out the door?
☆ Who influences their decisions?
☆ How emotional are they?
☆ What kinds of words do they use in their business, with friends, with their parents?

That's right, develop more than you'll ever tell the reader. But if you can see your characters, if you can hear them, if you can crawl into their skins, then so will your reader. You'll have plausible characters. You'll have characters that can reach others. You'll have the start of a good story or article.

Now, how are you going to show the reader these traits? How are you going to introduce the reader to your imaginary friends? How much are you going to reveal? How much will you leave for the reader's own vision? How are you going to invite the reader to get personally involved in the story?

Here are some ways to introduce your characters to your readers:

Dialogue	Plot	Setting
Foils	Events	Timing
Action		

A fun game to play is to actually cast the parts. Pretend you are the casting director and this story is going to be made into a mini-series. Millions of people will watch it. You want just the right person to play each part. Now, with your knowledge of actors, actresses, characters from history, and people you know — cast the parts.

☆ Would your dad play the lead?
☆ Would Harrison Ford play the hero?
☆ Would your little sister make a good Melanie?
☆ How about your piano teacher? Would she make a great Mrs. Sweetvoice?
☆ Do you want someone like Walter Cronkite or Robin Williams to play the part of the Sunday School teacher?
☆ Would you cast your grandmother, or Helen Hayes, as the pastor's wife?
☆ Who would you hire to play *your* part in the story?
☆ Should the dog be Lassie, Benji, or Beethoven?
☆ Should you hire the Sheriff of Nottingham or Omar Sharif as the rogue?
☆ Errol, Arnold, or Ernest?
☆ Shari, Cher, or Chevy?

Worksheets 3 and 4 (pages 289-291) gives you room to develop your characters. Make a separate sheet for each character. Cut pictures out of magazines that go with the character. Draw things that the character would carry, have, or want. Write down words that the character would use: "The Hero's Vocabulary."

Make your characters real.

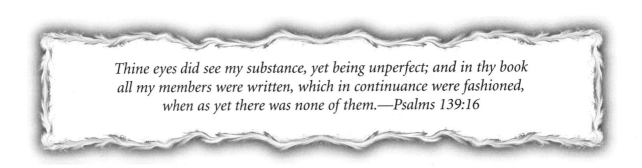

Thine eyes did see my substance, yet being unperfect; and in thy book all my members were written, which in continuance were fashioned, when as yet there was none of them.—Psalms 139:16

Writing to God's Glory / Student's Pages

© Jill Bond / Homeschool Press, PO Box 254, Elkton, MD 21922

Setting

Drifting out in space
Drifting in a torrent of white water
Drifting to sleep on a pile of mattresses balanced on one small pea

In an overstuffed chair marred with cigarette-burns
In a bean-bag chair striped with neon-green and fluorescent-orange
In a Louis XIV-style chair upholstered in fine needlepoint canvas

A home with columns of glass bricks and 80's art deco
A musty old warehouse filled with dust-covered bi-plane parts
A baseball stadium alive with cheering fans and redolent with the aroma of hotdogs

Sea, raging with the hurricane named Andrew
Sea, cold, frigid, icebergs threatening the ship's pilot
Sea, aquamarine and peaceful, calmed from the torrent by His command

Is your mind "drifting in a sea" of possible settings?

As much fun as it would be to write of knights and round tables, can you pull it off? Is it the best setting for your characters? Could your characters grow better in another garden?

Some need shade, some need full sun — what about your idea, your story, your concept?

Where are you going with this story? Not so much "what are you driving at," but more where do you want to place the personalities you've developed?

You are the master set designer on this shoot. If you want snow, poof, s-n-o-w, you have snow. If you want a Hawaiian sunset, you can have it. Are you there? Can you smell the flowers? Can you feel the salty air in your lungs? Does the gentle breeze invite any emotions? Travel without a flight attendant — take your reader with you.

Are you breathless with anticipation, poised in the middle of the street? Can you smell the fear? The bulls are about to be released in the annual Running of the Bulls in Spain.

Click the remote control of your imagination and you're viewing the next possible setting, a bohio in tropical Panama serving as a church building. The heat is stifling. The volunteer missionaries are carrying blocks, brought by an old, beat-up truck, across the stream and up the steep footpath to build a new church at the top of the hill.

Now, paint your favorite room in your home with words. Describe it. Bring it into focus for everyone. Is it the kitchen, where Mom pleases your palate? Or is it your room where you have your baseball trophy on display? Is it the family room, where you and Dad wrestle on the worn carpet?

Take us there with you. Tell us — what does it smell like? What do you hear? Is it hot, cool, comfortable, or cold? Is everything straight or does it need some attention? Tell us about the old couch that Mom wants to replace when the budget allows. Did either you or your brother ever confess to who spilt the cranberry juice on the carpeting? Dad never could get the stain completely out. What are those marks on the door frame? Were you really that tall at age five? Tell us about the family portrait you don't like — the one that Mom keeps out for everyone to see. Bring us home. Invite us to dinner with your family. Let us hear what you hear, see what you see, taste your Mom's cooking, and smell your faithful dog, Tex. Let us feel the velvet seat covers. Be hospitable and invite us home.

If it helps, make a prop list. Pretend you're the stage-grip and you have to go to the prop room at the studio and bring the props for the next scene. What do you need?

The list says a glass for the main character to use when he utters his third line. Is the glass important to the plot, or will any glass do? If it's for *Indiana Jones and the Last Crusade*, it *is* important which glass you choose for the prop. If it's for the wedding scene in *Fiddler on the Roof*, it had better be authentic looking. If it's for a child's birthday party, better pick up the plastic tumbler. Or it might play no role in the development of the story, so the standard ice-tea glass will do fine.

Think through your setting. From stage front to stage back, place the items needed to pull this scene off. Now, what about the lighting?

God created man in His mind before He created the world (Ephesians 1:4). He then spoke into existence our spectacular planet. He then developed man into a physical form and breathed life into him. He placed man in the garden. God was exact. He wasn't flippant, haphazard, or lackadaisical. God was deliberate. He was perfect. He worked out every detail of the scene. From the DNA of the moss on the trees to the number of Adam's hairs, God created everything. He has given us a lovely setting in which to live. He hasn't randomly given us this family or that family. He knows what he wants each of His characters to become and has placed us in the perfect setting to bring out of us fruit to His Glory. In comparison to His creation, our work is a one-celled amoeba — but we must, like Him, place our characters in a setting that will draw out of them the story we want them to tell, to His Glory.

There is a mine for the silver, and a place where gold is refined.—Job 28:1

Timing

When?

When does your story take place?

You might have decided that when you chose your characters and setting. Don't be too predictable. Mark Twain had fun throwing a "modern" man in with King Arthur. Timing is more than defining the period or the era of the piece.

Timing centers around placement and movement of characters. For a short story, the time frame should be very short: in a 3,000-word story you don't have the time to develop a character's eighty years of life. Choose one time, one particular time, and develop it well. How much time will elapse in your story? Is it a 20-minute snapshot of an event, or is it going to be a slow-motion, skip-frame rendering?

You're the master editor. You have reams and reams of developed film, enough for hours and hours of a movie. You must cut and splice, cut and splice, and render the film into a well-developed movie — all within your time frame.

Make a calendar for your story. Where were your characters on the *night in question*? What are their alibis? Where were they when the lights went out?

When are the pieces going to come together?

God is never haphazard in his timing. In God's World there are no coincidences. Your microcosm must reflect His example.

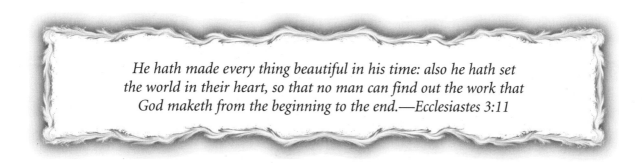

He hath made every thing beautiful in his time: also he hath set the world in their heart, so that no man can find out the work that God maketh from the beginning to the end.—Ecclesiastes 3:11

Editing

No one's writing is perfect. At least not today (and I'm not including Scripture). So, our writing must be edited. It's time you learned some standard editing marks:

Marking	Using it	Explanation
⊙	house⊙I said	a period goes here
⌄	of course⌄	a comma goes here
∧	and ^the^ author said	insert word(s)
∧	and the a^u^thor said	insert letter
/	and the a/u/thor said	substitute letter
⌒⌒⌐	and the (said) (author)	transpose words
∿	and the author siad	transpose letters
⁋	⁋ Tomorrow is	start a new paragraph here
⌒	But today is	no new paragraph
≡	the ≡bible≡ was	capitalize letter
/	the Bible /Was	use lower case
⌒	the Bi⌒ble was	remove spaces
#/	#/allright	separate words
⌄⌄ ⌄⌄	⌄⌄All right, she said.	insert quotation marks
—	positively unique	delete word(s)
⭕	Phil. or ⑤	spell it out
ꝰ	do we ꝰa want it?	delete
‖	(beside a string or listing)	parallel construction is faulty, re-do
#/	#/God loves you	insert a space

There are many other "codes" that various editors use. Some use abbreviations like:

"Ab" — faulty abbreviation

"Pass" — passive voice: re-do it

"Sp" or "Spl" — double-check your spelling

"Log" — faulty logic

"Stet" — leave as is

"AUQ" — author query

There are dozens of different marks editors use.

What I found interesting is that 95% of the marks in the various listings I found were all negative. Well, that's what copy editors do for a living. They take writing and catch typos and mis-printings. Their job is to make the writing perfect.

When you edit each other's works, please fill the pages with comment marks like:

☺ — you like it

✝ — makes you think about God

☑ — good stuff

🕐 — very timely

Be creative with your praise to encourage one another. I use all sorts of circles with "faces" to show confusion, understanding, laughter, joy, surprise. I use stamps with "super job," etc.

There are several "editing" exercises in the *Favorites* section.

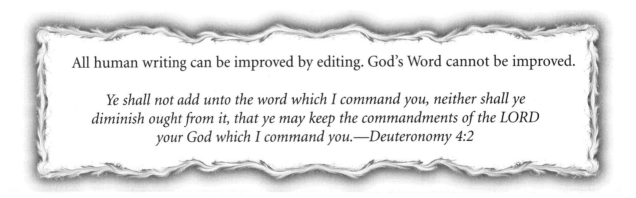

All human writing can be improved by editing. God's Word cannot be improved.

Ye shall not add unto the word which I command you, neither shall ye diminish ought from it, that ye may keep the commandments of the LORD your God which I command you.—Deuteronomy 4:2

Writing to God's Glory

Student's Pages

Writing Well: The Features

Checkmate in 5000 Words or Less

(Story Telling)

The chess match begins.

White moves his pawn to king's knight 4.

Black moves knight to queen's bishop 3.

White moves bishop to king's rook 3.

Black lays down his king and, conceding defeat, announces, "I see your checkmate in 58 moves. Brilliant game!"

The tournament is complete and the audience applauds, but somehow they feel cheated. They had paid more than five hundred dollars each for their gallery tickets. The final round of the World Chess Championship had promised to be as exciting as any sports event.

Now it is over. The whole round has lasted less than three minutes. Sir Reginald comments to his chum, "Brilliant game, don't you think?"

"I'm sure," the Duke replies.

"I don't know," the Countess adds. "I'm just not sure about move 47. Was it the rook or the bishop?"

"Well, the bishop, of course," Sir Reginald is quick to demonstrate his prowess with the game.

"No, no, no, my friend. It was definitely the rook," Duke Reinhardt rebukes.

"We'll never know, will we?" the Countess teases them both.

As tedious as plot development is, we must play each move. Though we know all 58 moves in our minds, we must steer the players (characters) to their appropriate squares (scenes) at the appropriate time. We must develop the plot, much like a chess game. We want the boy to get the girl, the villain to be locked away for 2.3 life sentences, and the teenager to realize that his dad really does love him. But how do we move the characters to that finale?

One way is to use minor characters like pawns. Their fate is meaningless, but they afford you interesting maneuvers in character development and plot exposition. The main characters, of course, will have more movement in your story. Be cautious that you don't lose your readers' interest by taking your characters on some tangential expedition. Always have the goal of moving every one of your characters toward the conclusion. Don't waste moves. But do make all the moves necessary. Then you'll have checkmate in 5000 words or less.

As you develop your short stories, plays, or novels, role play as the world's best chess master. You're in control of the board. Move your pieces wisely, with forethought. Make each move. Don't skip any. Then, when you're ready for the climax, your readers will be with you, rooting for their champion and savoring each word.

On separate paper, map out your strategy for your story, including locations and characters. Put it in black and white. (See Worksheet 7, page 297)

When Christ died on the cross and rose three days later, God said to satan, "Checkmate!" in so many moves. We know the outcome by reading Bible prophecy. Satan loses his kingdom and the White-As-Snow side wins. Yet, God has us play out each move in our lives. I'm so thankful to be a pawn in His Tournament of Champions.

Come now, and let us reason together, saith the LORD: though your sins be as scarlet, they shall be as white as snow; though they be red like crimson, they shall be as wool.—Isaiah 1:18

© Jill Bond / Homeschool Press, PO Box 254, Elkton, MD 21922

Emotions: Can You Use Them?

You must compel your readers to be interested in your characters. Like the Democrats said in the 1992 election, "Caring is everything." You want your readers to care. You want them to feel your hero's pain.

At some level you must invoke their emotions. It doesn't always have to be a call to arms (The Red Coats are coming!), but it must touch their feelings, or your story will be ignored.

There are several ways you can evoke your readers' emotions. One of the best is through good character development.

Identifying. If you can fashion a character with whom your reader can identify, you're home free.

If you write about a ten-year-old boy who is struggling with growing up, you'll have ten-year-old boys role-playing as your character. You'll have grown men remembering back to the struggles they had as a boy.

If you write about a young woman who isn't sure if she should say yes to a marriage proposal, you'll have grandmothers remembering their own courting days. You'll have young girls looking to the future, walking in the high heels of your heroine. You'll have young women identifying with your main character because you're touching them where they are.

Not only do your characters have to have the demographics to pair with your readers, but you have to make them lovable. Why should the reader care if Jim Hawkins finds the treasure? Because we care about Jim. We either become Jim Hawkins in the adventure with Long John Silver, or we adopt Jim as a son.

Characters must have to have a strength and a weakness.

Produce all your characters so your readers will love, hate, envy, loathe, empathize, pity, like, adore, or tolerate them.

- ☆ Will they identify with Laura as she wears old clothes to school?
- ☆ Will they like Melanie, in contrast to Scarlett?
- ☆ Will they hate Captain Hook?
- ☆ Will they cheer for Phineas Fogg?
- ☆ Will they fear for Mowgli in the wild jungle?
- ☆ Will they hope with Edmond Dantès in *The Count of Monte Cristo*?

What emotions do you encourage in your readers?

Beyond the characters themselves, the events in their lives should evoke an emotional response in your readers:

☆ Will they feel pain with Laura when Alonzo is hurt?
☆ Will they cry when Melanie dies?
☆ Will they want Peter Pan to feed Hook to the crocodile?
☆ Will they gasp as Phineas Fogg's balloon is damaged?
☆ Will they want to protect Mowgli from Shere Khan?
☆ Will their empathy change to disgust as Edmond Dantès seeks revenge?

The mechanism by which our emotions are evoked in *The Count of Monte Cristo* is an excellent device in literature. The reader matures with the character, but then the character acts beyond the reader's own sensibilities and the reader "turns" on the hero. Such is classic tragedy.

If you want to write well, you must elicit your reader's emotions as you develop your characters.

Ask yourself:

☆ What do I want the reader to feel?
☆ What do I want the reader to feel about Susan Peabody, my main character?
☆ What do I want the reader to feel about murder?
☆ What do I want the reader to feel about lying?
☆ What do I want the reader to feel about virtue?

As you develop your fiction or non-fiction, remember that we are emotional beings. If you can excite an emotion, you can encourage action.

Yes, you can use emotions to your advantage as a writer.

The next time you read your Bible, look for emotions in the people involved. How do those emotions play out?

Remember that "love" is not just an emotion but an action. Love felt but not acted upon isn't love. Christ performed the ultimate act of love: He died on the cross for our sins.

He that hath my commandments, and keepeth them, he it is that loveth me; and he that loveth me shall be loved of my Father, and I will love him, and will manifest myself to him.—John 14:21

© Jill Bond / Homeschool Press, PO Box 254, Elkton, MD 21922

Story, She Wrote

(Exposition)

Every story is a mystery.

Or else it isn't — it isn't very good or interesting.

You, the author, know the plot line, but the reader doesn't.

Don't confuse "who-done-it" with mystery.

Build your story like a "who-done-it." Have your verbal camera zoom in on the clues. Place little hints along the way. This ploy, called plot or character exposition, involves the reader. He feels he's a part of the story. You're giving him credit for being intelligent. He's prognosticating the ending. Give him enough leads so he can figure possible plot twists. Give him enough information so he'll know your character without having to read all the details.

Yes, even if your story is a basic narrative, you need to keep him reading.

Exposition is balanced by surprises. Don't be too obvious. You don't want him to figure it out and stop reading in chapter one or in the first paragraph.

Intertwine clues with action. He'll read on.

If your witness is going to be part of a major change in your hero, then introduce him, subtly, early in the narrative. If Billy's coach is going to be the one who gives him the Gospel, give your reader an inkling of who the coach is or what is going to happen.

The exposition can be a sentence, a few paragraphs, or a vignette inside another development. In the movies, you see flashes of other scenes. The camera zooms in to show the person in the crowd who will show up again in scene two. You can do the same thing with your skilled writing.

I'll say it again: exposition must be balanced by surprises. Don't spell out the plot line in your exposition, just give clues.

Think of it as a "written introduction."

"Reader, this is my main character, Henry. He has been King of England for twenty-three years now and is unhappy that he doesn't have a son...."

Your reader would be insulted if you did that to him. Instead, you must reveal those facts about your character when the reader needs to know those facts. Involve the reader, so he wants to know more. Some writers accomplish exposition by using the flashback technique.

You don't have to be too obvious. You don't have to be hysterical. You don't have to have the reader on the edge of his seat — just have him "sitting on ready" to flip the page.

Remember balance. Tell just enough ahead to spark the reader's curiosity. Hide just enough to keep him wanting more.

This isn't easy to do. It separates good writers from great writers. It is difficult to calculate since, as the creator, you know all the outcomes. I suggest you find some friends who will read your work. Fresh eyes can really help. They aren't too close to it. They aren't prejudiced in any way.

No author does exposition better than the LORD does in the Bible. In the Bible, it is called prophecy. One of the first expositions is in Genesis 3:15:

And I will put enmity between you and the woman, and between your offspring and hers; he will crush his head, and you will strike his heel.

The Lord tells us enough about the future to give us hope and to allow us to rest securely in His Holy Hand. The Lord doesn't tell us more than we need to know. He doesn't tell us the precise date of Christ's return. Obviously, we don't need to know. Yet, He does tell much about Christ's return so we can hope, we can live our lives properly, and we can witness. God has no problem perfecting the right balance of prophecy and mystery.

© Jill Bond / Homeschool Press, PO Box 254, Elkton, MD 21922

Conflict

I've heard from many of my students that, for them, CONFLICT is the most difficult aspect of writng.

I understand.

As Christians we seek peace. We like to think calmness. We don't look for conflict. It somehow seems more "Christian" not to have conflict.

I understand all those arguments. But without conflict you simply don't have a story.

Period.

It's conflict that makes the story a story.

You might need to adjust what your idea of *conflict* is.

You don't have to turn your characters into egomaniacal brats who go around picking fights (unless of course that is your plotline).

Conflict is simply the real or imagined tension that is woven into the characters or plotline of the story.

It is Biblical.

Pull out your Bible and read Ephesians 6:10-21.

Now, try to tell me that there isn't conflict "built into" any situation on this side of Paradise.

The Bible is filled with conflict. Cogitate (think carefully) for a minute and list five areas of conflict you can discover in its pages:

1. _____

2. _____

3. _____

4. _____

5. _____

That probably only took you a minute or two.

Conflict can be between two humans; a human and an animal; a human and circumstances; a human and the environment; a human and his own conscience or motives; a human and demonic influences; a human and government or authority; a human and God Himself or His messengers; and God and Satan. Can you think of any other kinds of conflicts?

Did any of the items on your list above fit any of these categories?

> Two humans—Saul & David, Jacob & Esau, Haman & Mordecai
> Human and Animal—Samson & the lion, Balaam & the donkey, David & the bear
> Human and circumstances—Job, Samson
> Human and the enviornment—Famines, Floods
> Human and himself—Paul, Peter, David
> Human and demonic forces—Demoniac, Mary, King Saul, Eve & the serpent
> Human and authority—Stephen, Daniel, Paul, and Silas
> Human and God—Jacob/Israel, Adam, King Nebuchadnezzar
> God and Satan—Job, The Temptation in the Wilderness

The conflict in your stories doesn't have to be dramatic (Moses versus Pharoah or David versus Goliath) — but it can be. It can also be subtle like the parable of the lost coins.

As you develop your plotline be sure to develop a believable conflict.

Your story can have more than one conflict in it. Think of all the conflicts in King David's life. Discuss the different conflicts with your teacher. How many did you recognize?

Don't avoid conflict in your writing. It is the conflict that makes your story a story. It is the conflict and its resolution that will propel the reader to understand your theme.

Use conflict to your advantage and remember the Bible is full of conflict — *all* resolved God's way.

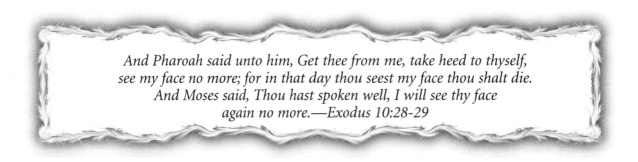

And Pharoah said unto him, Get thee from me, take heed to thyself,
see my face no more; for in that day thou seest my face thou shalt die.
And Moses said, Thou hast spoken well, I will see thy face
again no more.—Exodus 10:28-29

Subplot

Depending on how long a piece you're writing, you might want to introduce a subplot into your narrative.

Of course, every story has a plot. That is the main framework of the story. The subplot is like a story within a story.

Most good plays will have a subplot or side-story woven into the different acts. I'm not a fan of "sit-coms," but several of them that I have seen have a subplot. It's the "minor-action" involving the "minor-characters." It adds dimension to the story line.

Think about your life. How often do you have only *one* story line happening in your schedule?

Think about real lawyers. Are they really only working on *one* case, as the television shows would have you believe? No, they may have one major case they are involved with, but they have other cases which are at various stages of resolution.

If you were to write a story about your day, *your* day would be the plot, but you'd have your brother coming in and out with *his* day. His day would be your subplot.

Are you starting to understand?

Good.

Let's look at an example in the Bible:

Jonah would carry the plotline, but you could develop a story around two sailors and how the casting of lots pointing to Jonah and the calming of the storm convert them to Jonah's God. Can you imagine their dialogue? The sailors' story would be your subplot.

Could you develop another subplot from a different story in the Bible? Talk about it with your siblings and teacher.

When you write a book, your subplots are usually so involved they could be short stories on their own.

In a short story the subplots are very minor or absent entirely. It depends on how many words you have to devote to a subplot. You don't want your main story to suffer because you're spending too much time on your subplot. If you have a really great subplot, make it the main plot of your next short story.

Analyze the next novel you read for the manner in which the author develops the subplot.

- ✎ What is its purpose?
- ✎ Is there a sub-theme?
- ✎ How many characters were needed to carry the subplot?
- ✎ Was there overlap (characters, actions, circumstances)?
- ✎ How soon in the narrative was the subplot introduced?
- ✎ How soon did you recognize it as a subplot?
- ✎ When was the subplot resolved?
- ✎ How many subplots were there?
- ✎ Was there ever a link between the subplot and the main plot?
- ✎ How would you have done anything differently?
- ✎ Could you think of another subplot that could have been added to the story line?

Why am I having you analyze writing? You may be thinking, "This *is* a writing program, not a literature program, isn't it?" You're right. But until you can appreciate good writing, your own writing will suffer. You must be able to recognize the format, the style, and the flair of other authors, so you can develop your own. The more you read excellent writing, the better your writing will become.

And a woman having an issue of blood twelve years, which had spent all her living upon physicians, neither could be healed of any, came behind him, and touched the border of his garment: and immediately her issue of blood stanched. And Jesus said, Who touched me? When all denied, Peter and they that were with him said, Master, the multitude throng thee and press thee, and sayest thou, Who touched me?—Luke 8:43-45

None of us are "subplots" in God's scheme of events — that's something to rejoice about. This passage might be considered a "subplot" to the *Jairus and His Daughter* story, though to that woman it was a main plot in her life.

Shredding
(Re-writing)

Your first draft will not be perfect.

It may seem rude of me to say such a thing. But it's true. You'll have to fix it.

One of the major aspects of fixing a written piece is reducing its size.

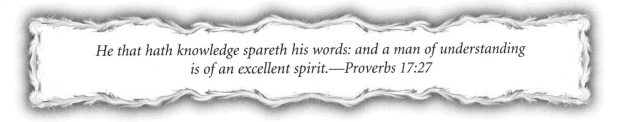

It may feel like you're shredding your work to pieces. It may feel like someone has kidnapped your kitten. It may feel like someone wants to amputate your toes.

But you'll get over it.

I have.

And I have lived to tell about it.

As I interview different friends who are writers, their problem isn't with blank pages and finding words to fill them, it's adapting their thoughts to the limited amount of space in which they are allowed to write — especially writers of short magazine pieces and news articles, etc.

The hardest thing I write each year is my Christmas letter. It seems I never have enough pages to retell all the wonderful things God has done in our lives each year.

But shred I must. And shred I do. So will you.

At about the third draft of one of your *five-course-dinner* writing pieces, count the words. Agree with yourself that your final version will have 10% fewer words. That may sound drastic. But after years of reading thousands of entries, submitted articles, and my own works, I am convinced that every piece could be improved if it were just cut, shredded, and properly edited.

So, I'll cut fifty per cent of this section and only allow the first page in.

He that hath knowledge spareth his words: and a man of understanding is of an excellent spirit.—Proverbs 17:27

Follow-Through
(Denouement and Epilogue)

During a golf lesson, the instructor kept telling me the follow-through was more important than the line-up.

I didn't understand him.

It didn't make sense.

After I had made contact with the ball, what difference did it make what I did with the club? I could just drop my arms straight down, right? Why did I have to bring the club on around over my shoulder? I thought it was just some golfers' ritual. But he was the pro, so I paid attention. It was amazing.

My puny little drives almost doubled when I mastered the follow-through.

How many of you have ever swung a bat? You already know that what you do with the bat after impact affects the power of the swing.

Let's think about this together. Really, it's what you are doing before impact that is going to affect the ball and enable you to have a successful follow-through.

If you don't plan for a fantastic follow-through, you don't have as much power in your swing — you bunt. Basically.

No power. No distance. No pizzazz. No home run.

This applies to your writing.

Technically, English-types call the follow-through the denouement (pronounce it "day-new-**maw**"). You need to know that word when you have to take a test, or if you want to impress someone the next time you go to a play.

But think of it as the "after-swing," the follow-through, the difference between a home run and a bunt. It's what happens after the big moment. After the impact with the ball — what happens? After the climax — what happens?

In fairy tales the denouement usually is quite simple: "and they lived happily ever after."

In the old Perry Mason television shows it's the part after the killer confesses and the defendant, Paul Drake, Della Street, and Mr. Mason sit around, finding out the one missing clue of how Perry knew who did it.

In the old police dramas, the follow-through is the part that says: Joe Grunch is now serving life imprisonment in the federal prison. His accomplice, Hilda Bouffant was given a reduced sentence and probation for turning State's Evidence. Policeman Billy Hoffa recovered from his gun shot wounds and is still on the beat. Music. Fade to credits. Commercials.

(Note that this part might actually be an epilogue, but we won't split hairs here.)

Think of the denouement of the last book you read. Was it just a paragraph, or a few pages?

You owe it to your reader to tie up any loose ends in the story, to link any of the un-linkable parts of the story, and to close it.

The follow-through of your writing is important. Remember, your readers now care about your hero, his dog, and his thirty-four goldfish. Give the readers a clue, a hope, a light to know what happens to your characters for the rest of their lives — or until the sequel.

I want you to notice the follow-through in the next ten stories or books you read or shows you watch. Discuss them with your teacher. Do you see why they are important?

Readers want closure.

As for me, I like to think it's Lassie's wave: as children, my siblings and I couldn't change the channel or turn off the television until Lassie waved at the end of the credits. We just had to see Lassie wave. It was closure.

You can't imagine my delight when we discovered the new Lassie shows. As I was telling my children about the "wave" tradition, we waited through the new credits and — "Life is Good" — Lassie waved at the end. All was right with the world once again!

So, in your stories, remember Lassie's wave, the golf-swing, the home run, the "and they lived happily ever after."

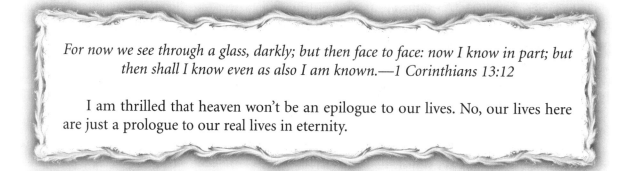

For now we see through a glass, darkly; but then face to face: now I know in part; but then shall I know even as also I am known.—1 Corinthians 13:12

I am thrilled that heaven won't be an epilogue to our lives. No, our lives here are just a prologue to our real lives in eternity.

© Jill Bond / Homeschool Press, PO Box 254, Elkton, MD 21922

Angle

"Flight 457 requesting approach to DFW."

"Okay Flight 457, runway two-eight-niner is clear, level off and come in at the heading mark five three degrees."

"Copy."

Just as an airplane pilot requests his approach, you need to request your approach to your story.

"Lord, requesting approach to story about bombing in Oklahoma City."

"Okay, take it from the prayer support angle on people in your town."

"Roger that, Lord."

I don't mean to be in any way disrespectful, but you must clear your writing with the Tower of Strength. You must seek His angle on the story.

What is the angle? Let's look at the story of David and Goliath. Your editor has told you to get the story on the battlefield. Your possible angles include:

Omnipotent reporter—overlooking the situation, "Yeah, it looks like a battle all right."
King Saul— "What am I going to do?"
David's brothers (before the killing)—to David: "What do you want, little guy?"
David—"God can handle this!"
Goliath—"I'm big, bad and ugly!"
One of the pebbles—"But I like the stream...."
The sling shot—"I'm David's best friend. We're tight, man. I mean tight."
The battlefield—"After all this trampling, it'll be years until I'll grow a decent thatch."
Goliath's sword—"I never really liked him anyway."
David's brothers (after the killing)—"And he's our *little* brother—can you imagine what we could do?"
Goliath's brothers—"We're out of here."

Try role playing. Each of you. Choose one of those possible angles or one of your own and tell the story of the giant killer totally from one of those perspectives. It's fun.

You're starting to understand angle. Here's another way to consider angle.

The big NFL game. It's the same game. But it isn't. Each one of these spectators is "seeing" a totally different football game because each is bringing in his own perspective to the game:

⇨ The little boy and his father—they have been planning this trip for three years. It will be a memory that they will share for a lifetime. They could only afford end-zone seats—but the little boy doesn't care. He's finally here at THE GAME.

⇨ The cheerleader who just visited her friend's church this morning. She's wondering about some things the pastor said. Is her skirt too short? She is starting to see the game — and her life — differently.

⇨ The quarterback whose contract is up for negotiation—he's desparate. His son has been diagnosed with a rare disease. His arm is getting as old as the rest of him. What if they don't want him next year? What will he do? He's got to throw the best game of his life.

⇨ The linebacker who can't believe he's finally playing pro ball—it took alot of tutoring to get him through college. They said he was dumb. Well, look at him now. He's Freezer-man. They just tell him to "sic' em," and he does.

⇨ The wealthy season ticket holder who gets ten seats on the fifty-yard line each year—even his car is custom painted the team colors. If his team loses, he's depressed the rest of the week. But if his team wins, *all's right with the world.*

⇨ The play-by-play announcer for the television network—he knows exactly where the ball is.

⇨ The "color" announcer who is checking his lap-top computer to make sure he has all the latest details—he can add color and background information on any guy who might touch the ball.

⇨ The producer in the control-center truck watching ten screens—he's making split-second decisions about angle, which camera, leads, etc.

⇨ The spoiled daughter of the team owner who is up in the glass-walled, first-class room—she couldn't be more bored. She'll have to "charm" all the VIP's her father invited to this game. Why did he have to buy a football team? How droll. After all, Elizabeth's father just bought a polo team.

⇨ The football—"Ow! That hurts. But then, I am the game."

Approach your writing from a distinct angle. Realize all the potential you have to make a story unique—depending on the angle you give it.

Now tell one of your favorite Bible stories from a different angle.

But the LORD said unto Samuel, Look not on his countenance,
or on the height of his stature; because I have refused him: for the LORD
seeth not as man seeth; for man looketh on the outward appearance,
but the LORD looketh on the heart.—1 Samuel 16:7

© Jill Bond / Homeschool Press, PO Box 254, Elkton, MD 21922

The Foreshadow Knows

(Foreshadowing)

When it's well done, it makes a work exceptional. When it's done poorly, it makes a work very amateurish.

You can make your work professional by mastering the writing tactic called "foreshadowing."

It is a way of clueing in your reader without giving the story away too early.

It is a great deal like walking on eggshells.

In a way it is like you're prophesying upcoming events.

You, as the writer, know what is going to happen in twenty pages. Could you involve your readers if you hinted at it now on page four?

Now, just a hint. Don't overdo it. Just get their minds clicking and thinking ahead. They'll keep reading to see if they have figured it out.

Honestly, do you appreciate it when a writer drops clues along the pages?

It gets you involved. The writer is giving you some credit for having intelligence.

The Bible is full of foreshadowing — except in the Bible, it is God who knows what is going to happen thousands of years ahead. He gave us the promise of Jesus as early as the curse on Adam and Eve.

Our writing is unimportant by comparison. But one thing about it, and I do want to make the connection, is this: Every prophecy of God either has come or will come true.

You must keep track (even on a separate sheet) of all the foreshadowing you do, to make sure you tie up all those loose ends throughout your work. You have to deliver on each of those promises. Your reader will know.

Foreshadowing can be very subtle. It might be a reference to a look the cousin gave to the minister. It sets the reader wondering if there might be more to the situation than we know. Or it can be more blatant — as a time-travel maneuver — you tell the ending first, then go back and catch the reader up from the beginning to the ending. Remember, a shadow just gives a milky, murky hint of the true form. A foreshadow is just that: a shadow that goes before.

Have you studied any of Shakespeare's work? He was a master at this. In his play, *Julius Caesar*, he foreshadows by using a soothsayer who warns "Big Julie" about the Ides of March, tipping off the reader that something is going to happen.

Old melodramas involved the audience by warning the hero about the impending danger. "Don't go in the sawmill. The villain is waiting for you. It's a trap." Of course, the actor couldn't hear the warning and was "captured." The audience was hooked.

In today's television, the newscasters tease you with "News at Eleven" headlines: "Major earthquake rocks planet, find out the details by tuning in to *our* news at eleven." You stay up to hear the news and are disappointed (or relieved) to find out that the "earthquake" was on Mars, according to some recent scientific discovery.

As you read, hunt for foreshadowing. Start keeping a log of examples of foreshadowing. As you note them, you'll start to improve your ability in this area.

It is a compliment to your reader to foreshadow.

Compliment your reader.

The Prophecy:
They part my garments among them, and cast lots upon my vesture.—Psalms 22:18

The Fulfillment:
And they crucified him, and parted his garments, casting lots: that it might be fulfilled which was spoken by the prophet, They parted my garments among them, and upon my vesture did they cast lots.—Matthew 27:35

One of the most exciting Bible studies is to match all the promises God made about the Messiah, our Lord, with the fulfillment of those promises — One Hundred Percent accuracy — OF COURSE! *What joy!*

The Ingredients—Words

I want you to bake a cake. But you can't have any flour.

Or eggs.

Or baking soda, or powder.

You can't have any milk, water, or juice.

Now go.

Ah, I'm giving you an impossible task — right?

Well, trying to write well without the proper ingredients — words — is like baking a cake with air. It's just — what's the word? — well, it's just impossible.

You have to build up your vocabulary.

You have to.

No way around it.

There is an entire section in *Favorites* ("Words, Words, Words," on page 315) to help you build your vocabulary and to help you keep track of your growth and your own personal lexicon.

Not only do you need to know what a word means, but more importantly, for *super* writing, you have to learn its connotation.

Do you know what that is?

A girl walks in the room who is 5'8" and she weighs 102 pounds.

Describe her.

Depending on the words you choose you can make her attractive or ugly.

> She could be svelte, model-like, slender, willowy, or slim;
>   OR
> she is scrawny, shriveled, gaunt, lanky, emaciated, or anorexic.

Writing to God's Glory / Student's Pages

Each of those groups of words has connotations. Each group basically "means" the same thing. But the images we carry along with us when we read those words paint quite different emotions.

A dictionary and a thesaurus will help you build your meaning vocabulary, but to really build your connotation vocabulary, you must read.

Exercise 1: Listen to a newscast (or read a newspaper) and note any "loaded" words the "impartial" journalist uses. It's rare to listen for more than one minute before you hear a word which carries a connotation to help steer the listener to an opinion. Yes, journalists are just supposed to report the facts. But, I challenge you to find one that *just* states the facts. You'll notice words with strong connotations like "terrorist." Notice the different connotation of "pro-life" or "anti-abortion."

Exercise 2: Fill in this chart with words or phrases with the same meaning, but different connotations:

Negative	Neutral	Positive
	huge	
	provincial	
	reprimand	
	hungry	
	knowledgable	
	involved	
	energetic	
	fan	
	commanding	

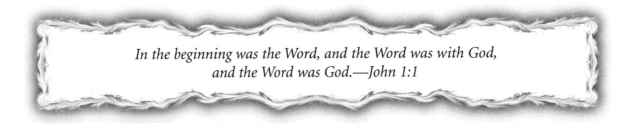

In the beginning was the Word, and the Word was with God, and the Word was God.—John 1:1

The Batter—Sentences and Paragraphs

If words are our ingredients, sentences and paragraphs are our batter.

It's the mixing of the ingredients in precise combination and order that make for different batters and proper batters to give us our finished product.

Chefs know that basically the same ingredients go in cakes and cookies. It is the amount of each ingredient and the combination of those ingredients that determine if we're making a cake or a batch of cookies.

The same is true with our writing.

All English-speaking writers start with the same ingredients: the English language, made up of our English words.

Yet, it's the combining of those words into different forms and in different orders that produces millions of different end-products, from novels to plays to comic books.

The content and the reading level are greatly affected by not only the word choice, but the word combining. If you're writing a story for third graders you would decrease the letter count of your words, but you'd also use simpler sentence structures than if you were writing for graduate students.

You could study sentence structure for months. Diagramming sentences is one of those things that seems to be a crucial life skill, or at least that is what English majors would have you believe. I've written and published thousands of sentences and yet the only time I ever diagrammed a sentence was in grade school. I think it is a way school-room teachers can "automate" teaching. It's a way of mass-marketing writing skills. It is easier grading when all thirty students must have exactly the same answer: check mark or no check mark. Easy. But our writing must be unique. No uniformity allowed. The "grading" is much more difficult when students "diagram" their own sentences by writing them — but it is much more true to life and true to the nature of writing.

Yes, go ahead and study all the mundane rules of sentence structure so you'll know them for any standardized test you might take. Store them in some accessible file in your brain. But, please don't make them affect your writing style. Some of the most stilted writing on this planet that I've ever read was written by those "grammatical whiz kids."

Think about a natural ball player. Yes, he knows the basics of the game. He drills. He practices. But he would never score dozens of baskets in a game if he mechanically walked through each of the basics before his lay-up. The basics are in him, but they are submerged so that the naturalness of his movements can produce *power results*.

Likewise, use the basics to make your sentences comprehensible, but don't use them to impede your words.

Sports announcers like to remind us that a diver will go through his dive completely — in his mind — before he moves far from the ladder. He doesn't go over the mechanics *while* he is diving. It's done before. Afterwards, he and his coach will watch the tapes to improve his next dives.

Likewise with writing. Learn the rules, yes. But not while you're actually creating. I've seen this over and over again. As you create, use the "creative side of your brain;" then go back and edit with the "logical side of your brain" — like a *one-two punch*.

Pick up any good book on your shelf. Choose any two pages. Count the number of words per sentence, and the number of sentences per paragraph. Average these figures.

I asked my son to do this counting exercise on one of the drafts of these two pages (pages 173-174; all 15 paragraphs). Here are his answers:

Paragraph Number	# words per sentence	# of sentences	Average # words per sentence
1	11	1	11
2	25	1	25
3	12, 25	2	18
4	7	1	7
5	18	1	18
6	28	1	28
7	19, 32	2	29
8	7, 27, 21, 12, 8, 22, 1, 6, 3, 30	10	14
9	24, 9, 9, 20	4	16
10	6, 8, 2, 2, 23, 20	6	10
11	17	1	17
12	25, 10, 3, 14	4	13
13	3, 4, 6, 7, 27	5	9
14	8, 4, 14, 3	4	7
15	22, 4	2	13

Average words per sentence: 12. Average sentences per paragraphs: 3
(FYI: Flesch-Kincaid grade level: 6.1; Coleman-Liau grade level: 9.5.)

I purposely wrote several different paragraphs: different in length, style, reading level, and meter. I did this so you'd start to get a feel for sentence and paragraph structure.

Do this same exercise with two pages from books you thoroughly enjoy and from books you don't like. Do you notice a pattern? Does the book's readability have anything to do with the pacing of the phrasing?

Many people enjoy reading when the writer varies the sentence lengths. Short ones. Medium ones. And then for effect, one that is a little more drawn out. It is somehow more pleasurable to the "eyegate" and for comprehension.

At first you might have to force yourself to vary the length of your sentences (and paragraphs) but then it will become quite natural. Also, the more you read good material the more natural it will become.

Depending on what you are writing, you'll want to stage your paragraphs. Have you ever been in a play? One of the first steps in producing the play is the "blocking." That's when the director and the actors just walk through the play, deciding who will stand where and when. For instance, in Act One, Scene One, the main character will enter at stage right and cross to back left for three lines, then move to right front, and on and on. It can be a very tedious procedure. But it keeps the movement on the stage lively, entertaining, and logical.

Likewise, you must block or stage your sentences and paragraphs. Place them on the page to be lively, entertaining, and logical. Their movement needs to be "graceful." There must be a flow and a cohesion among them.

Sometimes this cohesion is obvious with paragraph hooks and trailers. They are the linking sentences or words that deliberately tie two paragraphs together. Can you find any on these three pages?…That's right, the word "Likewise" ties the *idea* presented in one paragraph to the *point* in the next paragraph. Depending on what you are writing, hooks can be very effective. It is like giving your reader a tool with which to organize what he's learning.

Some writers like to summarize their thoughts at the close of each paragraph or section. This reinforces what the reader has learned. This works for non-fiction. It would be humorous and a bit odd in fiction.

You aren't treating your readers as dumb when you use hooks and summary clauses if you work it well and don't demean them. It is a very popular writing device. Look for hooks and summary clauses in a few books you are reading. Did you find some that were well-done? Did you find any that were amateurish? Were they helpful or a waste of type?

Jesus wept.—John 11:35

Expanding Universes
(Creativity)

Think big —

  As tall as you can reach —

    The top of the oak tree —

      The moon —

        The stars —

          The galaxy —

Ever growing, ever getting larger. How large can you think?

Think about God. Think how large He is. Picture how big just one billionth of God is — He's even larger than that. Our limited minds can't even imagine how big He is.

Is an elephant big? Is your house big? Is your church big?

Now picture your church. Do you see a building? Or doo you see a building with the grounds, parking lot, walkways, and flowers? Or do you see people? Where is your church now? How big is your church?

Now try this exercise. First of all, it can be done! Start anywhere on this page and without lifting your pencil, draw four lines which connect all nine dots. Only four straight lines without lifting your pencil. (Your teacher has the answer.)

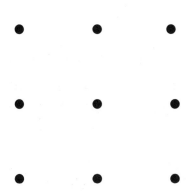

I didn't place that "mind-game" in this exercise to trick you. It serves the purpose of trying to get you to see beyond the imaginary limits we put on our thoughts, ideas, and creativity. Some of you figured it out, but most of you tried very hard, yet didn't go beyond the "false" limits of the imaginary nine-dot cube.

How does this apply to writing? Ah, you're starting to get it. Our writing must go beyond the nine-dot cube. It has to be expansive. Remember, we're writing after the mind of Christ for His Glory, and His Glory is *big*. As you write, go beyond the obvious: write the extraordinary. See things and possibilities others miss. Get your mind working.

Here's a fun exercise which you can do to get your mind going — kind of a jump-start to creativity.

Have someone tell you of two seemingly unrelated objects and you invent, create, or dream up some scenario, sentence, or link between the two things. Try these for starters (pairs 7-12 are for your own ideas):

Pair 1	sandpaper	lightbulbs
Pair 2	braids	avocados
Pair 3	feathers	bubbles
Pair 4	mountains	wedding ring
Pair 5	broken glass	wood
Pair 6	laughter	trouble
Pair 7		
Pair 8		
Pair 9		
Pair 10		
Pair 11		
Pair 12		

This is a game you can play in the car or as a filler in your day. It is writing. Just play "Pairs" by giving your sister a pair of words. Have her come up with a story, sentence, or link between the two. It is a way of expanding your writing universe.

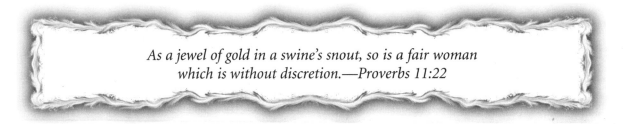

As a jewel of gold in a swine's snout, so is a fair woman which is without discretion.—Proverbs 11:22

© Jill Bond / Homeschool Press, PO Box 254, Elkton, MD 21922

Adjectives and Preservatives
(Why Write?)

"Write it down. If you want to remember it, write it down." How many times have you heard that?

It's true. Be it your next orthodontic appointment, or the address of the company where you are to get sized for your soccer uniform, if you write the information down, you're more likely to get it right.

Do you like to get mail?

I think everyone likes to get a personal letter from a friend or loved one.

What is your favorite book?

Yes, mine, too. Besides the Bible, what is your favorite story or novel?

 What was Columbus thinking as he crossed the Atlantic?

We know because he wrote it down.

Writing may seem tedious and a waste of time. I agree — because sometimes it is.

But, my friend, many times it isn't.

Do you remember all the events, exciting things, scores of your games, or how you felt when your little sister was born?

Have you forgotten anything you'd like to remember?

One of the most treasured items you'll have as an adult is your journal.

Honestly, I regret I didn't write more in my journals. I know I've mentally misplaced many stories, feelings, and happenings in my life which I'd like to retrace. If I had taken the time to write them down, I would never lose them.

Have you seen a photograph of something that happened when you were small? You were instantly transported back to that day and you can remember something about it. Do you feel strong emotions about the photograph? Can you remember your new haircut before the sitting? Did you want to wear a different shirt? Or was it a quick snapshot of a time you and your dad wrestled on the floor?

Could you do the same thing with your writing? Make a snapshot or formal portrait of something that happened this month in your life.

When my son Reed was six he wrote (with the help of an adult friend) "A Morning with My Mommy." I treasure it. He just told what his mornings with me were like and how he perceived them. It was a snapshot. It was one of the best gifts I've ever received.

I've reused pieces of my journals for magazine articles and sections of my books. I can re-read sections and remember a story for an anecdote, to see how I've grown spiritually, and to appreciate the parents and the family my Lord has given me. It also is very useful in keeping track of date. It is easy to mix up years and months. If you're writing a personal experience story (which is very popular and one of the easiest genres with which to be published), you'll have facts. You'll be able to involve the reader emotionally because you'll recall how you felt.

So much history is lost because no one wrote it down.

My great-aunt told me a story several times. How I wish I had taped it or written it down. It's lost now. She told of how she, a city girl, had visited a country family. She painted a picture of wash tubs, candles, and wood stoves that I had only read about in history books. She brought it to life. If only I could remember….

At least once a week for an hour, write down something. Get a spiral notebook, and jot down words, phrases, notes, and maybe even a few sentences or paragraphs.

Don't do it because someone made you do it. Do it because it's a very smart and rewarding thing to do.

Don't worry about grammar or spelling. It's for you. Be truthful. Mark fiction as such. I've tried to decipher some of my earliest writings — my handwriting has improved some, my spelling a hundredfold. Yet, as snapshots, they've very clear and exact pictures of where I was at the time.

Write it down.

Adjectives, nouns, verbs, articles — all serve you as preservatives.

They preserve your feelings, thoughts, opinions, memories, and growth.

Keep a journal and write it down.

Assignment:

1) Write a note or letter to a relative in another town on scratch paper, proof it, and then copy it on nice paper and mail it. Save the rough draft and file it.

2) Write a thank you note to your Sunday School teacher, pastor, pastor's wife or someone at your church to thank them for all they do (rough draft, proof, copy, mail, and file draft).

3) Write in your journal about a fun afternoon with your family.

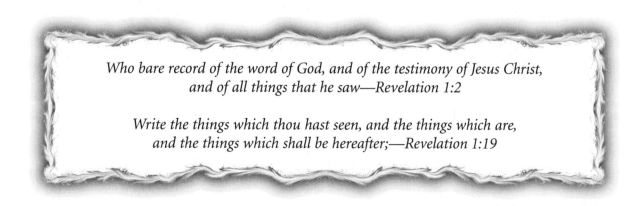

*Who bare record of the word of God, and of the testimony of Jesus Christ,
and of all things that he saw—Revelation 1:2*

*Write the things which thou hast seen, and the things which are,
and the things which shall be hereafter;—Revelation 1:19*

Writing to God's Glory / Student's Pages

Above Reproach

(Footnoting, etc.)

Don't copy someone else's work.

That seems simple enough.

That seems fair enough.

But is it?

There are volumes and volumes of case law concerning copyrights and infringements.

As Christians we should be above reproach. We should be able to testify to our work. We should give credit where credit is due.

As you do your research, keep very accurate records. Quote and give credit to the source.

If the idea isn't yours, give the originator the credit.

It seems so simple. Remember it.

Even if you change someone else's work around a little bit, they should receive some acknowledgment.

Also, your article will have more credibility if you make reference to experts, cite sources, and establish the facts. Instead of making your writing weak, your integrity will be validated.

If you want to quote someone, ask his permission. To give you an example, we have permission in writing from the people quoted in my book, *Dinner's in the Freezer!*.

Yes, it was very time consuming. Yes, it took a great deal of correspondence and detective work to track down each person. Yes, it added almost half a year to the production schedule. Yes, it was worth it.

There are quotes you can use which are in the public domain. A little research at the public library can help you determine if the material really is public domain, or if it's not, help you find out to whom the rights belong.

Don't assume the author has the rights to his work. In many cases you'll need to contact his publisher rather than the writer himself.

Would you enter a carpenter's home and remove a chair he had made, take it home and call it your own without paying for it? Certainly not. We call that stealing.

Yet I know Christians who think nothing of buying a book or curriculum and going to a copy machine and duplicating pages for their friends. This is just as much stealing as taking the carpenter's chair.

When you buy a book, only a portion of the price represents the cost of the printing and paper. What you are buying is the author's words, his ideas, and his way of writing things. A writer's writing is just as much a product as the carpenter's chair is.

You, as a writer, must respect other writers' words.

Because of who we are in Christ, when we write we must be above reproach.

Blessed are ye, when men shall hate you, and when they shall separate you from their company, and shall reproach you, and cast out your name as evil, for the Son of man's sake.—Luke 6:22

The only reproaches we should ever justifiably deserve are those from worldly accusers for the sake of our Lord.

Why?
(Purposeful Writing)

"Mommy, why is the grass green?"

"Mommy, why does the fork go here?"

"Mommy, why do we have door knobs?"

"Mommy, why is Daddy bigger than you?"

And several other thousands of questions fill the days of three- and four-year-olds.

They are wonderful as they search for answers to life's mysteries, like, "Why is milk white?"

They also want answers. They want reasons, explanations, and causes.

As you write, you should play the role of an inquisitive child and ask yourself questions. Every scene, character, image, and sentence should have a reason. Or else it shouldn't be part of your story.

Ask yourself some questions:

- Does this scene develop plot?
- Does this character add to the story line?
- Is this paragraph really necessary?
- Does this segment add to the suspense?
- Why should I include this detail?
- Does it help build the story?
- Is it superfluous?
- Would the story make as much sense without including it?
- Does it help create the proper mood?
- Will my reader be able to see the setting through this description?
- What else should I add to enhance the reader's comprehension of this situation?
- What would I want to have added to understand the plot's twists and turns?
- Is this sentence really necessary?
- Why did I write this page?

If you don't have a good reason for including a sentence, line, or paragraph, then strike it out.

If you sense a segment will sound confusing to your reader, clear away the rubble, and build a better paragraph. Your reader must be cognizant of your purpose.

Ask yourself "WHY?" and adjust your writing appropriately.

"And saying, Sirs, why do ye these things?" Acts 14:15
The Lord looks on the heart. He wants to know "why" we do what we do.

Writing to God's Glory / Student's Pages

© Jill Bond / Homeschool Press, PO Box 254, Elkton, MD 21922

SAM—Simile, Allegory, Metaphor

"As the sands on the Panama City beach, so are the numbers between one and two."

"Happier than a turnip in a compost bin."

"Christian left the City of Destruction and headed for the Celestial City."

Writers use three tools or techniques to paint visual pictures of ideas for their readers:

> S—Simile—explicit comparison (using *like* or *as*)
> A—Allegory—entire story based on a comparison or word picture
> M—Metaphor—implied comparison

Basically, you take something familiar to the reader and use it as a "word picture" to explain what you're saying.

These techniques are inspirational at their best and hilarious at their worst.

Can you think of any examples of *SAM* in anything you've read in the last month? Tell you teacher about it.

Write two sentences using either a metaphor or a simile:

1. _____

2. _____

It's difficult to pull an idea out of thin air, isn't it? Do you need a boost to get your mental rockets going? Okay, compare something (anything) to the space shuttle:

_____

Compare some action to eating spinach: _____

_____

Compare someone to Abraham Lincoln: _____

_____

Compare your home to something: _____

_____

Compare your father to someone else: _____

_____

Compare your last physical exercise (running, tennis match, whatever) to some other activity. Make your reader feel your exertion:

_____

Of course, you can go overboard with your imagery. It can make your reader drown in all your cleverness. If you keep it up, he'll feel like he's going down for the third time.

Reading will help you discern when to include your clever word pictures and when to use straight talk. Read good writing. Read *The Pilgrim's Progress*. Again.

As you record entries in your *Favorites* log, note (use a star or some other code) those passages which use simile or metaphor. Note allegories you appreciate.

Now for the fun stuff — as you read your Bible, start to keep a list of all the "comparisons" God uses. For starters, think about these metaphors and how they increase our comprehension.

⇨ Vine   ⇨ Root of Jesse   ⇨ Bride
⇨ Branches   ⇨ Breaking of Bread   ⇨ Body

Assignment: Start your own listing.

> *Come now, let us reason together, saith the LORD: though your sins be as scarlet, they shall be as white as snow; though they be red like crimson, they shall be as wool.*—Isaiah 1:18

Fact or Fiction

Read a fictional story. Read a non-fiction story.

Now, notice the similarities between the two.

Do they each have a catchy beginning?

Do they both build the story with interesting characterizations?

What about plot?

Do they both have a theme or point?

Do they have a timed closing?

I realize that colleges teach composition and creative writing as two completely distinct subjects. They approach these genres of writing as if they were mutually exclusive.

There is some logic in that "scheduling" technique, but I think it is misguided.

As an undergraduate, when I tutored students I discovered that they believed non-fiction had to be dry and boring, that a writer should only be "creative" in creative writing. They had the idea that only when the story was completely "play-pretend" did a writer have to involve the flowing side of his brain. This misconception produced BORING papers, reports, and theses.

It's as if composition was for the so-called *right brain-types* and creative writing was for the so-called *left brain-types*.

It was an exciting proposition to assist those students in being just as creative in their non-fiction reports as they ever had been in their fictional works. Likewise, I want you to benefit from the marvelous design God has placed in your body — use both sides of your brain when you write anything.

If a word picture would help you to understand this concept, think of it as "busing." You're integrating your thought patterns to produce a more well-rounded writing environment. The logic side will organize and make your writing reasonable, but left alone, very dull. The fun and fanciful side of your brain will create wild imagery, but it could be so disjointed that no reader could follow your logic.

I admonish you — whether you are writing fiction or non-fiction, your words must flow and draw the reader in.

So, don't look at this *Writing to God's Glory* course as only for would-be novelists. Use it to make *anything* you write more alive and vibrant.

Assignment: Write your autobiography. Your teacher will give you the parameters for this task. Use as much imagination with this non-fiction piece as you would if you were writing a story about a galaxy far, far away.

There is neither Jew nor Greek, there is neither bond nor free, there is neither male nor female: for ye are all one in Christ Jesus.—Galatians 3:28

I praise His Name that we are not segregated in His Kingdom.

© Jill Bond / Homeschool Press, PO Box 254, Elkton, MD 21922

Oink, Oink, Purr, Purr

(Onomatopoeia, Alliteration, Parallelism)

Carpenters plane, carve, and rout.

Chefs carve, sauté, and whip.

Writers have a variety of techniques also. They use onomatopoeia, alliteration, and parallelism.

Onomatopoeia

Using onomatopoeia can be fun. It can also be too cute. Onomatopoeia is the use of words which when pronounced make the actual sound (or close enough) of the word they refer to. Confused? Here are a few examples:

Oink, purr, swish, burp, meow, moo — you don't have to have a super-talented reader to be able to make those words sound like the words they mean. You can say "*oink*" so that it sounds just like a pig's grunting. You can say "*purr*" so that it sounds just like a kitten with his motor going.

One of the best places to find onomatopoeic writing is in children's literature. Preschoolers love the sound of words. They like it when Daddy reads that the cow says, "Moo," and draws out the o's so they can almost hear the cow's voice.

Don't go overboard with this technique when writing for adults. It's one thing to *burp* and *meow* through a story for your little brother; it's another thing to do it for your Great Uncle Harry.

Alliteration

Listen to your pastor's next sermon. He might just use alliteration to help you to remember the points of his sermon.

Alliteration is the use of words which begin with the same sounds. Proper use of this technique makes prose easier to read and to remember. Misuse of alliteration is annoying and trite.

"Sally and Susan sipped sassafras tea and salivated over salsa after they slept through the siesta."

Parallelism

While the two techniques explained above are optional and should be used sparingly, this technique is not an option. You must use it each and every time you write corresponding clauses.

By parallelism, I mean structuring your sentences so that if you are writing a list, each item of that list is in the identical (or equivalent) form. If you want to make a list, use all verbs *or* adverbs *or* nouns *or* adjectives. Don't mix the listing.

Here they are in sentences:

Yes	No
apples,	eating apples,
bananas,	yellow bananas,
pears, and	pears which are green, and
nectarines	nectarines

Yes	No
hopping,	hops,
jumping,	excited,
skipping, and	ready to party, and
laughing	laughs

Neladene likes apples, bananas, pears, and nectarines. (parallel)
Neladene likes eating apples, yellow bananas, pears which are green, and nectarines. (not parallel)

The children were hopping, jumping, skipping, and laughing. (parallel)
The children were jumping hops, excited, ready to party, and laughing. (not parallel)

Test your sentences to make certain you wrote your series or lists in parallel form.

Assignments:

1) Start a list of onomatopoeic words. Add five new ones this week.

2) Go on an alliteration hunt and find examples of its use in spoken and written words.

3) Find at least five examples of parallel construction in this or any other book.

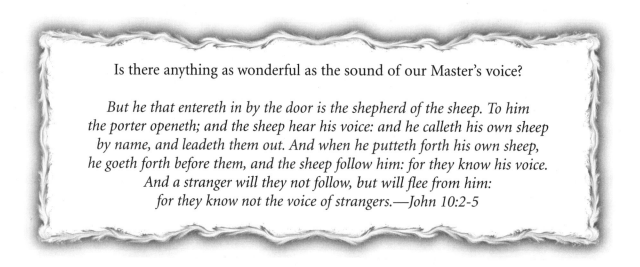

Is there anything as wonderful as the sound of our Master's voice?

But he that entereth in by the door is the shepherd of the sheep. To him the porter openeth; and the sheep hear his voice: and he calleth his own sheep by name, and leadeth them out. And when he putteth forth his own sheep, he goeth forth before them, and the sheep follow him: for they know his voice. And a stranger will they not follow, but will flee from him: for they know not the voice of strangers.—John 10:2-5

© Jill Bond / Homeschool Press, PO Box 254, Elkton, MD 21922

Style

Look around you. Notice the style of your home. How is it decorated?

Are there Jersey cow figurines, quilts, and wooden plaques?

Or, are there needlepoint chairs, Queen Anne cabinets, and Gainsboroughesque paintings?

Or, are there glass bricks, pink flamingos, and angular tables?

Or, are there wicker chairs, plants, and floral prints?

Or, are there bookcases loaded with books, mix-matched furniture, and family photographs?

Or, are there leather couches, jungle print pillows, and tiger wall hangings?

Or, are there baby swings, toys on the floor, and crayon-colored walls?

Is it warm and inviting? Or, is it cold and like a museum? Are guests instantly at ease? Or, do they feel at awe? Is it a home or a showplace?

Does it say, *"We live the way we like?"* Or, does it say, *"We live to impress others?"* Does it say, *"We are neat and tidy?"* Or, does it say, *"I'll straighten up later?"*

What is the spirit in your home? Is it restful? Or, is it frantic and hurried? Or, is it full of laughter? Does it reflect the Master of the house?

Just as your home has a style, your writing does also.

I've heard beginning writers declare, "I have to develop a writing style!"

All writers have a style. They develop it over time.

Just as your home is the result of years of "decorating," so your writing will begin to reflect your personality. It will flow from who you are.

God is working in all of us. He has made each of us a "custom creation." Don't try to deny that by trying to imitate your favorite author. It won't work.

If you keep yourself humble before the Lord, He'll work His work through you.

As some homes are modern, formal, cute, stand-offish, warm, wild, inviting, casual, unkempt, child-friendly, or even seemingly bereft of style — so are writers' styles.

At this stage of your writing development, you should be able to recognize different styles and appreciate how appropriate a style is to a work.

Assignments:

1)
- Make a list of ten different rooms you've been in recently (e.g., public library, church sanctuary, Grandma's kitchen, baby's nursery.)
- Choose a few words to describe the style of those rooms.
- Match those rooms to books or articles you've read — style-to-style.

2)
- Look through magazines, catalogues, and advertisements and clip the pictures of different rooms.
- Paste them on paper and number them as to the one which matches your "style" the best to the one which doesn't fit your style at all.
- Think of a character (anyone you know personally or a character from a story) who would live in a room like that and would "write" like the style of that room.

3)
- As you travel around town, notice different cars, trucks, and vans.
- Play a deducing game: If each vehicle were a writer, what would its style be? What would it write? How would it write it?
- Write a few sentences like "Buick" would write. How would "garbage truck" write? What about "Lambourghini"?

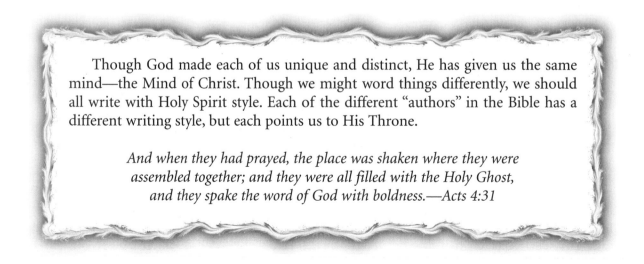

Though God made each of us unique and distinct, He has given us the same mind—the Mind of Christ. Though we might word things differently, we should all write with Holy Spirit style. Each of the different "authors" in the Bible has a different writing style, but each points us to His Throne.

And when they had prayed, the place was shaken where they were assembled together; and they were all filled with the Holy Ghost, and they spake the word of God with boldness.—Acts 4:31

© Jill Bond / Homeschool Press, PO Box 254, Elkton, MD 21922

Don't Feed the Flesh

Have you ever been to the zoo?

We have visited several zoos and they all seem to have one thing in common — signs which say:

"Don't feed the animals."

Some unsaved people have chosen to make a living by tempting others into sin. It is wrong to do this.

We, as Christians, must be careful that we don't "feed the flesh-natures" of our readers.

Obviously, we aren't going to write smut or untoward comments. That would be as obvious as smuggling a raw steak into the zoo and tossing it to the lion when no one is looking. I pray none of us would be tempted to such blatant sin.

It's the subtle feeding we must protect ourselves against — the picking up of a piece of popcorn and tossing it to the birds. In writing, that subtle feeding corresponds with anything we might write that would give any of our readers an "opening to sin."

The best protection against this is to post "Don't feed the Flesh" signs all over your mind, just like the zoo displays its signs in viewable areas. If you need to, write it in **bold** on the inside cover of your notebook, and pray that God will help you keep your writing pure.

Notice that the Bible discusses some "adult" topics, but at all times it is still rated "G." Likewise, as Christians, our work should be rated "G." The "G" should stand for even more than "General Audiences." It should stand for *Godly*.

Keep in mind Paul's warning that we must not present any situation to a weaker brother which may cause him to stumble. That applies to our writing also.

Earlier in this program we looked at characterizations and dialogue. We can describe a sinner and sin without "relishing the sin," and giving full details. You can get your point across without being explicit.

Ask Lord Jesus to be your first reader, and ask Him to test every word for its appropriateness. As your spirit becomes more sensitive to Him, you'll know when your writing is in jeopardy of feeding a reader's flesh-nature.

For instance, if you were writing for a diet club newsletter, you wouldn't want to describe the food they should be avoiding in a manner that encourages the readers to cheat on their dietary program and gorge themselves on "Death by Chocolate."

Just as we shouldn't "Feed the Flesh," we should, in our writing, promote proper behaviour and Godly living.

Assignment:

1) Write a sentence which encourages nutritious eating.

2) Write a sentence which discourages gluttony.

3) Write a sentence which encourages activity.

4) Write a sentence which discourages slothfulness.

5) Write a sentence which encourages cleanliness.

6) Write a sentence which discourages filthiness.

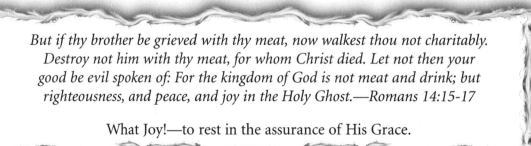

But if thy brother be grieved with thy meat, now walkest thou not charitably. Destroy not him with thy meat, for whom Christ died. Let not then your good be evil spoken of: For the kingdom of God is not meat and drink; but righteousness, and peace, and joy in the Holy Ghost.—Romans 14:15-17

What Joy!—to rest in the assurance of His Grace.

Thick Skin and Open Heart
(Writing as a Profession)

This is addressed to those of you considering any aspect of writing as a career or even as a part-time vocation. After some consideration and many questions from others, I've decided to answer some questions for you.

Who makes a good writer?

That is a tough one. On the surface it appears that a good writer is someone who writes well enough to be published. But there is more to it than that.

It reminds me of the little boy who wants to be a doctor when he grows up. His uncle says, "So, you want to practice medicine?" "No, I just want to have all the things a doctor has: prestige, money, golf, and respect." But he doesn't want to have to deal with sick people to get there.

Sometimes we see careers portrayed in movies and we see the "enjoyable" part of the job — it would be too boring to show the hours and hours of studying and detail work that careers take. Can you imagine a police show where we watch a policeman fill out the paperwork for two hours? No, we see the exciting part of his job.

Would the television show *Murder, She Wrote* be popular if we watched Jessica Fletcher typing for 43 minutes of each show? Probably not. So, we see her at publicity events, doing research, traveling, and having conferences with her publisher — the "fun" side of the career.

But there would be no television interview if there hadn't been hundreds of lonely hours at a keyboard.

Ultimately, just as a doctor has to work with sick people to be a doctor, a writer has to write to be a writer.

Sure, you want to be a writer: you'd love to travel around the country doing the talk-show circuit, autographing your books, working on the set when they make your book into a movie — but the reality is that the "fun stuff" is only a very small percentage of the time a writer spends "working."

There are hours and hours of writing, re-writing, going over manuscripts, and proofing blue lines. Not to mention all the hours of pre-writing, praying, and research. Not to mention all the hours submitting manuscripts and waiting for replies.

© Jill Bond / Homeschool Press, PO Box 254, Elkton, MD 21922

Lifestyle and $$

I'm not trying to talk you out of a career as a writer. I just want you to realize that writing is writing. And if God is calling you to be a writer, nothing I can say will dissuade you.

Writing can be a wonderful career. I wouldn't choose any other. It fits my lifestyle. *For me* it is the ideal "job" for a stay-at-home mom. But I don't have to make a living at it. My husband provides for our family.

As much as I want you to write, I don't want you to choose writing for the wrong reasons. Writing isn't glamorous, but then we shouldn't be seeking glamour.

For most writers, writing isn't financially rewarding. Very few writers actually make a living by writing. Many work freelance and are very grateful for the checks when they come in.

That's why when we heard of a four-million-dollar book advance it was such a big deal. They are rare! Rare indeed!

In 1981, the *New York Times* News Service covered a survey done by Columbia University. More than two thousand published authors were surveyed. The average writer earned $4,775 a year. The average hourly pay was $4.90 — below the current minimum wage. [Facts from *Write to Publish* in the Religious Market by Lucien Coleman © 1987 Lucien Coleman; page 3.]

> Yet, we should be writing because God has told us to. Our reward is in our faithfulness to Him. We're answerable to Him. We're accountable to Him.

Responses

I hold on to the fact that we're accountable to God because I'm not thick-skinned. This introduces another aspect of writing you should consider. Not everyone is going to adore your work as much as your mother does. Not everyone is going to love you.

When you write, even if it is fictional, you pour your very being into the work. It's you, your thoughts, your outlook. You leave yourself open to criticism. One of the first things a writer should do, I'm told, is to develop a thick skin. I haven't yet. But, then I am not known for going with the popular trends.

Fan mail is wonderful. I get letters which are better than anything I could have ever dreamed about. Letters of how I've changed people's lives with my words. That is gratifying. I can run for months on a letter like the one from the lady who said she was going to look me up in heaven to say "thank you." It had never before occurred to me that anyone would "stand in my line" to say "thank you" to me. Have you heard the song *Thank*

You by Christian singer Ray Boltz? I figured I'd spend the first trillion years at the feet of Jesus, then when He told me to go on, I'd stand in the lines of the thousands of people who have touched my life. Then this letter arrived. It had a profound effect on me. It made me really consider my "hobby" as even more of a gift from God.

Think about it. Someone looking you up in heaven to say "thank you" for how your writing helped him to figure out something in his life! That, my friend, is a gift from God! That is why we're writing. Not so we can be A WRITER, but so He can touch lives through us.

Those letters affect me. They sing to my spirit. God replenishes me through them.

To keep me humble, once or twice a year I get a doozy of a letter. I haven't yet developed the thick skin to shake it off. I received a rebuke one day. Some of it was deserved, some of it was off base. It was enough to make me crawl in God's lap and seek His face. Because, friend, our self-worth doesn't come from fan mail. It comes from Him. He thought enough of us to give His Son for us. Our worth is the value He puts on our lives.

As writers, we have to stay focused on Him. You'll get hate mail, or else you aren't impacting the world for Him. That comes with writing to His Glory. My husband just reads those letters, says the return address is from Satan and doesn't give them to me. Early in my career he let me read one: the woman assaulted me on three "quotes" of mine which I never said. She had attributed opinions to me which I don't hold and have never espoused. In closing, she demanded I stop talking about family and leave "children" out of my ministry! Alan was right — the return address might as well have read:

```
┌─────────────────────────────────────────────┐
│  Beelzebub                          ┌───┐   │
│  666 Sheol Way                      │   │   │
│  Gehenna                            └───┘   │
│                                             │
│                                             │
│                                             │
│                                             │
└─────────────────────────────────────────────┘
```

What is going to make some of you great writers is that your hearts *are* so sensitive. You can feel the emotions of others, so your characters have depth. You understand things in such a way that cold people totally miss. That is to your advantage. It takes being a caring person to develop a caring plot.

Yet, at the same time, that wonderful talent you have to empathize also makes you vulnerable, so guard your heart. Keep your eyes on Jesus and those fiery darts won't penetrate your armor. You'll recognize the enemy and treat him the way he deserves to be treated.

Another kind of response to consider is those letters from other Christians, truly written in love, to encourage you to be that much better. I love those — letters from others who care and come to me in love, sharing ideas, suggestions, and ways I could do better. Those are wonderful. Those are gifts. I look forward to receiving constructive feedback. I pray you'll be able to discern the difference between those from within and those from without.

Competition

I don't worry about competition with my writing. I don't see any evidence of competition in the Body of Christ. If we each are faithful to God with the talents He has given us, we don't and shouldn't consider the "sales volume" of others' works. If your friend wins a contest — that's wonderful! God wanted her work to win. If your work was printed in a magazine which only has a circulation of a few thousand — be thrilled! God knows who He wants to read your work.

The world would pit one book against another. The world would get all wrapped up with best-seller lists. Personally, I think God has his own lists. He doesn't look at "More than one million books in print" and get impressed. He looks at five-year-old Becky and the letter she wrote to Grandma, and says, "Well done, thou good and faithful servant."

That is what we should be looking forward to. Not how impressive our earthly resumé is — but the one He is typesetting for us.

The Resumé

Am I proposing that you shouldn't do your best and be organized? Not at all.

Yes, you should keep track of your writing. See the whole section, *Outlet Journal*, pages 273-281. I was just stating that your resumé doesn't fully describe the impact you really are having. God is keeping the most accurate tabs on your growth.

"I hate this!" the seminary student was so frustrated. I was also. I was working as the assistant manager of a printing firm near the graduate school. I was working with the student developing his "professional resumé." The more he worked, the "cheaper" he felt. It was as if he had to prove he wasn't a good Christian *to* prove he was a good Christian. He felt he was just being prideful, boastful, insincere, worldly, and ambitious: "I should be your pastor because I'm one of the most humble men alive today!" It almost was funny. Sad, but funny.

I understand that about resumés. Yet, you can control your own. You could present your impressive list of writing accomplishments in a way that toots His horn, not yours.

Many of the editors I know aren't looking for an impressive listing of published articles, certificates of achievements, and honorable mentions. They are looking for background information so they can write a biographical sketch about you to accompany your article.

As your writing develops, you will come across the editor who is more interested in your resumé, or "Who's Who" of magazines, than he is about what you wrote. That's sad. But that's part of the business.

Why even bother with those types of magazines? Because some of us are called to reach out beyond the fort — to evangelize. Yes, we are called to equip and encourage the saints. But we also might be called to reach beyond the "Christian marketplace" and touch lives through the secular media.

So, start keeping track of your writing. Start building your resumé. It could broaden your impact. But keep in mind it is not a tool to inflate your ego.

What Else Besides "Writer"?

There are several jobs related to writing that can provide income and satisfaction for you. Some of you might have a talent with words, but just aren't creative about coming up with your own ideas. Some of you have a talent for grammar and syntax. Some of you love reading and know just what others would like to read. There are ways you can use your talents. Here are a few to consider:

Co-Author or Ghost Writer: I know of writers who don't have to come up with the ideas for books, articles, etc. They team up with an "idea" person and write the words out for them. I know of a friend of a friend who was offered $10,000 to write up the stories of a soldier but she had to do it in one week. She worked hard for that $10,000.

Copyeditor: Once I've written a piece, cross-checked it, re-typed it, re-done it through draft after draft, put in my husband's corrections — I'm too close to it to see it anymore. Even editors who live with a work for weeks become almost blind to the typos. So, they hire copyeditors — fresh eyes — to read a work for typos, grammatical errors, and other problems that the writer and editors might miss. This can be a great free-lance job. You might need to start on a volunteer basis first to build up your skill and reputation:

☆ maybe your church secretary could use a proofreader for the weekly bulletin;
☆ the local printer might need someone to double-check layouts;
☆ your support group newsletter editor might love extra help.

Any of those could work into a part-time or free lance job. Then, when you're really good and have a track record, contact the editor of your favorite magazine and offer to proof their next issue for $25. Continue building your skill and resumé. Then approach a publishing house. Ask for a style sheet and a proofreading or copyediting test. Who knows — you could earn a few extra thousand dollars a year — finding those "i"s that weren't capitalized.

Editor: The word editor means so many different things to different people. There is the editor-in-chief at the newspaper who might not even read text, but mainly manages people. There are the book editors who work one-on-one with an author to get a suitable work completed. There are all-in-one-editors who edit and publish their own magazines. You'll find this common in the homeschool and small-press newsletter business — the editor is also the main writer.

This was only a brief look at possible jobs for those of you who like words and would like to do something with words beyond just writing. There are dozens of variations. Even when I worked as an assistant manager of a printing firm I was helping clients with the wording of a flyer, a resume, or a brochure.

And of course there are hundreds of writing options. Not all writers are authors. Just think of the possibilities....

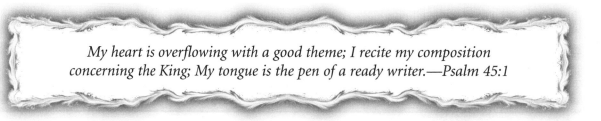

My heart is overflowing with a good theme; I recite my composition concerning the King; My tongue is the pen of a ready writer.—Psalm 45:1

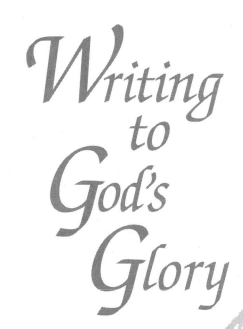

Writing to God's Glory

Craftsmen

More Power

(Use Verbs)

"Fred was going to work."

This sentence is much too weak to power any storyline vehicle. What it needs is more power. We need to boost it with high octane words, bursting with potential. As it stands now, it is lifeless. Empty. Wanting.

All too often sentences idle. They house latent power, but the driver just isn't gunning it with creative fuel. Let's learn how to put the pedal to the metal of our words.

How many sentences have you read that took you as far as the period, and left you waiting for the light to turn green?

Verbs give sentences life. Verbs excite the reader. Verbs propel your message around corners and into hearts.

Train yourself, force yourself, discipline yourself to say it with verbs.

As you battle bore-bees, alkaline adjectives, and ponderosa participles, you need more power — verbs.

Let's talk about Fred. We could list a string of adjectives, but let's give our reader credit for a little intelligence and let's show him Fred.

Fred #1:
Fred beamed as he kissed his wife goodbye, confident because among all the candidates, he had won the vice presidency at Acme Space Astronuts and Bolts.

Fred #2:
Tapping his foot, Fred waited for the beep, then grabbed his coffee out of the microwave, barreled his way out the door, fumbled with his keys, started his car, and gunned it out of the driveway, knowing full well that he was going to be late, again.

Fred #3:
Would he come back home tonight? Fred wondered as he strapped his gun belt on, buttoned up his jacket, and checked outside the door for any problems — the types of problems that arrested men in Fred's line of work.

By using verbs we now know a little more about Fred and his going to work.

Now it's your turn. Use only one sentence to make up your own versions of Fred:

Fred #4:

_____

_____

_____

Fred #5:

_____

_____

_____

Fred #6:

_____

_____

_____

As you work and toil to infuse your sentences with more power, avail yourself of the Source of all power. He is omnipotent, all powerful. If you're writing to His Glory, in His will, tap into His power source and juice up your narrative with His inspiration.

And they were all amazed at the mighty power of God.—Luke 9:43

© Jill Bond / Homeschool Press, PO Box 254, Elkton, MD 21922

Beware of the Bore-Bees

(Nix the "To Be" Verbs)

Hunt high and low, for they sneak in and render your writing "blah."

They worm in among your words causing your reader to retreat in terror from the maddening boredom.

With the diligence of Lancelot, Robin Hood, and General Norman Schwarzkopf, seek out these dreaded enemies and destroy them. This is your mission.

Activate your heat-seeking, retro-guidance erasers and mutilate them beyond recognition.

Launch your "scrub" missiles and rout those little misers out of your mind space.

To help you recognize them on the spot, the bore-bees' code names are:

AM
IS
ARE
WAS
WERE

They work for the dull writing department of 2-B.

Before we send you into the field on this tough assignment, we're giving you some target practice. Students, prepare yourselves. GO. Rewrite these insipid sentences. Bring them to life with active verbs.

1. She is too talkative.

_____

2. He was kind to the dog by petting the canine on the head.

_____

3. I am too tired to write another sentence.

_____

4. They were going to think of something to say.

_____

5. John is lazy.

_____

6. Bill and Gary were going fishing.

_____

7. Holidays are busy times for our family.

_____

8. Horses are big.

_____

> *I am convinced that I know* that the only One that does use the phrase "I am" effectively and precisely every time is
>
> ### The Great I AM—Yahweh GOD!
>
> *And God said unto Moses, I AM THAT I AM: and he said, Thus thou say unto the children of Israel, I AM hath sent me unto you.*—Exodus 3:14
>
> (The opening phrase in this box is a crass example of the improper use of I am.)
>
> Let's not deter our writing from His Glory by diluting the phrase "I am."

Writing to God's Glory / Student's Pages

© Jill Bond / Homeschool Press, PO Box 254, Elkton, MD 21922

Less is More
(Compact Your Writing)

"More or less considering less or more than more or less," was a difficult line to utter correctly in the play, *Deadwood Dick*. The student actor, though, delivered it with perfect accuracy each time. The play was fun and a parody of itself. The old western melodrama sprang to life with tried and true characters, corny lines, and a ridiculous plot. Try memorizing that line from the play and then listen to it.

Less is more when you're writing.

Droning on and on and on is boring. Say it. Don't resay it. Don't say it again and again. Just say it the first time, once and for all. Don't just say the same thing again with a few different words. Don't say it like I said it in this paragraph.

Give your readers a little credit. They're not as dull as your writing could be.

After you write a piece, count the words. Decide to reduce the word count by at least 10%. Then do it. Use one powerhouse word, instead of two featherweights. Remove those bore-bees and let the action verbs carry the weight. Only leave in "that" when it is vital to comprehension. Obliterate any extra words. Don't be redundant.

Banish military treatises and bureaucratese from your mental data banks. Like parasites, they'll feed off your better judgment and fill your phrasing tapes with horrible examples of stretching a good ten-word sentence into a sixty-five-word sleeping pill.

Make your writing tight and forceful. Let it flow with the energy of its own words; don't let it get bogged down in useless dribble.

Don't overexplain. Is it necessary for the reader to know that Uncle George went to college in New Hampshire where he met your mother's sister, Susan, who was visiting her best friend from high school, whose name was Sylvia Carnegie (no relation to *the* Carnegies), who had been the homecoming queen the year your mother entered high school in that quaint little town named after Francis Marion who was also known as the Swamp Fox? If all the reader needs to know is that Uncle George dropped Billy off at Little League practice and the whole story is about Billy, *don't* give us the life history of Uncle George.

It is a temptation to tell all we know. Be an iceberg. Keep most of your knowledge under the surface of your writing. Otherwise your writing will leave your readers cold.

© Jill Bond / Homeschool Press, PO Box 254, Elkton, MD 21922

The challenge: rewrite with fewer words.

1) Joyce was able to announce_____

2) long-standing traditions_____

3) Perhaps, after due consideration you would be so kind to inform us of your decision.

_____

4) In the event of uncalled for disturbances in the patterns of climatic influences, forcing unprecedented precipitation, it is advised by this council, and highly recommended, though not mandated, that the person of nearest proximity to the locale in question avail himself to reconfigure any window which is not in a closed and secure position.

_____

_____

5) Our research indicates that a high preponderance of domestic engineers would procure adequate staples for their family's sustenance at said location, if it was proven that said facility could drastically improve the viability of their staying within the stringent demands of their financial control mechanism.

_____

_____

6) Heather was happy, joyful, and thrilled with the idea.

_____

7) Harvey was an imaginary rabbit of huge proportions, completely a figment of Jimmy Stewart's imagination.

_____

8) Patton was a military general in the army.

_____

9) President Ronald Reagan was the oldest man ever to serve America, his country, as president.

_____

10) I helped my mother fix dinner last night by setting the table, putting out the silverware, forks, spoons, knives, napkins, plates, spices, salt and pepper, glasses and drinks.

_____

When we read the Bible, notice how God doesn't waste words. His words are beautiful.

The heavens declare the glory of God.—Psalms 19:1

Let the heavens rejoice, and let the earth be glad; let the sea roar, and the fulness thereof.—Psalms 96:11

He doesn't tell us too much or too little. Likewise, in our lives we need His balance.

Railroad Crossings
(Nix the Word "That")

Railroad crossing, watch out for cars. Can you spell that without any "R's"? —

T.H.A.T.

. . . and we were so very clever when we tried the joke on our daddy.

Yet, how much our writing would improve if we hadn't learned how to spell that so well.

Like a that out of Hades, we let it flit and flop all over our sentences. That we may be less understood. That we might impress our teachers. That we might achieve the all-important word count, if we stick in a few extra thats.

It could be *that* more than ninety percent of the thats I come across are totally worthless.

Your sentence is racing down the communication track; the verb engine is doing all the work, the noun cars keep their passengers content, the adjective car contains the next sentence's harvest. Then you, the engineer, do it. You neglect all your training and on the track you lay a that. Crash! Bamm! The carnage is newsworthy. The casualties lie bleeding, seeking triage. At the intersection of two wonderful modes of communication, the signal lights fail and that causes the premature death of a great sentence.

That should be avoided.

Before you allow a that to dwell on your computer screen, hang on your erasable board, or drip on your notebook paper, make sure that it is needed. A sentence is a terrible thing to waste.

The coal, full of energy, rests peacefully in the bin, waiting for the signal, *your* signal to start the engines. You are your sentence's engineer. Open the throttle, ease off the brake, holler to the fireman to start shoveling coal, engage the engine, and roll forward. Keep in mind, more accidents happen at railroad crossings than on the straight track. Stay alert for those railroad crossings without any "R's" — THAT.

Cross out all the unnecessary uses of ~~that~~ in the following (or re-word the sentence):

I was hoping that you'd be interested in coming over to my house for dinner Thursday night. That night we're going to show an old movie video of *The Man Who Came to Dinner*. Or, is it *Guess Who's Coming to Dinner*? I get those two movies confused, though they have nothing in common, except that they both have that word dinner in them. Does that confuse you, also? I've also invited George and Heidi, that couple we met at that ski resort on that vacation we took that year we first met at that convention in Toledo. I hope that they like old movies, too. I'm not sure what June is cooking for dinner. That will be a surprise. Is that Okay with you?

I'd better close now and get this e-mail letter transmitted because that boss of mine is starting to monitor our time. I don't want to get my terminal time terminated. Heh, I made a joke. Wasn't that funny? Zip me your answer so that I can tell June how many to cook up that surprise dinner for. That's about it for now.

It might be a scary thought at first, to know we are accountable for each idle word we speak (or write). Yet, we can rest in the knowledge *that* He loves us deeply, sincerely, and faithfully.

But I say unto you, That every idle word that men shall speak, they shall give account thereof in the day of judgment.—Matthew 12:36

(Notice: "that" is in the verse.)

Time Travel
(Tense Agreement)

Time travel stories are fun. H.G. Wells wove an exciting story of time travel in 1895: *The Time Machine*. Eager children traveled with Doug and Tony through *The Time Tunnel*, a black-and-white television show which aired in the early sixties. Doc Brown and Marty McFly catapulted through centuries via their souped-up DeLorean in the *Back to the Future* movie series. Mr. Whitaker, the patriarch of the *Adventures in Odyssey* series, invented an imagination station where children travel to other times and places.

Yes, the idea of time travel is exciting. Trips through the future monopolize an entire genre of writing: science fiction. Consider the popularity of the *Star Trek*® series of television shows and movies. I agree with you: your creativity can have fun developing plots among the weaves of the space-time continuum.

However, and here's the catch, we don't want the narrator to travel through time in the same paragraph. We want his perspective to have a consistency of tense.

Choose your time frame and stick with it. Either write in past or present tense.

You can blend time frames through narration and flashbacks. Be careful and stay true to your time framework.

Read this introduction to a story and try to stay with its currents of time:

Captain Kirk walked on the bridge and says to Lt. Data, "Marty McFly was arriving on the locomotive DeLorean at high noon. Prepare an Away Team to greet him." Doug looked over and says, "H.G., We're going to have fun meeting other time travelers here on the Spaceship Intraprize."

Doc Brown sat down and pets his dog, Einstein. "Oh, yes, it'll be grand to see Marty again."

Whit asks if anyone would like a banana split.

The tractor beam locks onto the DeLorean and pulled the tired traveler on board. "It was worth the trip," Marty had said when he saw the doc. "When did you arrive?"

Doc Brown, looks at his chronometer and says, "Tomorrow."

As much fun as we could have in developing such a story by mixing time travelers together, it is awkward to read if the narrator is jumping in from various time frames.

Time travel is part of stories. We want the characters to move through some space of time. Yet, we must give the reader a comfortable chair from which to view the action. Will we place him on the bench, watching the action as it takes place? Will we set him in a recliner chair of the future looking back at the action like looking through an old photo album? Will we place him in a chair and face him toward tomorrow? You the author must place him in his framework and be, oh, so careful not to whip him around through tense manipulation at a warp speed beyond human comprehension.

Go through the story introduction above and correct all the time-frame errors. (English teachers refer to them as tense errors.) Fix all of the narrative to match a particular perspective. Or rewrite some other paragraph. (Use separate sheets of paper.)

1) Write it using past tense. (The writer is telling the story as if it all happened in the past.)

2) Write it using future tense. (The writer is telling the story predicting future events. This is almost impossible to do well.)

3) Write it using present tense. (The writer is telling the reader what is happening now as a current spectator.)

4) Write it using past perfect. (The writer is telling the reader the story in the most boring way possible using the "a good time was had by all" style.)

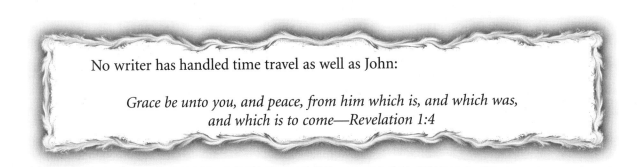

No writer has handled time travel as well as John:

Grace be unto you, and peace, from him which is, and which was, and which is to come—Revelation 1:4

The Boy who cried "!"

(Don't Waste Your "!")

"Turn from your wicked ways!"

"Repent!"

"Behold!"

Emphasis is needed and supplied with a ball and bat "!".

Interjections are useful and add drama to our sentences.

They add import. They add accent and weight to certain phrases and sentences.

"Attention!" Like reveille, the exclamation point alerts the reader to attention.

The caution you must heed, is not in using it, but in the frequency with which you use it.

Remember the story of "The Boy Who Cried Wolf"? He shouted for *help!* too many times. When the real time for "!" came, he had lulled his townspeople in to thinking that "!" was meaningless.

Imagine yourself sitting in church listening to a visiting pastor. If he announced the ladies quilting bee with a "!" voice and then read the Scripture with a "!" tone, and then told a baseball illustration with a "!" style, and then gave the salvation story with a "!" emphasis, you would have already tuned him out.

If it helps, picture the *bat and ball* as made of solid gold. It is expensive. It is worthy, but it costs a great deal to use. You want to use it sparingly. Otherwise, what you really want to emphasize becomes common. Stay clear of constant hyperbole. Stand clear of histrionics.

Give your writing more credibility by saving your "!" for when the wolf is really at the door.

Remember, if you construct your paragraphs well, the writing alone will have the reader at the edge of his seat.

Read these sentences and weigh for yourself if the "!" is needed, or if you could reword the sentence so the "!" is part of the words, not the punctuation. [Remember, it is better to say it with words than with punctuation.]

1) Help!

2) Call 911!

3) The bake sale is on Saturday!

4) You'll have a great time!

5) Jane Smith won the race! Billy Jones came in second! Wallace Winthrop came in third!

6) Holly jumped through the hoop!

7) The elephants charged!

8) I finally got the children down for bedtime!

9) I finished my homework!

10) The Bible is the best book every written!

For an interesting study, the next time you read your Bible, look for "!'s" and watch for their use.

To illustrate: The entire book of Ephesians (KJV) is written without using an exclamation point. Paul gave us the emphasis in Ephesians with words. The excitement is there. The validity is there. He didn't write weakly and then draft and "!" to make his points.

...be strong in the Lord, and in the power of his might. Put on the whole armour of God....—Ephesians 6:10, 11

Auntie Cindy

(Antecedents)

"If I only had a brain," he sang.

"A heart," he sang.

"The nerve," he sang.

"A home," she sang.

In the children's classic, *The Wizard of Oz*, L. Frank Baum created a story line filled with characters — each on a quest: the scarecrow decided he needed a brain; the tin man felt he needed a heart; the lion desperately wanted courage; and the "fearless leader," Dorothy, just wanted to go home to her Auntie Em.

Now how does this apply to grammar? It's all about antecedents.

Antecedents aren't a fun topic. I agree. So, picture the yellow-brick-road travelers as you write pronouns. The pronoun "she" is looking for her Auntie Cindy, "her" antecedent.

Since we're the creator, the master storyteller, the writer, we know exactly who the "he" is when we write a sentence. Yet, if we aren't careful, we can confuse our readers. We'll have little boys putting leashes around their own necks, as in:

> Stuart, after washing his dog, put a leash around his neck, **and** went for a walk.

That isn't as confusing as some of our sentences can become. We could argue that anyone knows the leash went around the dog's neck. I agree, but let's not make our reader travel the whole length of the yellow brick road to grasp our meaning. Let's be more direct and let Dorothy click her heels together at the very beginning. Let's give each pronoun a clear antecedent.

If it is any comfort, faulty reference is a very common problem for writers. Once you've written your piece, reread it for those lost pronouns. If any phrasing could be misconstrued, reconstruct it. After all, we want to be understood, don't we?

Help out the "wayword" pronouns and references in the following:

1) Susan and Billy went on a field trip to Sea World in Orlando where they have killer whales and dolphins. They are mammals and give birth to live babies. They nurse just like we do. They ate fish for lunch. They had fun at the park.

2) One of the Smithsonian Museums is the National Air and Space Museum. They have the Wright Brothers' first plane. They flew it on December 17, 1903 at Kitty Hawk, North Carolina. The museum tour guide pointed out the Spirit of St. Louis, flown by Charles Lindbergh. He made the first solo flight across the Atlantic. They all cheered when he finished 33-1/2 hours later. We liked the Air and Space Museum. You should go there, too.

3) "Doctor, Doctor," the nurse urged, "his vital signs are dropping." "Hand me the paddles," the intern ordered. "All clear," he commanded. His chest heaved under the charge of the electric current. His breathing was erratic. "Again," he said. This time the monitor shot up and down showing a regular heart beat. "He's going to make it," the nurse said. "He's going to pass this cardiac test."

The Bible is always clear about its references and antecedents. Likewise, we must be very careful when we are writing about our LORD so we don't confuse His characteristics and masterful touch with a human pronoun. One way we can always differentiate his (human reference) from His (God's) is by capitalizing all pronouns and nouns referring to God. Yet, we must not rely totally on the capitalizing device to do our work for us (several Bible translations don't capitalize the divine pronouns). We must make our writing clear. Remember, we have the most important message in the world.

That I may publish with the voice of thanksgiving, and tell of all thy wondrous works.—Psalms 26:7

Writing to God's Glory / Student's Pages

Peace Talks

(Verb Agreement)

"Mr. President, I think you might want to reconsider your position," Secretary of State Kissinger stated in his distinct accent.

"Okay, I'll go to China," President Nixon decided.

Peace talks on the level of world affairs are critical. Each national leader comes to the table with his own position and beliefs. Each wants to win for his side. Yet, if the talks are successful, some agreement is made. They create a level of harmony, albeit sometimes miniscule.

Play-act that you're a head of state and you're seeking agreement. Except you're not at a summit meeting, you're convening in your own writing. You're seeking harmony in your wording.

Instead of counting missiles and troop numbers, you're concerned with number, the property of a verb which shows whether it is singular or plural.

As you write creatively, it is sometimes very easy to mix singular nouns with plural verbs and vice versa. As you, a head of state, rewrite, check through your sentences to make sure the noun nation and the verb country reach agreement.

Here's a dress rehearsal:

1) Billy ride in his father's new car.

_____

2) They plays on the computer game.

_____

3) You writes well.

_____

4) Susan and Jane goes to church together.

_____

5) The Harris family have seven children.

_____

Fill in the chart:

Plural Noun	Plural Verb	Singular Noun	Singular Verb
They	write		
		The boy	sang
Horses			whinnies
Bunnies	hop		
	gloat	The politician	
		The preacher	laughs
Doctors	operate		
Girls			plays
	sing	A parent	

True peace is not the absence of war. We know from studying Scripture that summit talks don't create peace.

For the kingdom of God is not meat and drink; but righteousness, and peace, and joy in the Holy Ghost.—Romans 14:17

Writing to God's Glory / Student's Pages

© Jill Bond / Homeschool Press, PO Box 254, Elkton, MD 21922

Article Attractions

(Articles and Adjectives)

"Billy Jones, you just won the National Spelling Bee. What are you going to do now?"

"I'm going to Disney World!"

Yes, the Walt Disney World attraction is very attractive.

People are naturally drawn to fun places. They want to be there. They feel happy and comfortable there. They belong there (even if it is for a too-short vacation).

Do you know what an article is? An article of clothing? An article in the newspaper? Articles of Faith?

Those are all good, but we're concentrating on improving your writing. Here we're talking about articles of speech: **a, an,** and **the.**

Though we call them articles, we use them like adjectives. They modify or limit their nouns, as adjectives do. If we were into the tedious process of diagramming sentences, we'd diagram articles in the same way as adjectives. Now, aren't you a better person for knowing that?

What good comes from learning about articles?

Better communication.

A pencil, but **an** orange. **A** clock, but **an** hour. Using **a** and **an** can be easily mastered by listening to the first sound of the noun that follows it. If the first sound is a consonant, use the **a** form, or else use the **an.**

I think you can handle that. But one aspect of using articles that may confuse the best of writers is where to place the *article* in relation to the noun in a string. Consider:

> Reed has a blue pair of jeans.
> Reed has a pair of blue jeans.

Your reader will understand the sentence better if you place the adjective closer to the noun.

Give the following sentences a trip to your favorite attraction and allow the adjectives to ride close to the nouns. "Parents, kindly grab your children by the hand and secure all personal belongings while boarding the tram," is a line repeated over and over again by amusement park attendants. Likewise, you need to kindly place the adjectives and nouns securely together, and make certain all articles match their nouns.

Fix the following sentences:

1) Susan went shopping at an store and bought a purple pair of shoes.

_____

2) Mark drank a steaming hot cup of tea.

_____

3) Hope devoured an delicious plate of food.

_____

4) Robin ripped open the pretty box of wrappings to find her present.

_____

5) I'm not sure, did you mean to say you loved the green rows of plants?

_____

Aren't you delighted that God never gets us confused? He detailed us with exactly the right adjectives and attributes. He has planned us to the finest detail. And He loves us dearly.

But the very hairs of your head are all numbered.
—Matthew 10:30

Alkaline Adjectives

(Proper Use of Adjectives)

Do you have a garden? Have you helped your parents weed a flower bed? Have you ever tested the soil for pH levels? Have you ever noticed the chemical coding on bags of fertilizer (e.g., 12-15-8)?

Different plants need different soils. A skilled gardener would never plants roses in acidic soil. The plants would die a premature death in the soil of the wrong chemical make-up. Azaleas grow well in acidic soil. They thrive in oak-leaf compost. I think hydrangeas are fascinating because they change color according to the chemical composition of the soil.

Many plants change color depending on the level of sun they receive. For instance, if crotons get too much shade, they'll be all green. Sunlight brings out their colors and gives them beautiful variegated leaves.

Bear with me. We'll tie all this into writing. As writers, we're like gardeners, trying to plant words to produce a spectacular garden of meaning.

What can ruin our efforts — inappropriate soil for our adjectives, or planting more adjectives than the "sentence soil" can nourish.

Adjectives are easy to plant. We can think of adjectives quickly. Adjectives can be fun and quite effective.

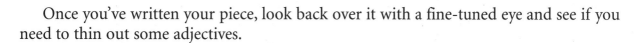

On the flip side, they can become weeds and take over our gardens.

Once you've written your piece, look back over it with a fine-tuned eye and see if you need to thin out some adjectives.

Too many adjectives weaken the impact of your work. Reassess your sentences. Are they filled with adjectives? Could you rework them so that verbs carry the weight?

Could you adjust the soil of the sentence structure so the adjectives can really flourish?

"Susan is very intelligent."

That sentence might work well as dialogue, but it makes for weak writing if it is used in the narrative. It would be better to show her intelligence than to come right out and tell the reader. Give the reader some credit for intelligence, as you write;

"Susan scored 1550 on her SAT." Or,

"The high I.Q. Society, Mensa, has asked Susan if she'd like to join." Or,

"Susan sits in the first seat since she's the smartest student in class."

In all these sentences we're conveying the same thought: Susan is intelligent. But in the last three, we showed the reader instead of told him.

Adjectives are good. Your work needs them. Just don't allow them to overcome all the other flowers in your garden. Remember it this way: adjectives offer opinions, verbs state facts.

Consider each of these sentences. Pretend they are in paragraphs filled with adjectives. Try to change them to give the paragraphs balance. Reword them without the strong dependence on the adjective to convey the meaning. There is nothing incorrect with them as they are now, but they could be improved.

1) Bill told a whopper of a lie.

_____

2) She was lovely.

_____

3) The sunset was beautiful.

_____

4) Abe was honest.

_____

5) Bill moved the large box.

_____

6) She was a happy girl.

_____

Doesn't it give you comfort to know the Master Gardener has planted us in exactly the right soil? He didn't throw you on the path or allow the weeds to choke you. He has given you the perfect balance to produce the flower of His fruit.

But other fell into good ground, and brought forth fruit, some
an hundredfold, some sixtyfold, some thirtyfold.
—Matthew 13:8

Writing to God's Glory / Student's Pages

© Jill Bond / Homeschool Press, PO Box 254, Elkton, MD 21922

Ponderosa Participles
(Dangling and Misplaced Participles)

"Hoss, hitch up the team. We're headed to town," Pa announced at breakfast.

Hoss did what he was told.

Like Hoss, we must learn to harness up the team for the purpose it was designed. How far would the Cartwrights get, if Hoss didn't secure all the harnesses and tethers?

You've heard the expression "dangling participles." Think of participles as wild horses that you have to constrain by reins and leads. Otherwise, they'll run off and leave your reader stranded in the wagon.

Related to the wild-horse participle is its cousin, the gerund mule. The gerund is a great worker once you get it going and motivated. Remember, mules don't reproduce. They're a hybrid, a cross between a horse and a donkey. You have to crossbreed them into your work, then keep them working. Don't allow them to bolt, resort to laziness, or wander off aimlessly. (Gerunds can be recognized by their tails: "ing.")[1] For example, "While cooking dinner, the phone rang and Mother answered it." Let me get this straight, the phone was cooking dinner? That's not what was meant, but that's what it says. Here it is in better form: "While cooking dinner, Mother answered the phone." (It is obvious that it rang if she answered it.)

Correct these examples of dangling and misplaced participles and gerunds:

1) A graph was drawn by Mother showing the history of the kings of Judah.

_____

2) After finishing all the homework, the television set was turned on.

_____

3) Running at full speed, we saw him win the race.

_____

---

1. Gerunds almost always end in "ing." For example, "singing" can be used as a noun — The singing was beautiful. Gerunds are verbs turned into nouns, usually by adding "ing."

4) Calculating her bank balance, the deposit was for the wrong amount.

_____

5) Wanting to drink her blood, Bethany was bitten by a mosquito.

_____

6) By salting the food at the table, less salt is consumed.

_____

7) Kissing her son, he wiped it off.

_____

8) Checking the temperature of the candy, the burner had to be turned down.

_____

The Lord loves us too much to ever let us go off and get lost. He holds us close and draws us back to His Watchcare. We might think we're untethered, but it is our shortsightedness. He has never lost track of us.

And when he cometh home, he calleth together his friends and neighbors, saying unto them, Rejoice with me; for I have found my sheep which was lost. I say unto you, that likewise joy shall be in heaven over one sinner that repenteth, more than over ninety and nine just persons, which need no repentance.—Luke 15:6, 7

Writing to God's Glory / Student's Pages

© Jill Bond / Homeschool Press, PO Box 254, Elkton, MD 21922

Whoot-n-nanny

("Who" and "Whom")

> "Swing your partner 'round and 'round,
> Jump up in the air and touch the ground,
> Grab that pretty lady 'round the waist
> now promenade out in due haste."

"Who's that calling tonight, ma?" Billy Bob asked.

"That's Billy Ray Charles, son. But whose fiddle is he a'plunkerin'?" Ma quizzed back.

"Who knows? But it sure sounds purty." Aunt Lula Mae was ripe to the challenge. "I'll find out for ye."

"I heard tell it was Billy Floyd whom he got it from, " Slyvia Downswallow was up on the latest gossip.

"Now, where'd on earth did Billy Floyd get such a plum-nearly perfect fiddle? Who can I ask?" Aunt Lula Mae was thinking out loud.

And so the monthly Whoot-n-nanny and Cider Drinking Party was off to a great start.

Do you know when to use who or whom, who's or whose? Many people don't And many people have to stop and think about it. I have to double check my work, like you do. Here are some helps:

> Use *who* in place of he, she, or they.
> Use *whom* if you could substitute with him, her, or them.
> Use *Who's* in place of who is.
> Use *whose* in place of his, her, or their.

Here's a walk-through.

"_____is going to win the pig calling contest?" Should we use who or whom? Which would you use: he or him? "He is going to win the pig calling contest" or "Him is going to win the pig calling contest"? You're right! "Who!"

"_____is it?" Should we use who's or whose? Would you say, "It is hers"? Or would you say, "It is she's"?

"_____going to town for the corn-squeezing carnival?" Do you use who's or whose? "He is going" or "his is going"?

"_____cow posed for that billboard ad?" Would it be, "she is cow…" or "her cow"?
Now try it for yourself:

1) Billy Ray Bob has a new sweetie. Do you know _____she is?

2) Sally June is _____.

3) Her brother, Charlie Duke, _____ won the county track meet, is chaperoning her real close like.

4) _____ did Charlie beat out for the title?

5) _____ his cousin?

6) Joe Taylor is _____.

7) You mean the Joe Taylor _____used to court Sally June?

8) The very one. _____would have thought it possible?

9) It sure is a small world. By the way, from _____ did you get all your information?

10) The Gossip Gazette! _____ paper is it anyhow?

11) The MacGillicutty sisters, _____ uncle is a big city publisher.

12) If you think we tell secrets here in the mountains, you oughta hear what they chatter about in those tabloids. They don't leave out any _____, what, where, or _____with for that matter.

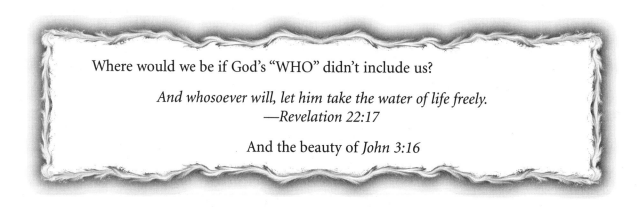

Where would we be if God's "WHO" didn't include us?

And whosoever will, let him take the water of life freely.
—*Revelation 22:17*

And the beauty of *John 3:16*

© Jill Bond / Homeschool Press, PO Box 254, Elkton, MD 21922

And of Green Gables
(Too Many "Ands")

There is nothing really wrong with the word. She just needs the proper environment. She's an orphan, you see.

We must place her in the perfect home.

In the proper family, she can thrive, give, and grow.

In the wrong home, she'll wilt and distract from the family.

Sweet, alive "And" — she has so much to offer. She can jazz up ideas. She can combine thoughts and bring flare to other words. But only if she is placed properly.

She's so like her brothers "Then" and "That."

The family resemblance is true. She can be a real nuisance if left on her own without the appropriate nurturing and care.

And you know exactly what I mean.

And if you don't try very hard, you'll be able to remember a time, not so long ago, when you started every other sentence with "and." Or you strung together a paragraph of sentences with "ands."

Here — I'm handing you some "ANDs." Place them properly among these words and punctuate to make sentences:

_____Susan_____wasn't_____certain_____about_____the_____new_____girl_____
after_____all_____her_____hair_____was_____the_____most_____ridiculous_____
shade_____of_____red_____her_____clothes_____were_____anything_____
but_____subtle_____yet_____she_____did_____wear_____the_____friendliest_____
smile_____Susan_____ever_____saw_____anyone_____have_____before_____
could_____she_____be_____a_____friend_____what_____would_____the_____
others_____say_____Susan_____wished_____life_____were_____easier_____
less_____troublesome_____why_____couldn't_____someone_____just_____
like_____someone_____just_____because_____you_____liked_____them_____
not_____worry_____what_____other_____people_____you_____liked_____
thought_____of_____you_____liking_____this_____new_____person_____

It makes my heart so very glad to know that God is the Father to the fatherless[1] and no one in Christ is an orphan.

The LORD preserveth the strangers; he relieveth the fatherless and widow: but the way of the wicked he turneth upside down—Psalms 146:9

1. Psalms 68:5

Writing to God's Glory / Student's Pages

© Jill Bond / Homeschool Press, PO Box 254, Elkton, MD 21922

Moreover

(Use "More Than," not "Over")

"He ain't got a name yet," the little red-haired boy declared about his mutt of a dog.

Mrs. Tomlin quickly answered, "There's only one place to go for a good name," as she reached for her Bible.

"Are there any dog names in the Bible?" his eager face implored.

Mrs. Tomlin started searching the Bible for references to dogs and found, "a living dog is better than a dead lion. Moreover, a dog has …"

"That's it," Mrs. Tomlin's son was filled with joyful anticipation. "We'll call him Moreover…."

This cute little exchange occurs in an old Disney movie, *The Biscuit Eater*. The story continues as two young boys train the mutt into a champion.

If you can picture a fuzzy-faced dog named "Moreover," you're halfway there to learning the proper use of more and over. In many cases **more** should be used, not **over**.

It won't take you long to find misuse of the word **over**. It's commonly used in advertisements by "writers" who are notorious for misusing the English language.

When talking about quantities, use "more than." Save **over** for positional uses.

"Over 300 hamburgers sold" is really saying:

The correct wording would be, "More than 300 hamburgers sold."

Over is used for something that is above — physically over. Or **over** may be used to show a span of time. "Over a period of twelve years" is permissible. However, "during" would be easier to understand.

Read the following sentences and decide if the sentence is proper as it is written. If it isn't, correct it.

1) Tex helped Lonny load and haul over twenty logs. (Did he haul them over to the wood shed, or did he haul more than twenty logs?)

_____

2) Yesterday, Pa shot over ten quail. (Did he shoot over the heads of ten quail, or did he shoot more than ten quail?)

_____

3) Over the last decade, my children have grown ten years older.

_____

4) My truck gets over twenty-one miles to the gallon. (Does it "get over" — runs on top of — twenty-one miles, or does it get more than twenty-one miles to the gallon?)

_____

5) Mom has asked that we memorize over two Bible verses a week.

_____

Now write five sentences of your own using **more** and **over** properly.

1) _____

2) _____

3) _____

4) _____

5) _____

> *Then said Hezekiah to Isaiah, Good is the word of the LORD which thou hast spoken. He said moreover, For there shall be peace and truth in my days.—Isaiah 39:8.*
>
> Jesus did a mighty work on the cross for us — more than we're able to fully realize on this side of eternity. Over the years, I've understood this more and more — His work was complete.

The Then Man
(Rarely do You Need the Word "Then")

Back in the 1930s audiences were thrilled with a series of movies about a detective: *The Thin Man*. He would outwit the police and the bad guys and solve the mysteries. His demeanor was calm and slightly "snobby."

I want you to be a detective. You are going to hunt through your work and others' work and become that famous detective: THE THEN MAN.

Your job is to ferret out any misuses of the word **then** in your writing.

Here is your first case. Grab your magnifying glass and fingerprint dusting kit and solve:

> Just as Sergeant Billergast opened his car door, he heard a woman scream. Then he unlatched the safety on his gun and signaled his partner to go around to the back. Then he slowly, and with caution, approached the front door of the mansion. Just as he reached to open the massive door, the butler came rushing out with blood all over his uniform. Then the Sergeant asked him, "What's going on in there?"

Did you find all the unneccessary **then**s? Like superfluous clues, they don't help the story at all. Every **then** was useless in that story. It follows that if you're writing the next sentence and it follows the preceding sentence, as most sentences do, THEN you don't need to write **then**. The reader will automatically know the action is next.

Here now, solve a few more cases as that world-famous detective, The Then Man:

> 1. "But, I don't know who done it," the upstairs maid answered with her cockney accent. Then the cook shouted, "Oh, she does know. My, the way she spies on everyone around 'ere." Then the maid lunged at the cook, "Oh, what do you know, you old fat slob." This remark did not please the cook. If the investigator hadn't silenced them, I don't know but they would have started quite a row. Then, the investigator turned to me and said, "And what do you know about all this?"

2. Deep in the African jungle, Sir Gareth Von Tribal turned to his guide and asked, "How much longer must we wade through this slime?" His able guide, Gutii, replied, "Until we reach the dry land, sir. It should only be a few more yards." Just then, as they were about to pass out of the slough, one of the workers in the back of the caravan screamed. Then everyone turned to find out what the commotion was all about. But he was gone. The worker carrying all the gifts had disappeared. "Then what should we do when we meet the chief. I mean without gifts, will he even deal with us?" the portly Sir Von Tribal asked. Then Gutii asked, "Don't you even care about Bombdu and what's become of him?"

3. Even the air inside the shanty smelled of the sea. Brunt and Baccus played cards on the makeshift table. "How much longer, boss?" Shifty Smith asked the man wearing the custom-tailored suit relaxing in the corner. Then Brunt cursed and instantly threw his knife. Then Baccus didn't move as the knife landed between his ring and pinky fingers and sliced the ace of hearts in two. Then the boss shouted, "You two stop it. We can't have you killing each other over a silly game of cards. I need you for the heist tonight." Then the old door swung open, and there she stood — the most elegant woman ever to grace the waterfront. Then, she breathlessly said, "Now!" Then each man moved to his position. They were ready.

Notice that the then in this verse is needed. It is perfectly placed. It is not superfluous.

So when this corruptible shall have put on incorruption, and this mortal shall have put on immortality, then shall be brought to pass the saying that is written, Death is swallowed up in victory.—1 Corinthians 15:54

Capital Idea

(When to Capitalize)

"Are you a true capitalist? Or are you one of those pinko commie spies?" the senator asked.

In 1954, Wisconsin Senator Joseph McCarthy chaired a series of investigating committees to discover the level of Communist influence and infiltration into government, education, defense industries, and other fields.

Many authors have developed stories focusing on the ideological war between capitalism and Communism.

With the *savoir-faire* of a James Bond, the foresight of a Ronald Reagan, the presence of a John Birch, and the fortitude of a Douglas MacArthur, you need to support the CAPITALIST idea in your writing.

Know who your capitalist friends are. And know when to use them.

We'll only discuss here the more covert operatives, the obvious ones have already blown their cover *(like all proper names and the first letter of each sentence and the pronoun I)*. Everyone already knows them. Call these covert operatives into Headquarters when you need them. Use your double-action pencil with the multi-functional eraser on the tip.

Op 001. All the names of countries, states, cities, counties, and all proper adjectives derived from them: France and French (but you mustn't capitalize words no longer associated with their place of origin that are common nouns: china [for dishes] or india ink).

Op 002. Don't capitalize school subjects, unless they are derived from a proper noun or have a specific course number: English, United States history, biology, Chemistry II.

Op 003. Capitalize departments of government: Department of Labor.

Op 004. Do not capitalize names of directions, unless they refer to specific geographical locations: travel north for three miles; she comes from the South.

Op 005. Capitalize historical documents, treaties, etc.: Declaration of Independence.

Op 006. Capitalize titles of family relationship when used with the proper name or in its place. Don't capitalize them if preceded by a possessive pronoun or are not followed by a proper name: Aunt Eloise, Mother, her father, my cousin.

Op 007. Not only should you capitalize holidays, but periods of history: Christmas, The Roaring Twenties.

Op 008. Don't forget to capitalize all the acronyms of organizations (the letters stand for words which would be capitalized if they were not abbreviated): C.I.A., K.G.B., O.S.I., P.L.O., F.M.L.N. [Note: CIA, NATO, FBI may be written without the periods — if in doubt double-check in a dictionary. Some acronyms become so popular and common, it is no longer necessary to separate with periods.]

Now pull out your secret-agent-decoder ring and double-action pencil and ascertain which "capitalization operatives" you need for each of these paragraphs and then follow through on your mission — capitalize the words correctly:

"we have a mission for you, james," m stated rather matter-of-factly. "agent 99 just sent us this message from the south of france," he handed the torn paper to james.

"could this be code, m?" james asked "'aunt martha has met her mother in the observatory.'"

"of course, jimmy, my boy. no one speaks english any more," m was rather put out.

"i know its code, but is it coded code?" james hated being treated like a child. "you know like the case of the bloated whale, a code within a code within a code?"

"you'll have to see q about that," m signaled q to join the conversation.

"over here, james," q called out. "i have a new gadget for you. It looks like a bowling ball — and weighs as much actually — but if you put all three fingers in, like so, it sends an f.m. radio signal for transmitting flight plan verification data to american awac aircraft overhead. the tricky part, however, is to not take your fingers out while flying — otherwise the clearance is void — and no telling what could happen."

"i've always wanted to take bowling lessons, q, but i'm afraid the bureau of communications would disapprove. after all, courses like ee 341, electrical espionage for blithering idiots, would be far more appropriate, don't you think?"

"that's enough nonsense, both of you," m commanded. "james, i need you to take this copy of the magna carta with you to paris for the bastille day celebration. i've arranged for you to meet with the chief of o.s.i. in a bus just north of a green telephone booth. he will be dressed as your aunt martha. there you will read the document in your best albanian dialect over the loud speakers. is that clear?"

God's love for us is not secretive. We don't have to search covertly to realize the magnitude of His love for us. We need no special training to receive this love. It is offered:

While we were yet sinners, Christ died for us.—Romans 5:8b

Who's That

(Use "Who" for People, not "That")

Yes, we've already completed a lesson on the proper use of who and who's. We even *zunckered out* "thats" a few lessons back. Now here we are, looking at them again, but this time with a new application:

"Peoples is peoples." Things are things.

God made people important — more important than things.

Recently, I saw a bumper sticker stating: "I don't ❤ anything." In the first second, I thought, "What a lousy attitude. That driver doesn't care about anything at all. Doesn't he love anything?" Then a second later, I gulped and agreed with him — I don't ❤ anyTHING either. I ❤ people. Not things.

Have you ever heard the expression: "Too many people love things and use people instead of loving people and using things"?

As Christians, we know how much more importance God placed on man compared with other creations. We need to demonstrate this in our writing.

When you're describing a person, use **who**.

When you're describing a thing, use **that**.

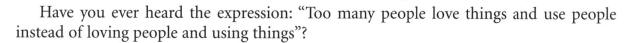

"If you are teaching a student that is not your child, we must have their parent's or legal guardian's signature to be able to accept their work."

Did you catch it? To be honest with you, we didn't. We apologize. That statement somehow got past us in the rules for our "God Bless America" writing contest. It should read:

"If you are teaching a student *who* is not…"

A student is a person, and so more important than a thing which just deserves a **that**.

Are you getting it?

Test these sentences (from a mock "letter to the editor") and correct the "**thats**" or leave them as they are:

1. Mrs. Peddleton, that lady across the street, backed into our garbage cans again this morning.

2. Though we were upset, we just moved the cans, that are made of plastic, back to the shed.

3. Our garbage handlers insist that we move the cans out to the sidewalk each day that they come by to get the trash.

4. I remember growing up in a small town where the trash men would go to the cans in your yard, in your shed, or in your garage, and unload them and then return the cans to where they belonged.

5. I think the old method the handlers used is better because the neighborhood looks so much better and there are people that can't physically carry their cans to the curb.

6. The neighborhood that is normally so pretty is so unsightly on trash day with everyone's garbage at the curbs.

7. In Sun City, Arizona, the garbage cans are set into holes in the ground near the curb with a trap door-type lid. This system keeps the neighborhood looking good and keeps back the dogs who love to rip open garbage bags.

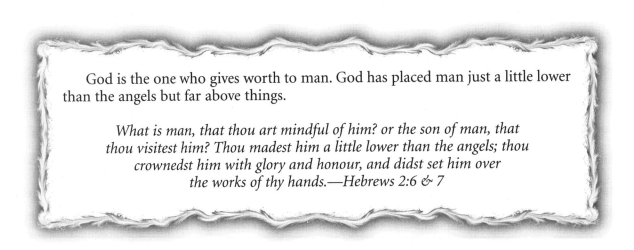

God is the one who gives worth to man. God has placed man just a little lower than the angels but far above things.

What is man, that thou art mindful of him? or the son of man, that thou visitest him? Thou madest him a little lower than the angels; thou crownedst him with glory and honour, and didst set him over the works of thy hands.—Hebrews 2:6 & 7

It's Us or Them

(When to Use "We" or "Us," "I" or "Me")

The coach paced back and forth in front of his team. His team. The team he had been waiting for all his career. This was the team that could do it. Of all the boys he'd coached, this was the one year he had every position filled with a star. This was his team.

And he'd be hornswoggled if he'd allow anyone to rob him of his championship trophy.

This was his moment to shine. He gave his boys the pep-talk to end all pep-talks. They knew what was expected of them. He summed it all up with these words:

"Remember, boys, it's us or them and this year it's going to be US!"

And with a whoop, the team headed out for the junior Olympic pig-calling contest.

The coach knew when to use "us" and when to use "them." Do you? Do you know when to use we or us, I or me?

Here are the guidelines:

With compound sentences, mentally omit the compound and then test the sentence for correctness.

Here's an example:

Mother and _____ (I or me) cooked dinner.

Try it without (Mother and) and you'll quickly see the answer is "I."

Here's another one:

(We or Us) _____ boys study our Bibles every night.

Would you say, "We study our Bibles every night" or "Us study our Bibles every night"?

Here's one more for practice:

Our pastor encouraged _____ (we or us) girls to meekness.

Would you say "Our pastor encouraged we" or "Our pastor encouraged us"?

Good, you're getting it.

Circle the correct word in the following:

1. Mother taught Rebekah and (I, me) how to sew.

2. Uncle Edmund, Dad, and (I, me) went to a prayer retreat last weekend.

3. Before we leave on the mission trip, our support group is giving George and (she, her) a going-away party combination prayer meeting.

4. You and (he, him) are invited to the prayer meeting.

5. (We, us) Smiths always sit together during the worship service.

6. We gave Bibles to Scott and (he, him).

7. They gave thank you notes to (we, us) Smiths.

We are called out to be a peculiar people. We're hand selected to be on God's team. Paul often writes to us as a coach. He gives us pep-talks to keep us encouraged in our well-doing. Let's listen to Coach Paul and keep on keeping-on.

And let us not be weary in well doing: for in due season we shall reap,
if we faint not. As we have therefore opportunity, let us do good unto all men,
especially unto them who are of the household of faith.—Galatians 6:9 & 10

The Three *MUST*keteers
(*Positive, Comparative, Superlative*)

Young d'Artagnan checked the straps on his belt for the thirtieth time. He must not lose the fifteen crowns his father had given him. He had a long journey before him. It would be the longest of his life. It would be even longer than the trip to Madame de Combalet's villa.

He fingered the edges of the precious letter. The one that would make his future possible for him. He knew this page was more precious than any he had ever carried for his father before. He must not ruin it. He must make his father proud. His father would be prouder of him than of his brother. He had to make it so.

All of a sudden with a swoop and a yell, three musketeers sprang out of the bushes and assaulted him. He grabbed for his sword, but it was too late. The three were upon him and he was theirs.

He was done for, even before his journey began. He was positive it was for the best, because if he could be so easily fooled, what good would he ever be for his sovereign. His face registered defeat. The three Musketeers hooted for their victory and let down their guard for just a second. That was all d'Artagnan needed. This time he was on the offensive…*"En garde!"*

Now, you, young musketeer, must wage a battle with the three MUSTketeers to learn the proper comparison of adjectives. Just as d'Artagnan was armed only with the three gifts from his father: fifteen crowns, a horse, and a letter of introduction to de Treville, you have three rules: postive, comparative, and superlative.

Here are three rules to help you know how to use comparative adjectives:

1. Short adjectives (of one and sometimes two syllables) are compared by adding *er* or *est* to the positive form:

long	**longer**	**longest**

2. Longer adjectives of more than two syllables are usually compared by using the helping words more and most or less and least:

comprehensive	**more comprehensive**	**most comprehensive**
comprehensive	**less comprehensive**	**least comprehensive**

(Comprehensiver is not a word.)

3. You have to just know the irregular comparisons:

good **better** **best**

Now fill in this chart:

Rule #	Positive	Comparative	Superlative
1	red		
	precious		
3	much	more	
			highest
		longer	
	little		
	bad		
2		more concise[1]	
1	happy		
	free		
	elated		
			bravest
		more precise[1]	
	conspicuous		
		greater	

Remember, most good dictionaries will spell out the comparisons for you. If in doubt, look it up.

---

1. Note: Some two-syllable words fit under rule #2. When in doubt — check it in a dictionary

Greater love hath no man than this, that a man lay down his life for his friends.—John 15:13

Aren't you thrilled that God doesn't compare us with one another, and that we are made pure through the blood of Jesus. A "most excellent" solution to our problem of sin.

Racing to the Finish Line
(Be Positive)

"Gentlemen, start your engines!" the announcer's voice blared over the loudspeakers.

James' heart began to race as he pretended he was one of the drivers. He pressed his foot down on the concrete bleacher as he heard the engines revving 100 feet below him, down on the racetrack. He strained to see them through his imaginary windshield.

As the green flag was hurled, James shifted gears on his armrest. His father looked down at his son and smiled as he remembered the excitement he had felt the first time *his* father had taken him to the Daytona 500.

Had he made a mistake? Mr. Cobb wondered. Would his son remember why they had traveled to this race? They were part of a missionary team, there to witness to the thousands of racing enthusiasts who poured into the coastal town each President's Weekend.

Mr. Cobb patted his son's back as James stretched to see the lead car take the perfectly inclined curve. He thought about the endorphines pulsating through his son's system. "That racing thrill won't compare with what he'll feel when he leads someone to Christ," he mused. Mr. Cobb was confident as they both watched the cars race forward through lap twenty.

Racing forward. It's the way we should write. Moving forward, not backward.

One way we can accomplish this is to word our thoughts in the "positive" form rather than in the "negative" form. State something is "A," rather than as "not B."

It makes more sense to the reader to be told what "is" rather than to be told what "is not." Think for a minute, "how informative is this statement?":

"A is not B"
Well, that tells you A isn't B, but it could be C, D, E, … or Z. By knowing that A is not B, we don't know what A really "is."

"Mario is not an African-American."
Okay, but what is he?

"Jack's car is not a Formula 1."
Okay, but what type is it?

Rewrite the following sentences in their positive form (as needed):

1) Witnessing to someone is not like brushing your teeth.

2) Bob really wasn't scared when he started to tell his testimony.

3) It's not that he was nervous, but he did feel his pulse racing.

4) The roar of the race was not at all like he had imagined it would be.

5) They waved at Mr. Gareth. He smiled, not tired at all from walking back and forth wearing a sandwich billboard covered with words.

6) The billboard didn't quote modern philosphies.

7) It didn't offer any help for directions.

8) It didn't try to sell snacks or refreshments.

9) It didn't try to raise money for a local charity.

10) It didn't spell out the price of parking.

(It did tell of a loving Saviour.)

Finally, brethren, whatsoever things are true, whatsoever things are honest, whatsoever things are just, whatsoever things are pure, whatsoever things are lovely, whatsoever things are of good report; if there be any virtue, and if there be any praise, think on these things.—Philippians 4:8

Splitting Infinitives
(Don't Split Infinitives)

Massive. If ever completed it would be unprecedented in scope and cost.

The atom smasher.

Billions of dollars, taxpayers' dollars, spent so a few scientists can complete some very complicated experiments.

You've heard the axiom: "splitting hairs." Well, they want to split atoms (almost infinitively small).

Though many writers couldn't begin to explain to you the mechanics of atomic physics, they do know how to split things to cause an affect (an affected sentence, that is) — split infinitives:

Here's an example: *to carefully listen* should be written *to listen carefully.*

The infinitive verb should stay next to its **to** with the adverb following.

In most cases. A good writer can "hear" when it is okay to split the infinitive for a proper effect. But be forewarned, most times it is best to NOT separate the **to** and its verb.

Assignment:
Try these for yourself:

to ravenously eat _____

to clearly think _____

to objectively evaluate _____

to lovingly pat _____

to loudly cry _____

to sarcastically smirk _____

Here's a common split infinitive you might have heard that is grammatically incorrect, but it sounds right:

"To boldly go where no man has gone before." It would not have the impact if it were written, "To go boldly where no man has gone before."

> *He hath shewed thee, O man, what is good; and what doth the LORD require of thee, but to do justly, and to love mercy, and to walk humbly with thy God?—Micah 6:8*

Can you hear it? It just wouldn't have the same impact as to humbly walk with your God. Have you ever thought that humbly is the only way to walk with God? It is He who hath made us and not we ourselves.

© Jill Bond / Homeschool Press, PO Box 254, Elkton, MD 21922

Which Hunt
("That," "Who," "Which")

Some families think witches are cute. They allow their children to dress up and play-pretend to be witches. Today there is an outcry for tolerance, but consider the situation back in the 1690s:

In a small town called Salem, Massachusetts, the town fathers heeded the words of scripture: *Thou shalt not suffer a witch to live* — Exodus 22:18.

Not nearly of the same import, I want you to go on a "which hunt." I want you to look in your work for the word **which** and make certain it is the word you want to use. Here, let's clarify: **which** informs the reader only about a characteristic of the noun it follows. It doesn't distinguish as to "which" item the noun is. Now, wasn't that confusing?

Here's an example:

The broom that has an angled head is in the closet. (Tells the reader which broom we're referring to; not the broom with the flat head, but the one with the angled head. By using the word that the writer implies there is more than one broom.)

The broom, which has an angled head, is in the closet. (Tells the reader more information about the broom involved, even if there is or isn't another broom in the closet.)

So, be sure that you use **that** when you should and **which** when you should.

Here's another reason to go on a "which hunt" — many **which**es (and **who**s for that matter) are not needed.

Read this sentence as it stands, then remove the **which**, and test to see if it makes just as much sense. If the **which** is unnecessary — remove it.

Salem, which is in Massachusetts, was the home of Nathaniel Hawthorne.

Do you see how you could remove the **which** and improve the sentence?

Here are some sentences for you to check to see if they are written properly. If they are not, correct them (**hint**: there may be some other problems to fix — taught in other lessons):

1) Nathaniel Hawthorne, who is an author, wrote the *The House of Seven Gables*.

2) Tituba, who was a slave girl from West Indies, triggered the Salem witch trials when she told a group of young girls about voodoo.

3) The girls, who became so enticed by her stories, developed emotional problems.

4) The magistrate hammered his gavel, which was made of oak, to quiet the court room.

5) One of the girls' fathers, who had wept bitterly about the voodoo stories, stood up and demanded justice.

6) "Tituba and her two friends should be hanged for their sins," the father demanded, "which is what they deserve!"

7) The judge, who was a man of God, agreed with the father.

8) He sentenced the three women to death by hanging from the tree in the town square, which was in front of the courtroom.

9) This witch hunt continued for about one year in this little town in Massachusetts, which is remembered for its "intolerance" and not for its piety.

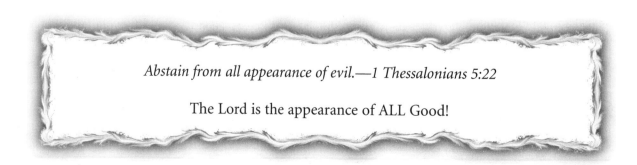

Abstain from all appearance of evil.—*1 Thessalonians 5:22*

The Lord is the appearance of ALL Good!

Writing to God's Glory / Student's Pages

© Jill Bond / Homeschool Press, PO Box 254, Elkton, MD 21922

Gone With the "Than"
(Proper Use of "Than")

"Fiddle-dee-dee, I'll think about that tomorrow." Scarlett was more complacent than she had been.

"But Miss Scarlett, what will we do?" Prissy was even more upset than she.

Are you confused? Sometimes even professional writers make the mistake of writing half a comparison.

Be careful whenever you use the word "THAN" not to allow the comparison to puzzle the reader. Don't permit your meaning to be "gone with the **than**."

Scarlett was more complacent than she had ever been before? Yesterday? Or was she more complacent than she had ever been happy (or another emotion)?

Was Prissy more upset than she had ever been before? Or was Prissy more upset than Scarlett was upset?

Check all your work for the word **than** and be certain you present the comparison very clearly to your reader.

For each of these sentences, write two (or more) alternative meanings:

1) Dagny looked more like a Labrador retriever than an Airedale.

a) _____

b) _____

2) Miss Melanie is more ladylike than Aunt Pittypat.

a) _____

b) _____

3) Scarlett was closer to Stuart than Brent Tarleton.

a) _____

b) _____

Now write three sentences of your own in which you make your comparison very clear to your reader.

1) _____

2) _____

3) _____

Our Lord does care about comparisons. No, He doesn't compare us one with the other, but He does compare how much we love Him compared to how much we love things. He wants our total love. Remember when he asked Simon Peter:

So when they had dined, Jesus saith to Simon Peter, Simon, son of Jonas, lovest thou me more than these?—John 21:15

Choosy Writers Choose
(Check the Definition)

You know the commercial, "Choosy mothers choose…" their peanut butter carefully.

The feminists are screaming for *choice* — though they usually mean anything *but* choice.

Have you heard any of the arguments for or against choice in education?

Do you have a hard time choosing which flavor of ice cream you want of the 33 or 53 or 99 flavors available?

Choices — we make them every time we choose one word instead of another.

May I suggest that choosy writers choose the best word — the correct word.

Here are a few examples of pairs of words many writers have trouble choosing between:

1. Among and between — If the choice involves more than two things use **among**. Use **between** when the choice is only between two things.
2. Precision and accuracy — **precision** means you can replicate the process exactly and **accuracy** indicates a high probability of making the goal.
3. Flaw and defect — A **flaw** is an imperfection — it may or may not be defective. A **defect** interferes with form, fit or function. Something can be flawed and not be defective.
4. Imply and infer — To **imply** something is to suggest it, while **infer** means to figure it out. You could infer something from what someone else has implied.
5. Farther and further — **Farther** should be used when writing about distance; **further** means more. Example: I have to travel further to get farther.
6. Continually and continuously — **Continually** connotes repeating an action over and over (usually indicates a long period of time without stopping or with short breaks); **continuously** means continuing without breaks (doesn't have to be a long period of time).
7. Literally and virtually — **Literally** means directly related to the words (to contrast something with an exaggeration) or it can mean unimaginative; **virtually** means in effect not in strict definition (Mr. A may be functioning as the president though the corporate structure places Mr. B in that position).
8. Alternate and Alternative — **Alternate** implies no choice, while **alternative** connotes a selection can be made.

You'll hear many other words misused. Add a page (or pages) to your *Favorites* section of your writing notebook, listing words you should be use carefully.

Choose one of the two words from each example above and write a sentence using it properly. (Advanced students should write a sentence for each of the words.) You might want to double-check their meanings in a dictionary.

1. _____

_____

2. _____

_____

3. _____

_____

4. _____

_____

5. _____

_____

6. _____

_____

7. _____

_____

8. _____

_____

Where would any of us be if God hadn't made the choice to include us in His plan?

And when there had been much disputing, Peter rose up, and said unto them, Men and brethren, ye know how that a good while ago God made choice among us, that the Gentiles by my mouth should hear the word of the gospel, and believe.—Acts 15:7

Writing to God's Glory / Student's Pages

Inventive Writers

(Making Up Words)

Edison leaned over and recalibrated his *rediomoter*. "It has to work," he mumbled half to himself and half to his assistant. It was late. Too late. And he was due home hours ago.

"If I just adjust the *microzipotoper*, it might just do it." He fiddled with another dial.

His assistant was starting to doze off. Jack was used to the routine: another late night while his genius boss fiddled and adjusted again and again. Jack liked his work because he knew the hours would pay off — a new invention to improve the quality of life for thousands.

Edison shouted, "Eureka! — as my hero, Archimedes, shouted when his work came together — Jack, we've done it…I think."

Inventing is fun at times; more often it is very hard work. I know first hand, as my father is an inventor and has "created" numerous products. Inventing has its place. But one place it doesn't have is in making up adverbs. When you're writing, be careful about creating new words out of thin-*letters*.

Putting ly to every other adjective might seem very creative, but what it will do is leave your reader bewildered and frustrated.

Yes, you can invent a word if it fits your character. It can be fun, like the words your author "invented" in this piece: *Microzipotoper* and *rediomoter*. But it was intentional. It was written for "effect."

Before you invent a word, test yourself to make sure it is a valid "invention." Its meaning should be patent!

Test these adverbs to see if they are correct, or if you should rewrite the sentence to use "real" words.

1. Jack yawned tiredly as he looked over at Edison.

2. Edison jumped agitatedly, "Can't you see it?"

3. Jack rubbed his eyes exhaustedly, "Sure, Sir, just give me a minute to focus."

4. "I was able to raise the temperature three degrees!" Edison said frustratedly. He was mad his assistant didn't grasp the significance of the sensor reading.

5. "Three?" Jack asked incredulously.

6. "Yes, three. Three whole degrees," Edison barked pompously.

7. "But is that enough?" Jack asked meekly.

8. "What a question — is that enough? Well, of course, it is enough," Edison stated as his voice wavered.

9. "Well, I think so. I think it is enough," he added discompassionately.

10. "Well, you know best, boss," Jack quickly stated sophomorically.

11. "Hang it all, let's go home. We'll start fresh tomorrow," Edison replied soporificly. "The world will have to wait one more day for hot-water-bag thermal-underwear."

Aren't you glad God "invented" you? He made you just as He wants you to be. You're not three degrees too tall or too short. You are a fine invention! That is patent in Psalm 139.

I will praise thee; for I am fearfully and wonderfully made: marvellous are thy works; and that my soul knoweth right well.—Psalms 139:14

Writing to God's Glory / Student's Pages

© Jill Bond / Homeschool Press, PO Box 254, Elkton, MD 21922

Gotcha

("Got" is not the Past Tense of "Have")

Do you have a little brother or sister OR a good memory? Do you ever play "Creepy Mouse," "Mr. Tickle," or "Elephant's Trunk" with your baby sister? Did your grandmother play "Gettie-gettie" with you?

Our Trent knows the game so well, his grandmother can just "sing the tune" to the "Elephant's Trunk" game (da-dum, da-dum) over the phone and he'll giggle.

Now that you're older, you might play "Tag" or "You're It."

"Hide-and-seek" is another fun game to try to elude the one who's IT.

I think we all know the feeling of being nabbed with the old "Gotcha."

Well, with your writing, you need to help with a ticklish situation. You need to play like you're IT and "Gotcha" to some **got**s.

I don't know how to say it any plainer but, dear ones:

GOT is not the past tense of **have**.

Got is another one of those words misused thousands of times every day. Just because you'll hear people everywhere using **got** as the past tense of **have**, don't you do it.

Check through your work for the word **got**. As in the game of "Hide-and-seek," you may count backwards from ten first, if you want to. Then seek out the **got**s and say "Gotcha" and get rid of them. Use the proper word in its place.

Got is a perfectly fine word. You have my permission to use it. Im' not saying to avoid the word **got**. I want you to mean **got** when you use **got**. Got is from the base word **get**, not the word have. To test if you're using the word **got** properly, convert your sentence to present tense and if the word **get** fits, then **got** would also. As you develop dialogue, you might want to use **got** in developing a character's style or for your phrasing to sound more *natural*.

☆ An outfielder is going to say, "I've got it!" as he dives to catch the baseball. Technically, he doesn't dave it yet, but it is a signal to the center-fielder that the left-fielder is going to get it. Wouldn't it sound funny for the ballplayer to say, "I'm going to get it in a few seconds"?

☆ A surfer isn't going to say, "Pardon me, but have you the time?" He's going to say, "What time have you got, Dude?"

☆ "Got a minute?" would be an appropriate phrasing for one office worker to ask his co-worker. When speaking to his boss he might be more formal and say, "Mr. Smith, do you have a few spare moments to discuss the McGruger case?"

Do you remember the "More Power" lesson when you created some "Freds"? Keep that lesson in mind as you develop your narrative. You might want to reconsider using **got** (a weak verb having more than 50 meanings) and use a more powerful word like procured, stole, snatched, caught, understood, or earned.

Play "Hide-and-seek" with these sentences and correct the **got** or leave it if it is okay.

1. I've got a lovely bunch of coconuts.

_____

2. What time have you got, Mate?

_____

3. Billy did do it and I've got the proof.

_____

4. It has been a long time since we've gotten any fresh fish.

_____

5. Perhaps, I never thought of it quite like that before, "What got her down?"

_____

6. It's got to get better tomorrow.

_____

7. It isn't fair. Jennifer got more than I did.

_____

8. John got caught with a second helping of dessert.

_____

I know the song goes "He's Got the Whole World in His Hands." Songwriters can get away with less-than-perfect grammer...sometimes. (For textbook-english it should be: "He has gotten the Whole World in His Hands" — but doesn't that sound silly?) Either way, I'm confident God does have all the universe in His control.

The LORD reigneth; let the earth rejoice; let the multitude of isles be glad thereof.—Psalms 97:1

Writing to God's Glory / Student's Pages

Love is Lovely

(Overuse of Words)

She was a frail young thing — naive, trusting, and beautiful.

He was rich, handsome, cruel, and independent.

That is, until *He* met *Her*.

Or so goes the plot of dime-store romances. The sales for this type of book are staggering: 48.6% of all mass market sales in 1992 (source: *Publisher's Weekly* / January 24, 1994). That translates into $885 million annually.

People are in love with love. They want it. They are hungry for it. And they search out and spend money for it.

Love.

What a power-word. Or, it can be. Yet, it can be so meaningless.

Consider:

1. I love green beans.
2. I love my dog.
3. I love the new mall.
4. I love my father.
5. I love her haircut.
6. I love ice cream.
7. I love my bike.
8. I love that new music album.
9. I love Jesus.

All nine times the word **love** was used to describe an "emotion" about something or someone. Yet, did you notice how different the level of the emotion was?

Be careful when you use the word **love**, that you mean LOVE and not just "fond of," "appreciate," "like," "enjoy," "savor," or "worship."

If you use **love** consistently, it loses its meaning. It tends to have no meaning. So, save the word **love** for when you really mean it.

Can you think of any other words which have lost their meaning by overuse or misuse?

_____   _____   _____

_____   _____   _____

Rework any of the sentences on the previous page in which you think **love** is not the best word to use.

1. _____

2. _____

3. _____

4. _____

5. _____

6. _____

7. _____

8. _____

9. _____

God doesn't have a flippant attitude about love. Consider John 3:16 and:

*If there be therefore any consolation in Christ, if any comfort in love,
if any fellowship of the Spirit, if any bowels and mercies, fulfill ye my joy,
that ye be likeminded, having the same love, being of one accord, of one mind.
Let nothing be done through strife or vainglory; but in lowliness of mind
let each esteem other better than themselves.—Philippians 2:1-3*

Nitro-Commas

(Proper Use of Commas)

Nitroglycerin.

Deadly or salubrious.

Dangerous or life-giving.

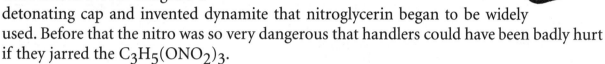

Nitroglycerin was considered too volatile when it was first discovered in 1846. It wasn't until Alfred Nobel designed a detonating cap and invented dynamite that nitroglycerin began to be widely used. Before that the nitro was so very dangerous that handlers could have been badly hurt if they jarred the $C_3H_5(ONO_2)_3$.

From blasting atoms at a rate of more than 3,000 times, it creates quite a destructive force. It explodes to 3,000 times its original volume at a rate 25 times faster than gunpowder, but now it can also be a "cure" for certain heart and blood-circulation diseases.

It's both. Deadly and life-sustaining — all depends on the control and use.

Now, commas aren't that serious. But they can change sentences to mean opposite thoughts. Consider:

The teacher wrote this sentence on the board:

    The principal, said the teacher, is not very smart.

The principal walked in the room, saw the board, erased the two commas and changed the total meaning of the statement.

    The principal said the teacher is not very smart.

Commas do matter. We must place them with care. We should never use more than we need or fewer than we need.

Commas should only be used when they are needed.

Treat commas with respect. Commas used incorrectly can blast your writing into meaningless dribble. Commas used precisely can invigorate your work with coherency.

Your assignment is to write (or find) sentences in which the comma's placement or removal changes the meaning. Here's another example:

She was overheard telling the pastor's wife who was gossiping about the church picnic…

She was overheard telling the pastor's wife, who was gossiping about the church picnic…

1)_____

_____

_____

2)_____

_____

_____

3)_____

_____

_____

4)_____

_____

_____

The Lord asks us to mind the little things. Consider the admonition in James:

*Even so the tongue is a little member, and boasteth great things.
Behold, how great a matter a little fire kindleth!—James 3:5*

The Incredible Shrinking Intellect

(Don't Be a Word Snob)

We must impress our readers, right? No, not really.

Do you know the meaning of these words?

funambulist
fossarian
sierodromophobia
allochtonous
pyknic
cacozelia
parepithymia

Sometimes we feel we must use a big word to show off what a fabulous command of the English language we have.

Think small. Think about the cell-sized adventures of characters in shows like *The Incredible Shrinking Woman*; *Tom Thumb*; *Honey, I Shrunk the Kids*; *Fantastic Voyage*; and *Land of the Giants*.

Yes, you might have a fantastic vocabulary. Consider it as you respect your readers. Sometimes the best way to communicate is to think small.

Writing so your reader will understand you is not the same as compromising your intellect; on the contrary, it is a strong indicator of it.

There are times to use the big word, the *sesquipedalian*. It can be fun to do in developing an egghead character.

If you do choose to use a word which might be beyond your readers' comprehension, define it with your writing. Helping your readers expand their vocabularies is a very positive aspect. To avoid making your readers feel like they have a shrinking intellect, bring them along with you in your narrative. If the big word is the best word to use, give them clues, leads, and definitions in your sentences.

Don't allow *your* intellect to shrink, either. Continue to add words to your vocabulary. One of the best ways to do this is to read, read, and *read*. In these exercises, look up the italicized word, and write a defining sentence to teach the word to your reader. Don't be obvious about your definition.

Example: *cogent* — Bill explained his opinion so I could understand it. He gave us a *cogent* argument for his pro-life position.

1. *anachronism* _____

_____

2. *dubious* _____

_____

3. *etymology* _____

_____

4. *mores* _____

_____

5. *moot* _____

_____

6. *myrmidon* _____

_____

7. *oxymoron* _____

_____

The Lord never leaves us wondering what He means — He tells us what we need to know. He even "defines" terms for us.

Now Faith is the substance of things hoped for, the evidence of things not seen.—Hebrews 11:1

And about the ninth hour Jesus cried with a loud voice, saying Eli, Eli, lama sabachthani? that is to say, My God, my God, why hast thou forsaken me?—Matthew 27:46

The Name Above All Names

(God, Capitalized)

Of course, we've saved the best for last — writing about our LORD.[1]

In an earlier exercise while you employed operatives to protect the "capitalist" ideal, did you notice an important rule of capitalizing was left out?

The standard rule is to capitalize words referring to the Deity (God), the Bible, and religions.

Yet, as Christians we are often compelled by our convictions to improve on this grammar rule. For emphasis and to distinguish the importance of God, we capitalize all references.

In our publications and other Christian publications, editors choose to capitalize words which are describing God or His Work: Work, Hand, Touch, Spirit, and others.

Some of us also choose to capitalize personal and possessive pronouns refering to God: He, His, Him.

Some publishers choose not to capitalize references to false gods and pagan idols. Whereas a hindu might want to emphasize rama or vishnu by writing them: Rama and Vishnu. Those publishers choose not to dignify the status by purposely leaving them lower case, as they are not "proper" names.

These rules are not hard and fast and many editors will disagree among themselves about whether or not to capitalize religious references.

Even two of our editors wholeheartedly disagree about whether to capitalize (B)iblical or not.

---

1. FYI: about LORD and Lord

God	Elohim
LORD, GOD	Jehovah (Blend of YHWH and vowels of Adonai)
Lord	Adonai
God Almighty	El Shaddai
Most High God	El Elyon
The Everlasting God	El Olam
The God Who Sees	El Roi

Source:
Strauss, Lehman; *The First Person, Devotional Studies on God the Father*; Loizeaux Brothers, Neptune New Jersey; Copyright 1967, sixth printing 1983.

When submitting work to a secular editor, he will (more than likely) only allow God, Jesus, or a direct reference to Him to be capitalized. A Christian editor might choose to capitalize even more words than you have.

We want to distinguish the differences between His Work and the work of others.

Now write twenty sentences about HIM and capitalize to emphasize who He is.

_____

_____

_____

_____

_____

_____

_____

_____

_____

_____

_____

_____

_____

That men may know that thou, whose name alone is JEHOVAH,
art the most high over all the earth.—Psalms 83:18

That, my friends is our mission: that men may know that Almighty God is THE most high over all the earth.

Writing to God's Glory / Student's Pages

Writing to God's Glory

Outlet Journal

Magazine Evaluation

Date: _____   Name: _____

Magazine: _____

Copies evaluated: _____

How often published: _____

Lead time: (if known) _____

Publisher and address: _____

_____

Any POC: (points of contact) _____

Referrals: _____

Circulation: _____ Subscription rate: _____

Types of articles: _____

_____

Fillers: _____

Titles: _____

Style: _____

Quotes: _____

Mission statement: _____

Leads: _____

Ideas: _____

Magazine Evaluation (Sample)

Date: July 4, 1995 _____ Name: Reed Bond _____

Magazine: CHERISH _____

Copies evaluated: 4 _____

How often published: quarterly _____

Lead time (if known): four weeks (for the finished article) _____

Publisher and address: Marten Family, _____

Route 1, Box 267; Dodge Center, MN 55927 _____

Any POC (Points of Contact): Mrs. Wanda Martens _____

Referrals: Jill Bond (Mom is a friend of Mrs. Martens) _____

Circulation: N/A _____ Subscription rate: donations _____

Types of articles: spiritual lessons, testimonials only, poetry, no fiction, any style submissions

Fillers: yes _____

Titles: submit with article, no preference for title style _____

Style: family-friendly, laid back, real life _____

Quotes?: no quotes, if possible, best to use first person articles, rather than research-type

Mission Statement?: To link families together _____

Leads: _____

Ideas: Reed wants to write a story about Trent and their special relationship

Query Letter (Sample)

Reed Bond
PO Box 254
Elkton, MD 21922-0254
410-392-5554

Wanda Martens, Editor
CHERISH
Rt 1, Box 267
Dodge Center, MN 55927

Dear Mrs. Martens,

"What's it like having a brother with autism?"

Many people have asked me that question. I reply, "It is one of the most wonderful things in the world — to have a brother with austism. It opens your mind up and shows you how nice life can be."

I would like to write an article for your magazine about my brother, Trent. God gave Trent a gift that not many people have. I want to write this article to tell people that children, men, and women with handicaps aren't terrible. Actually, they are blessings.

I think God has given me a talent to write and I want to use that talent to His Glory. I wrote *Betsy's Butter*, a published book. I have also written several articles for other international magazines and newsletters: the *Bonding Times* and *PREACCH*.

I am the eleven-year-old son of your friend, Jill Bond, and have completed the curriculum, *Writing to God's Glory.*™

I have enclosed a stamped, self-addressed envelope for your reply. Please let me know if you would be interested in this article. I can adapt it to your publishing needs. Is there a particular angle, word count, or format you would like me to use?

Thank you for your consideration. May God Bless your ministry.

Growing in Christ,

Reed Bond

Magazine Listing

Here are the addresses of some family-friendly magazines. They all accept and publish Christian children's writing. This listing is by all means incomplete. It was the last page I wrote of this book, knowing it would be out-of-date by the next day. Publishers change. Addresses change. Rates change. New magazines and newsletters come out weekly. But, at least, it is a starting point for you.

BIG Ideas/Small Budget
2201 High Road
Tallahassee, FL 32303
Monthly, $12 per year

CHERISH
Entire magazine
Route 1, Box 267
Dodge Center, MN 55927
Quarterly, suggested donation $10 per year

Heavenly Highlights
Entire magazine
345 E Hawksdale Dr
Grants Pass, OR 97526
$12 for 1 year (10 issues)

The Home School Family
Student's section: *"The Home School Student"*
PO Box 682
Nice, CA 95464
Bi-monthly, $15 per year

Kids At Home
PO Box 9148
Bend, OR 97708
Bi-monthly, $20 per year

Kids for Life
Entire newsletter
4960 Almaden Expwy, #172,
San Jose, CA 95118
Quarterly (donations)

NATHHAN NEWS
Children's section:
    "From the Hearts of Children"
5383 Alpine Rd SE, Olalla, WA 98359
Quarterly, $25 per year

PREACCH
(Parents Rearing and Educating Autistic
    Children in Christian Homes)
PO Box 736
Lake Hamilton, FL 33851
Quarterly, $15 per year

Sugar 'n Spice
Entire magazine
    (subsection for boys & preschoolers)
Editor: Jenny Gordon (13)
Rt 1 Box 89-A
Cairo, WV 26337
Bi-monthly, $5 per year

Also, don't confine yourself to writing only for children's sections or children's magazines. Many of you are writing so well you could submit an article as an adult. You're not being dishonest by not stressing that you are still a minor. Write your best article, submit it and let it stand on its quality. I've read articles by teenagers which were publishable in the "regular" section of a magazine. Never be deceitful — just don't underestimate what God might be doing with your writing.

Writing
to
God's
Glory

Ideas

Worksheet 1: The Master Plan

Working Title: _____

Date: _____ Name: _____

Bible References: *(log actual verses and references on separate paper)*

_____

Theme: *(best to use 2-3 words, but no more than 10-15)* _____

_____

Main Characters: *(separate worksheet)*_____

_____

Minor Characters: *(separate worksheet)* _____

_____

Time Frame: Start time _____

End time _____

Setting: Describe the settings and props needed for your story. *(separate worksheet)*
(25-50 words for each setting, can be in list fashion)

_____

Research: What do you need to do for research? *(separate worksheet)*

_____

Plotline: How are you going to develop your story? *(separate worksheet)*

_____

Worksheet 2: Bible References

Working Title: _____

Date: _____ Name: _____

Log actual verses you are using as the basis for your story:

1) _____

_____

_____

2) _____

_____

_____

3) _____

_____

_____

4) _____

_____

_____

5) _____

_____

_____

6) _____

_____

_____

7) _____

_____

_____

8) _____

_____

_____

9) _____

_____

_____

10) _____

_____

_____

Worksheet 3: Main Character Development

Working Title: _____

Date: _____ Name: _____

Main Characters: *(make up separate worksheets for each main character)*

Name: _____ (Nickname): _____

Is character saved or unsaved: _____

Age: _____ Sex: _____ Race: _____

Physical characteristics: _____

_____

Social and educational background: _____

_____

Religious experiences: _____

_____

Besetting sin: _____

Strengths, talents, gifts: *(if saved, list at least one Spiritual gift)* _____

_____

Growth: _____

_____

List at least ten other details about this character. (For ideas review: "Casting," page 143) Write what another character could say about this character. How else could you "reveal" this character to your readers? Are you going to "show" this character to us slowly, or will we know him immediately? How are you going to get us to care about this character?

1) _____

_____

2) _____

_____

3) _____

_____

4) _____

_____

5) _____

_____

6) _____

_____

7) _____

_____

8) _____

_____

9) _____

_____

10) _____

_____

Worksheet 4: Minor Character Development

Working Title: _____

Date: _____ Name: _____

Minor Characters: *(make up separate worksheets for each minor character)*
(only fill in the blanks which are applicable to your story's development.)

Name: _____ (Nickname): _____

Is character saved or unsaved: _____

Age: _____ Sex: _____ Race: _____

Physical characteristics: _____

_____

Social and educational background: _____

_____

Religious experiences: _____

_____

Besetting sin: _____

Strengths, talents, gifts: *(if saved, list at least one Spiritual gift)* _____

_____

Growth: _____

_____

List at least five other details about this character. (For ideas, review: "Casting," page 151) Write what another character could say about this character. How else could you "reveal" this character to your readers? Are you going to "show" this character to us slowly, or will we know him immediately? How are you going to get us to care about this character?

1) _____

_____

2) _____

_____

3) _____

_____

4) _____

_____

5) _____

_____

_____

Worksheet 5: Setting

Working Title: _____

Date: _____ Name: _____

Opening setting: *(key words, phrases; use all the senses to describe)*

_____

_____

_____

_____

_____

_____

Other settings:_____

_____

_____

_____

_____

_____

_____

Worksheet 6: Research Plan

Working Title: _____

Date: _____   Name: _____

What do you need to research: *(copied from Master Plan)*

_____

_____

Research strategies:

_____

_____

In addition to the Bible, what is your plan for research: *(check box, once completed)*

Primary research:

☐ _____

☐ _____

☐ _____

☐ _____

☐ _____

☐ _____

☐ _____

☐ _____

☐ _____

☐ _____

Secondary research:

☐ _____

☐ _____

☐ _____

☐ _____

☐ _____

☐ _____

Interviews: *(calls, face-to-face, letters)*

☐ _____

☐ _____

☐ _____

☐ _____

☐ _____

Quotes: *(to be added as research develops)*

☐ _____

☐ _____

☐ _____

Statistics: *(to be added as research develops)*

☐ _____

☐ _____

☐ _____

Worksheet 7: Plotline

Working Title: _____

Date: _____ Name: _____

Plotline: _____

Action to introduce characters: _____

Main plot: *(be brief)*_____

_____

_____

_____

Sub-Plot(s):_____

_____

_____

_____

Conflict: _____

_____

_____

_____

_____

Surprises: _____

_____

_____

Resolutions: _____

_____

_____

Divine Connections: *(obvious or subtle)* _____

_____

_____

_____

Climax: _____

_____

Denouement: _____

_____

Epilogue: _____

_____

Outline: *(use additional sheets, as needed)* _____

_____

_____

_____

_____

_____

_____

_____

Writer's Checklist

Name: _____   Working Title: _____

Draft number	Date	Req'd	1	2	3	4	5	6	7	8	9
Date of draft?											
Bible confirmation?											
Prayer?											
Theme?											
Word limit requirements?											
Above reproach?											
Where's the paint?											
Sense-able?											
Reader's language?											
Characters?											
Setting?											
Timing?											
Conflict?											
Subplot?											
Follow-through?											
Foreshadowing?											
Sentence count?											
Justifiable?											
Any SAMs?											

Draft number	Date	Req'd	1	2	3	4	5	6	7	8	9
Power words?											
Bore Bee check?											
Fewest words possible?											
Results given to God?											
"That" check?											
Tense agreement?											
"!" under control?											
Antecedents linked?											
Noun/verb agreement?											
Articles?											
Judicial use of adjectives?											
Participles okay?											
Who's proper?											
Too many "ands"?											
Over/under?											
Then?											
Capitals hunky-dory?											
Who or that?											
Pronouns correct?											
Comparatives correct?											
Positive wording?											
Any split infinitives?											
"Which"es hunted?											
Full comparisons?											
Double-check meanings?											
Any new words?											
Gotcha?											
Full meaning?											
Commas cared for?											
Pompous at all?											
Glory to God?											

Writing to God's Glory / Student's Pages

Writing
to
God's
Glory

Favorites

Welcome to Favorites

This section of your "working book" is for your collection of favorite writings.

Through the years this will grow and grow as you collect more and more examples of writing, phrasing, and words you like.

The difference between this section and the *Ideas* section is this one will contain others' works. Keep them separate because you don't want to accidentally use someone else's words as your own.

I like to note time, date, source, page number, author, circumstances, etc., along with the copied words.

A loose-leaf or spiral notebook works well.

Just do it.

In this section, you'll see pages for:

1) **Shorts** — little snippets of conversations, word couplings, phrases, and other cute SHORT sayings

2) **Stu's Blue** — an example of a story in process

3) **Vignettes** — more than a snippet, less than a story, vignettes are a series of sentences that present some thought, scene, character, idea: *Rainy Day Bonding* is an example

4) **First Lines** — for you to add to, first lines of some famous writings

5) **Words** — vocabulary building; words you don't want to forget or that you like for any reason

6) **Quotables and Stats** — on being precise and keeping track of sources

7) **Reed's story** — an editing practice

8) **Reed's Review** — to illustrate the superiority of writing a review rather than a book report

9) **Others' Words** — A collection of other children's ideas, stories, and answers to some of the exercises

Shorts

Have you ever thought, "I like that," about something someone said or wrote? "That's clever!" "I wish I had thought of that." "I hope I don't forget that."

Somewhere in the *Favorites* section of your writer's notebook should be your list of "Shorts."

I encourage you to keep a log of ideas, phrasing, etc.

Some things I have in my "Shorts" section:

☆ Bethany didn't know what my new bathroom scale was, so she came up with a term which fit in with the vocabulary she knew — "the clock on the floor in your bathroom." I might use that someday in a story.

☆ Someone told me that a child describing carbonated drinks said they taste fuzzy like when your foot falls asleep. "Isn't that cute?"

In this part of your notebook keep a listing of clever wordings, phrasing, and short sections that you might want to use someday. Add to it regularly. Follow around your favorite preschooler — preschoolers always say things with such a fresh approach. They aren't bogged down with, "Well, no one ever said it that way before." I'm careful to flag things as original or borrowed. Some of the ideas I can't use because they are someone else's work (or with permission I can quote them) and some of the ideas are "mine" to use. If I note it is from someone else, I try — to the best of my knowledge — to note who, when, etc. You might want to keep two lists: Borrowed Shorts and My Shorts. (I like to keep *my* ideas in the *Ideas* section of my notebook and others in the *Favorites* section.)

I like to jot down any circumstances about the situation that will help me later. I also like to date the entry.

You might find a particular wording you like in a book you're reading. List it on your "Shorts" list and note the date, place, author, and wording (in quotes).

You don't need to know "where" you'll put your ideas. What matters is that you're learning to play with words, feel their sounds, analyze their effects, and appreciate their combining.

Stu's Blue

Sometimes I think my second son, Stuart, is "allergic" to writing. It is not one of his favorite things to do. So, I "tested" the ideas in this book on him to see if I could get him more interested in writing. I asked him to give me a story about something I knew he liked: the color blue. His first try was basically:

Blue. I like Blue. Blue is blue. Yes, I like blue.

I love him, but it does need some work — don't you agree?

So, we tried the "downloading" idea. I grabbed a pen and a sheet of paper and I asked him to come up with anything that was blue, reminded him of blue, or was related to anything that was related to blue. I assured him there were no wrong answers.

We worked for about fifteen minutes and he came up with more than 75 words:

☆ Clothes: jeans, shirt, coat, jacket, shoes, sweaters, hats, socks
☆ Mood: sad, tears
☆ Skies: Air Force, Blue Angels, Wild Blue Yonder
☆ Blue screen
☆ Police: Boys in Blue
☆ Moon
☆ Jazz music
☆ Smile — (blue makes you smile)
☆ Chair — hair
☆ I.D. color
☆ Eyes
☆ Sea: ocean, fish, bluefish, blue whale
☆ Rainbow
☆ Flag — red, white & blue
☆ Blue light bulb
☆ Blue Christmas lights, blue stars
☆ Doctors wear blue
☆ Blue shades
☆ Blue gas — fire, natural gas
☆ Blue jet
☆ Big Blue: IBM
☆ Big Blue Marble
☆ Blue-chip Stocks
☆ Blue ribbon

We talked over his list and I asked him if he had a story or something else we could say about "blue." He immediately started "flying through the family room" dictating with complete sound effects:

> i pulled through the throttle and the blue jet rolled, spun about to go through upside down turned up through it and came down for a perfect landing everyone saw it and i was voted best stunt pilot sliced the rainbow in half too skinny wings too fat so blue stuck to my wings and like midas golden touch blue uniform all blue i found blue everywhere as i was doing to stunt it was for a movie they raced me to the hospital with blue lights flashing and finally we were there i was greeted by doctors and nurses all wearing blue jazz music during stunt home gas blue cooking the biggest ocean you've ever seen flew over the ocean and came back over upside down biggest blue whale of all time next to school of blue fish celebration gave waved red white and blue and gave blue ribbon biggest you ever saw played the blues gave me blue chip stocks with the big blue ibm reporter asked what it looked like i answered big blue marble a few months later i got married and my mother had blue tears my children learned to be a space driver don't worry i didn't really fly the jet it was for a movie and it was all blue screen

(Whew!) Lots of words, thoughts, ideas just flowed out of his mind. In less than an hour he had gone from "I like blue" to building a story about a pilot. Notice I didn't punctuate any of his words. I just took straight dictation — dumping words on paper.

A few weeks later, he wanted to dress up his *Blue* story, so I pulled it back out and he fixed it up to:

> I pulled on the throttle and the jet rolled and spun around a half circle, came down and went up. We had to postpone the flight for three hours because of the rain. Like I said before, the rain stopped.
>
> I did my maneuver I went up came up twisted up side ways twisted and went up like this [lots of hand movements] and as I was going when I just finished the flight the rainbow just appeared to me. I just went right through it and a little *[family interruption during writing]* Meanwhile there was another clown from the circus though he had resigned from the circus and he was employed with plane company and he thought it was his time to do his flight and when I was about 5,000 feet up he came around and hit my tail and made my whole plane spin around and land upside down and the plane then burst up into flames and then they took hoses to put out the flames and it took a little while fortunately the flames didn't touch me. Finally they got me out then they called the ambulance they rushed me to the hospital at top speed with the blue lights flashing. Then they took me

to the emergency room but to my surprise everyone was wearing blue and the lights were dark blue the last time I went in there four weeks later I got out of the hospital with one crutch and when I came to the airport they gave me a blue ribbon and a cash award of blue chip stock in the big blue — IBM oh one more thing it was all just for a movie and the stunt was all just blue screen. The end.

Stuart is improving.

Here's his last version. He decided to stop with it there. Of course, you can find areas that you could improve. Why don't you? Try your editing skills, using the notations in the "Editing" lesson, page 149. Improve it.

I'll type it in the standard "double spacing" style to give you room to edit it.

Blue
(Working Title)

I pulled the throttle and the blue jet rolled, spun about to go through

the sky. We had to delay the flight for three hours because of rain. I slid

upside down, turned up and came down for a perfect landing.

I was just finishing the flight when a rainbow appeared to me. I just

went right through it. While I was protracting the jet sliced the rainbow in

half. It was so skinny and the wings too fat, so, blue stuck to my wings. Like

Midas' golden touch my world became blue.

While I was flying I saw the biggest ocean you've ever seen. I flew over

the ocean and came back flying upside down. There was the biggest blue

whale of all time next to a school of blue fish.

Meanwhile, there was a clown from the circus, though he had resigned

from the circus. He was now employed with a plane company. He thought it was his time to do his flight. When I was about 5,000 feet up he came around and hit my tail and made my whole plane spin around and land upside down. The plane burst into flames. They took water hoses to put out the flames and it took a little while. Fortunately the flames didn't touch me and my all blue uniform and blue helmet. Finally, they were able to get me out. They called the ambulance and rushed me to the hospital at top speed with the blue lights flashing.

They took me to the emergency room. But to my surprise everyone was wearing blue and the lights were dark blue. The world had turned blue!

After I recovered, they gave me a celebration and waved the Red, White and Blue. They gave me a blue ribbon, the biggest you ever saw. They played the blues, jazz music, and gave me blue chip stocks with the big blue — IBM.

A reporter asked me what it looked like up in the sky. I answered: "Like a big blue marble."

Oh, but not to worry — I didn't really fly the jet. It was for a movie and it was all blue screen.

The End

Did you see any progress from his first attempt through his second, third, and fourth drafts? Do you notice the same kind of progress in your work?

Did you learn anything about editing? Notice how different a writing style an eight-year-old uses as compared to a four-year-old or a teenager.

Vignettes

After several days of constant rain, I decided to use the opportunity to ask my two older sons to tell me what they saw out the window. I didn't feed them any lines. I just took dictation, giving them each a turn to add a sentence. The first version was a mixture of tenses. We went back over their vignette and wrote it all in past tense. Then we made it present tense and they chose their favorite: present tense. That version was printed in the support group newsletter. I mention this so you'll get a feel for some of the fun writing exercises you can do that aren't frivolous.

Rainy Day Bonding (version 2)
Dictated by Reed (age 6) and Stuart (age 4) Bond

The sky was gray. The clouds were like a foggy white sheet of paper. They weren't like usual. They weren't fluffy. You couldn't play pretend shapes with them.

The air was like when Mommy runs the humidifier. It tickled my nose to breathe. The sun was hiding just as if it was playing hide-and-seek.

The rain was dripping to the ground. There looked like streams and the mud looked like land, creating a miniature world in the back yard.

The jungle gym was slippery and "slidey." We would slide very fast on that slide.

A flash of lightning — one-Mississippi, two-Mississippi, three-Mississippi, four-Mississippi — ROAR! The lightning was four miles away.

The water on our neighbors' roofs looked just as white as snow, but it was just wet. The wood shed was soaked. The wood looked darker when it was wet. The swing was moving and it looked like an invisible child was swinging, but it was just the wind.

Thank you, God for a rainy day.

Rainy Day Bonding (version 3)
   Dictated by Reed (age 6) and Stuart (age 4) Bond

   The sky is gray. The clouds are like a foggy white sheet of paper. They aren't like usual. They aren't fluffy. You can't play pretend shapes with them.

   The air is like when Mommy runs the humidifier. It tickles my nose to breathe. The sun is hiding just like it is playing hide 'n seek.

   The rain is dripping to the ground. There looks like streams and the mud looks like land creating a miniature world in the back yard.

   The jungle gym is slippery and "slidey." We'd slide very fast on that slide.

   A flash of lightning — one-Mississippi, two-Mississippi, three-Mississippi, four-Mississippi — ROAR! The lightning is four miles away.

   The water on our neighbors' roofs looks just as white as snow, but it is just wet. The wood shed is soaked. The wood looks darker when it's wet. The swing is moving and it looks like an invisible child is swinging, but it is just the wind.

   Thank you, God for a rainy day.

   The end

I realize it is a very simple piece of writing, but it was a great start. Notice the details they described.

Your writing can be great. Ask someone to be your scribe as you think through some situations. Jot down even "loose thoughts" and ideas. You'll come up with some very clever observations. I don't know if I had ever noticed that wet things are darker in color.

Keep a section of your *Favorites* for your thumbnail sketches, your "slice of life" paragraphs, your vignettes. You'll see your improvement, so be sure to date them.

© Jill Bond / Homeschool Press, PO Box 254, Elkton, MD 21922

First Lines

Some might say the most difficult words to write are the first lines.

They have to be wonderful. They have to "sell" the whole book.

What would you say is the most famous first line? I agree: *"In the Beginning."* What would you think for second place? Would it be "Four-score and seven"? I don't know. Perhaps: "It was the best of times, it was the worst of times." But it would be an interesting survey.

Think of any "beginnings" that have ever caught your eye or ear (the sounds of the words). Why did you like them? What about those words made you want to keep on reading? Think of the last book you read — can you remember how it started?

Think about magazine articles. Sometimes editors even set the first line off in special-type or oversized fonts. They want to draw you into the rest of the article. Are there some that turn you off from the "get-go"? Why?

Notice how the news programs "sell" the newscasts with intriguing words to tease the viewers. Don't you strongly dislike the ploy of those "check-out stand" magazines with sensational first lines? That is shoddy journalism. We're called to a higher ideal.

What about your writings?

Have you labored and labored over the first words while you stared at a blank page? Those first words. They can be "killers."

Here's a tip that works for me: Don't let writing the first lines keep you from writing. Start mid-stream and then go back and write the first lines — again and again and again....

I understand Charles Dickens rewrote the first line for *A Tale of Two Cities* over and over again. Shouldn't we do the same?

It's a good habit.

One interesting practice is to notice first lines. Record journal entries of first lines you like (and maybe reasons why) and ones you don't like (and why). You'll learn, not by the copying, but by figuring out why the author chose that particular beginning.

See if you recognize the first lines of these famous novels:

[Note: the '?' is placed in these exercises instead of the proper names, because if I typed in the proper names, there would be little challenge in this exercise. It would be too obvious.]

"'?' was not beautiful, but men seldom realized it when caught by her charm…"	
"My name is Ishmael…"	
"When I look back, my first memories are of a large rolling meadow…"	
"Squire Trelawney, Dr. Livesey, and the rest of these gentlemen having asked me to write down the whole particulars about '?', from the beginning to the end…."	
"When '?' was sent to Misselthwaite Manor to live with her uncle everybody said she was the most disagreeable-looking child ever seen…"	
"It was seven o'clock on a warm spring evening in the Seeonee Hills of India when Father Wolf woke…"	
"On the morning of January 6, 1842, the people of Paris were awakened by the deafening peals…."	
"In the year 1192, the people of England feared for the life of their beloved king…"	
"The eyes of the starving wolfpack gleamed like hot coals in the blackness of the frozen arctic forest…."	
"True!—nervous—very, very dreadfully nervous I had been and am; but why will you say that I am mad?"	
"Christmas won't be Christmas without any presents…"	
"Mr. '?' , who was usually very late in the mornings, save upon those infrequent occasions when he was up all night, was seated at the breakfast table…"	
"Looking back to all that has occurred to me since that eventful day, I am scarcely able to believe in the reality of my adventures…"	
"'?' was dead, to begin with."	
"If you want to find Cherry-Tree Lane all you have to do is ask the Policeman at the crossroad…"	

Words, Words, Words

Words are the ingredients for all of our writing. You need to improve your vocabulary. I need to improve my vocabulary. Your teacher needs to improve her vocabulary.

We need to be able to use words not only correctly, but precisely. Not only do we need to spell them correctly, but to employ them to work for us at their fullest capacity.

As I read books, I come across:

☆ words that I'm not overly familiar with;
☆ words I think I know the meaning of, but am not 100% certain;
☆ words I want to remember; and
☆ words I might want to use some day.

I record these words.

Often, if I own the book, I'll turn to one of the blank back pages and write down the words and the page number. When I have time, I'll look up those words and double-check their meaning.

I've found several errors. Even published authors and copyeditors make mistakes. Since we, at the *Bonding Times*, misused the word "penultimate," I've found it misused in the same fashion three times. (We had misused it to mean "the ultimate of the ultimate" instead of its correct meaning which is "next to the last." What a difference in meaning.)

I'm also collecting words that will fit into a certain genre of writing. (It might be a reference book I will write someday as a tool for other writers.) Unlike a thesaurus which gives us synonyms and antonyms, my "Words" list gives me words I'll use whenever I write about something in particular — that goes with one of my categories.

For example: My page about "pirates" has words that I'd use to describe the creak of the boat, the fullness of the sails, and the type of phrasing pirates used: Ahoy, Matey; Shiver Me Timbers; Keel Haul; etc.

I collect words that would cover all the senses, dialogue, characterization, and whatever else suits me. I could look up smells and find dozens of words to describe different scents.

Writing to God's Glory / Student's Pages

Start your own private *Words* list.

Assignment: Write the name of each topic listed below on a separate sheet of paper and put the sheets in your notebook. Throughout the year add words to the list that you could use if you were ever to write a story about that topic.

1) Pirates
2) Medieval Times
3) Space
4) High Tech
5) Old West

6) Bible Times
7) Your present homelife
8) Medical
9) Cops and Robbers
10) Jesus

Show your lists to your teacher one year from now. Your goal is to have at least 25 words per page. (Check with your teacher, she may adapt that assignment according to your age and ability — she may want a hundred words by tomorrow!) So, if you're ever asked to write a story about

☆ Sir Vance-a-Lot,
☆ Mars 2345,
☆ David and Abigail,
☆ Dr. Getbetter,
☆ That desperado Wild Will Hiccup,
☆ Officer Al Gethim, or
☆ Your Lord of Lords,

you'll have a ready-made list of words that will fit your story and you'll be able to use those words to give your writings an authentic feel.

To recap:

1) You should keep a list of words for vocabulary building.
2) You should keep a list of words under specific headings.

Even with your vocabulary words you might want to start subcategories and "file" them under different headings. (Words a town's matriarch might use; words the town's drunk would use; words a minister uses; etc.)

There will be overlap. You might put the word "exercise" under your listings of "education," "health," and "spiritual warfare (exorcise)."

Enjoy your words. Remember, writing is sculpting with words.

Your own list would go in your *Ideas* section of your workbook. Here is a portion of my lists:

Pregnancy (only page one of several)

Bigger than Life	Big Brother
But I'm not ready	Allergies
Swollen feet	Names
Proud Papa	Dreams
Rushing to the hospital	Emotions
Surprise	Crying
It's a Boy	Laughing
It's a Girl	Mood Swings
Cigars	Joy
Storks	Life
Baby clothes	Creation
Bonnets	Blessings
Prams	Changes
Strollers	Books
Nesting	Research
Beached Whale Syndrome	If one more person asks me...
Doctors	C-sections
Nurses	Complications
Waiting Rooms	What if?
Scales	Routes to the hospital
Samples	Rooming-in
Sonograms	Hospital route
Heartbeats	Waiting
Cold jelly	Pain
Morning Sickness	Dr. Jekyll — Mr. Hyde
"Where are my feet?"	A woman in labor is not a pretty sight
Waistline?	Prenatal stress
Stretch marks	Miracles
Vitamins	Ten toes
Green peppers and blueberry yogurt	Hoo-hoo-ha-ha
Walks	Breathe
Mommy	You breathe, I'm having a baby
Nursery	Labor rooms
Pink and Blue	Hard metal
Yellow	Hospital gowns
Stethoscope	First cry

Smells (anything relating to, first part of list)

Salty	Air
Noses	Pollution
Colds	Onions
Stuffy	Garlic
Balmy	Potty-training
Baking bread	Fresh-cut flowers
Babies	Compost
After the rain	Wheezing
Potpourri	Coughing
Gardenias	Burnt toast
Roses	Burnt rubber-plastic
Orchids (no smell)	Fire
New car	Barbecue
Air fresheners	Hickory-smoked
Apples	tangy
Springtime	Dogs
Orange blossoms	Bloodhounds
Minty	Picking up the scent
Cinnamon	Rescue
Christmas	Bob Hope
Tart	Clues
Horrible	Perfume
Rancid	Olfaction
Putrid	Whiff
Stinking	Whisper
Rank	Suggestion
Sour	Hint
Musty	Breeze
Malodorous	Shampoo
Rhinoplasty	Scent-free
Kleenex	Lemon-scented
Bouquet	Pine cleaner
Aroma	Scented markers
Chili	Bubble gum
Reek	Syrupy-sweet
Redolence	Maple

© Jill Bond / Homeschool Press, PO Box 254, Elkton, MD 21922

Green (anything relating to)

algae	emeralds
alive	envy
alligators	eyes
aloe vera	fields
amphibians	float
apples	flowers
army suits	foliage
Astro-turf	food coloring
Astros	football
avocadoes	four-leaf clover
bad shampoo	fresh
beans	frogs
bile	gak
blooming	gallbladder
bread mold	go
broccoli	go ahead
budding	grapes
burgeoning	grass
bushes	green back
callow	green ice (Panama Jack)
Calvin and Hobbs	green light
camouflage	greenies (environmentalists)
carpet	growing things
Celtics	guacamole dip
chlorine	hair
chlorophyll	herbage
Christmas Trees	holly
construction paper	honeydew
crabs	Hornet
crocodiles	Hulk
cukes	icee (popsicle)
cups	iguana
dark	ill
dollar bills	immature
Draping of the Greens	Ireland
dresses	ivy
elves	jade

Green (cont.)

jelly beans	pale	string
Jets	parrots	swamp water
Jiminy Cricket	peas	tadpoles
Joe Green	pencils	team colors
Jolly Green Giant	Peter Pan	teeth
Jolly Rancher	pickles	think green
Knomes	planet-friendly	thumb
kudzoo	poison ivy	tights
lake	Puck	trees
lawn	raw	turtle
leaches	relish	unhealthy
leaves	Robin Hood	unripe
Leprechaun	rosebushes	unripe tomato
lettuce	rotten eggs	unsophisticted
lime	salad	vegetation
lizards	scarfs	verdant
Marlins	scenery	verdure
mildew	seasick	vibrant
minerals	seaweed	vitamins
mint jelly (with lamb)	shamrock	wane
mints	shells	watches
mix	shirts	watermelon
moss	shoes	Wearing of the Green
Mountain Dew	slime	wet behind the ears
Mr. Greensleeves	snakes	word
naive	spray paint	Wreaths
Ninja turtles	Spring	young
notepads	Sprite bottles	youthful
O-D (Olive Drab)	St Patrick's day	Zucchini
paint	sticker bush	

Quotables and Stats

Gathering quotes and statistics may seem quite a waste of time. After all, you can just log on to your Multimedia Reference Library CD and have access to hundreds of quotes. Right?

Well, yes, but then again, maybe not....

It depends on the kind of writing you're going to do. Yes, many of the most "famous quotes" of "famous people" are in Bartlett's and other quote books and CD-ROM programs. But you'll find that these sources will not contain the words of some of the people you'll want to quote, for instance:

☆ Christopher Columbus (his Christian writings)
☆ Oswald Chambers
☆ Early martyrs of the Church
☆ Hannah Whitall Smith
☆ Horatio G. Spafford
☆ Fanny J. Crosby
☆ Your grandfather
☆ Your pastor
☆ Your parents

☆ Billy Graham
☆ James Dobson
☆ Rush Limbaugh
☆ Jocelyn Elders
☆ Yogi Berra
☆ Gary Bauer
☆ David Barton
☆ Thomas Jefferson (his ideas on crime)
☆ Francis Schaeffer

As a Christian, you'll want to write from a Christian's unique perspective. Many of our "sources" for material are not deemed "famous" by the editors of quote books. Also, some material you might want to use may be too recent to have been included in a book of quotations.

Suppose you want to write a letter to the editor about presidential appointments. You'll be glad you kept some of Jocelyn Elders' quotables such as the one about "safer bullets."

I realize statistics can be misused, but they can be very effective. For instance, "just yesterday," on the news, a study was announced about the increase in suicide rates. The announcers stumbled around trying to find answers. My sons thought it was amazing that the media couldn't see any relationship between the increase in suicides and teaching people that:
  1) they are only glorified monkeys,
  2) life has little value because abortion is "okay," and
  3) death with dignity is a "wonderful solution."

That is the beginning of an article, a letter to the editor, or a chapter for a book.

Most of the writers I know are "clippers." They clip articles from the paper and from magazines. Then they start building their files — for an article they'll write some day. In the same way crafty people collect ribbon, fabric, and material for a craft project they will do someday, writers collect ideas, quotes and stats.

I have a file cabinet full of folders on different topics. And I use many of them. Sometimes it is just to spark an idea or to remind me of a situation. Sometimes it is just for the "facts" in case I ever have to "name my sources."

I also like to keep a running list of quotes. These differ from "Shorts" in that they will actually be used as "quotes," not just ideas to be worked into a story line.

I add in things like:

- A lie told through the media as fact
- Stats (13% of all accidents happen in the home — not a real stat, so don't quote me)
- A bizarre statement made by some "modern guru"
- Recipes (I still write cookbooks and I get ideas all the time)
- Anything from my pastor's sermons
- An anecdote from a radio program (Did Adrian Rogers build a great story on *Love Worth Finding*? Write it down.)
- Jokes (I have the hardest time in the world remembering jokes)
- A "Life is like a . . ." quote from a grandfather
- Copies of magazine or newspaper articles I liked or hated

Always be sure to write down on the paper the date, source, and author of the quote — so you will give credit where credit is due.

Here's your assignment, gumshoes: by this same day next month, show your teacher your collection of at least ten quotes. They can be from the list above or your own private expanded list. Be able to state, in a few words, a possible use for each of your "quotables" (e.g., a letter to the editor about the value of speed bumps).

Reed's Dictation and Review

Here is a copy of an "unedited" work my son Reed wrote when he was ten years old for his then three-year-old sister. It is the straight, no caps, no commas, no frills editing. You'll find it is very difficult to read. Makes you appreciate grammar, huh? What would you capitalize? What would you reword? Where would you put the commas? It is double-spaced to give you room to make your notes.

It was an early spring day in April just about lunch time when the little girl put her doll and new toys in her basket a specially made basket one end of it connected to one side of the wall in a corner the other side would connect to the other wall and the back part would be hooked to the ceiling she skew it was very different to the doll and many of her friends because they had been used to sleeping on the bed or playing with her less and less she had thought she had heard the master the little girl's father that the girl was growing up and she didn't need little dolls or all those other toys she had the girl had already had many other beautiful toys but all they had in them were wires screws and bolts the only person who was real and made out of bolts and screws was kinks a toy make up of a wind-up mouse the top part of a plastic easter egg and some wires and levers and four little wheels from a toy car all the rest of them who were real were of stuffing but no wire bolts screws or nay of that sort because you see that would never do but as I was saying the girls was putting her toys away in the new basket which would be regrettably be the cause of all their misfortune that is a fact that tolkan the toucan did not like to be flown around in fact he did not like to be flown at all you see when he was first delivered he was a special toy bought by a Sears catalogue but when the mailman dropped him he was never the same that fall was to be the thing that shook up the little wire that made him fly so he never flew correctly every time he tried it looked promising like he might fly but always he would make some kind of turn or twist that would send him down with a thud now shall we look apon the dresser drawers where kites and tolkan was getting ready to fly tolkan getting on top of kites was very scared he had always hated heights and you would too if you were dropped by a mailman now kites you might ask who is he he is a handmade kite but you see he was made in the shape of a bat the very first time the girl flew kites the string broke and he went whizzing through the air gliding to the girl and landing at her feet he would never be a good kite because you see kites had to be free for if string were connected to him someone else was controlling him and he did not enjoy that so he would not do his best at flying so the girl only used him as a glider thing like a paper airplane but much nicer anyway kites is ready to jump off the dresser drawers with a very scared tolkan on his back here we go are you ready tolkan the poor bird was too scared to speak he just slightly nodded his head then here we go said kites as he jumps off the dresser drawers down and down they went tolkan thought all of a sudden kites had lost his marbles he's nuts he's bonkers he's cracky he's batty he's knatty he's a crackpot we're going down said tolkan covered his eyes with his feathers tolkan knew that not because he had his eyes open but because he could feel them going up wheeee that was fun tolkan said kites I always did want to try a little of going on the edge tolkan was very scared up we go into the basket oh look said the doll it's kites and tolkan and they're headed straight for us duck said kinks in a very scared voice and so they did whew in just the nick of time because kites went right over their heads and landed behind them kites said the doll tolkan said kinds tolkan was a little shaken up and a little bit dizzy so he walked up to the very edge of the basket but you see there were holes in the basket woven holes very small and tolkan's foot got caught in one of them whoa he said as he fell down right on the rim of the basket he looked down and let out a yell of fright for as you remember he was afraid of heights and he started falling up and down crashing into the sides of the basket he would hit one than the next one then the middle one then he would go on to the first one and get hit but somehow his foot got caught in one of the holes which I have told you about tolkan stop we'll get you out of there said the doll but he did not hear her he was trying to get out of it himself he was flapping his wings and going forward he thought of himself if I grab the second hook

I'll be able to pull my leg out of this hole he started pulling but unfortunately he was pulling the first hook out and when he grabbed the second hook it started to pull out too and the tension from both of them being pulled out caused the middle hook to come out as well down they went did I ever get to mention miss barbara (baarbaaraa) the girl's big stuffed lamb or should I say sheep the girl was getting a new bed and the part of the bed when you pull the mattress off the girl had set up two of them one standing where it was and other leaned vertically across it like a teeter-totter she had set barbara on one end it was right under the falling basket the basket hid the side of the teeter-totter and shot poor barbara up in the air she almost hit the ceiling but down she came she hit her end of the teeter-totter which was up and made it go down and shot the basket up through the window I understand what you are thinking why would the window be open well if you remember it is a spring day in April and spring days are always nice and of course you'd have the window open the force of the teeter-totter shot them very far across the back yard and over the neighbor's fence what do we do now said kinds I got an idea said the doll we'll use the girl's old handkerchief its very big well what do you expect said the doll its the girl's tolkan she said see if you can climb up to the very ends of the hooks and tie this around each hook as a parachute but unfortunately the dolls idea did not come out the exact right way you see instead of going down they went up you see the pressure of the wind hit the handkerchief and blew them up and up over the house oh my I've never been this high said kinks tolkan was so scared he was biting his nails and birds don't do that unless they are very scared now they were in florida and the house was near the kennedy space center where the space shuttle is over and over they went over the fence and over the guard it was amazing how they passed security right over them and know why the security was there the shuttle was about to launch

—more—

Now, I know Reed's ending. And it's very good. But what ending would you put on the story? Remember it's a story for a pre-schooler. They can believe anything can happen….

Writing to God's Glory / Student's Pages

© Jill Bond / Homeschool Press, PO Box 254, Elkton, MD 21922

Note:
Beginning a unit study on library science, we checked several books on the topic. *Helping Your Child Use the Library* was one of the texts which Reed (age 12) was assigned. After reading it cover to cover, he composed this review.

Helping Your Child Use the Library

by Kathryn Perkinson — Illustrated by Brian Griffin
Published by US Department of Education; © 1993

A Review by Reed Bond © 1996

Realizing that this book was published by the Department of Education, I can understand more why my parents are educating me at home. Yes, it was informative but the manner in which they presented the facts was exceedingly dull and unimaginative. It could be used as a reference book. Yet, it is not a book I'd recommend for enjoyment. Either I am well-versed about library science or this book is very base — I didn't learn anything new from it.

One aspect that I found personally intriguing was the section: *Services for Special Children*. The author applied the Americans With Disabilities Act of 1992 to the arena of public libraries. I learned that by law, the libraries have to accommodate children like my brother, Trent who is autistic. If your librarian isn't aware of these facts and wants ways to make his library accessible to special Americans, then suggest that he write to the Association of Library Services to Children/American Library Association, 50 East Huron Street, Chicago, IL 60611 (1-800-545-2433).

I found the "*For More Information*" section very disturbing. Was this federal endorsement of some books over others? When individuals do this it is discernment, but when governments do this, it's censorship. By choosing certain references they promote those books and by leaving off other equally good resources they are "disapproving" them or ignoring them. This borders on government sponsored advertising for certain select publishers, editors and authors.

It all comes together when you read the *Foreword* and *AMERICA 2000 Library Partnership* pages. It is another usurpation of the government into the boundaries of parent's authority. They openly confess that they are in league with the National Endowment for the Humanities working toward the National Education Goals[1] — producing cookie-cutter-kids. All in all — a politically-correct book.

I do not recommend it. You have better things to do with your time. Yet, it does serve as a prime example of the danger in the National Education Goals.

1. From the Foreword: "All of the books in this series tie in with the National Education Goals set by the President *[Clinton]* and the Governors. The goals state that, by the year 2000: every child will start school ready to learn *[whose definition?]*; at least 90 percent of all students will graduate from high school; each American student will leave 4th, 8th, and 12th grades demonstrating competence in core subjects *[core — according to whom?]* U.S. students will be first in the world in math and science achievement; every American adult will be literate, will have the skills necessary to compete in a global economy *[as in Revelations?]*, and will be able to exercise the rights and responsibilities of citizenship; and American schools will be liberated from drugs and violence *[and Christian influence, too?]* so they can focus on learning. *[The fear of the LORD is the beginning of knowledge — Proverbs 1:7] Italics mine.*

Writing to God's Glory / Student's Pages

© Jill Bond / Homeschool Press, PO Box 254, Elkton, MD 21922

Hero in the Skies

Here is a short story written by Ryan Doran, a student of mine (reprinted with permission). I'm also printing his mother's note because it states the wonderful effect your writing can have on the lives it touches.

Jill, I find this a wonderful, fictional piece with distinct traces of the father-and-son relationship I so cherish in our home. I loved this myth for I know my son has realized the sacrifice and love he has received during these training years. Seeing his ability to impact the same training in his own family at the correct time, gives me a sense of security for I know my husband. He's taught Ryan to be honorable and one day to be a father apt to teach the same.

Your class, Jill, has opened a door that can never be closed. Hope to be sending you more work we're all proud of.

Love,
Barbara Doran

"Hero in the Skies"
© Ryan Doran

He was not a man, but a merprince under King Waterlo. To understand the myth of Prince Patras, you must remember within your hidden dreams, the enchanted world of the mermaids. You see, contrary to the legends and myths about the mermaids, there were also mermen and merchildren.

These patriotic people loved and protected their beautiful world. They held both the king and prince in high esteem. There was just one problem; the king knew his young son, Patras, would never be brave enough to lead his people. This is how it all began.

"Son, son," Waterlo called. "What are doing?"

"I'm working in my room, Father!" Patras yelled, knowing his father's hearing range.

"Patras, go play with the other boys. They're playing a new game called finball!"

"I know, but I might get hurt," he said shyly.

"What will I do with that boy?" the king thought to himself. "I know! I'll take him on one of my shark hunts in Smooth Rock Canyon. No merman has ever been hurt, but it will make him feel strong and brave, almost hmmmmm…like he could take over the ocean," the king said with a bit of deceit, yet love in his voice.

Thinking long and hard the night before the great hunt, King Waterlo wanted to make a wise decision, but slowly his dreams caught up with him, and he fell into a deep sleep.

Upon awakening, Patras and Waterlo were filled with fear and excitement, impatient to begin their journey to Smooth Rock Canyon. The time had come: the beautiful chariots stood before Patras. Horns blew and the adrenaline burned through his body, for he did not know what to think of the quest. As the rush of chariots passed through the deep, Patras and his father began the chase.

The rocks and coral seemed to pass so quickly, it made Patras feel dizzy. Yet the sudden jolt of the vehicle kept him on his toes (or fins, if you may.)

While Patras and his father were finishing the hunt, they both felt a sense of bravery, for their chariot had caught the shark. You see this was not just any predator, this was Brutous, the strongest and most ruthless beast. (He once devoured a shipload of Odysseus' men in one of Poseidon's great storms.)

As the prince and king swam off the chariot, a dreadful thing happened: Brutous broke through the net he was kept in! With a thrust of his powerful tail, he blazed forward through the water, his deadly eyes glaring directly at Waterlo. The king, glimpsing the shark out of the corner of his eye, became white with fear. He felt completely helpless and for the first time in his life, totally powerless.

With instinct so intense, Patras burst forward with his spear in his hand, and without a thought, hurled the razor sharp weapon through the water into the muscular chest of the shark. Movement stopped immediately, and the vicious predator sank slowly to the dark, dirty ocean floor.

That evening, after Waterlo settled down enough to relax, he looked as if he was missing something he loved very much. You see, Waterlo knew what he must do with his son. Tears filled his eyes and hugging the child he began to explain his plan to Patras.

"I can't let anything happen to you, my son. I must keep you from harm." Waterlo explained how he would lift Patras high above the heavens, for there was no harm there.

Zeus, "god of the heavens," saw this time of despair and rewarded Patras with the brightest star for bravery, so all could see this great hero on a warm summer night. Zeus also gave Patras the two most beautiful stars, Bara and Boru, meaning life and death; for truly he stood in the way of both of them.

The End

Sample Answers to Craftsmen Exercises

Here are some sample answers to some of the *Craftsmen* exercises. Students of various ages and writing abilities wrote these "answers." They are neither "right" nor "wrong." I'm giving you these examples to encourage you and to give you some ideas. Most of the exercises could have dozens (perhaps thousands) of possible "correct" answers.

1) More Power

The German army was attacking and he only had one more anti-tank round, Fred prayed for courage as he climbed into the turret. (Tank driver in W.W.II)

Fred picked up his mop and shoved it into the barrel, made sure the sudsy water was clean, and put on his overalls with the paint smudges. (School janitor)

It was November 12 up in New York, and Fred looking out his window saw that the flags outside the Guard Room signaled "*as for class,*" put on his jacket and his cap as he headed out the door to "plebe" English. (West Point Cadet)

As Fred put on his white gloves and red hat, checking to make sure his uniform was unwrinkled, he thought, "Well, it's an up and down business, but at least the tips are good." (Bellhop)

"Well, it's another day and the captain always tells us to get our sky-flyers," Fred thought as he put on his helmet. (Student pilot)

Fred put on his rear-view mirror glasses as he climbed into his motorcycle then he went down the giant highway tube in the sky. (Futuristic biker)

2) Bore-Bees

1.
☆ She talks and talks and we wonder if she'll ever stop to listen.
☆ She talks too much.
☆ Details and details, she goes on and on with more details.
☆ And yesterday she talked for thirty minutes about some casserole she made back in 1953. And today she's going to tell us about a meatloaf from 1967. "Why did I volunteer to visit the elderly?"
☆ "Shut-up, woman!" her husband shouted on. "I can't stand your perpetual babbling about inane things."
☆ The pastor stated that gossip is a sin and suggested that certain ladies in the congregation could not hold their tongues. "The tongue is a small member but just as a large ship is steered with a tiny rudder . . ."

2.

☆ He petted his dog on her head and gently said, "Good Lady."

☆ Ginger wagged her tail as he petted her head.

☆ He couldn't help but feel kindly for God's small creatures. "They seem so helpless," he thought as he stroked the wounded collie and looked around the waiting room at the other animals.

☆ He loved his Airedale so much that he patted her head and scratched her between her ears.

☆ Knowing his beloved Shepherd was about to deliver, he gently stroked her head and whispered reassurance to her.

☆ "Good, Sheba," the blind man patted his companion on her head. "Forward when the traffic clears."

☆ "Nice dog, little boy," the stranger bent down to pat the terrier on it's head. "Would your mom like to buy a new vacuum cleaner?"

3.

☆ "I know Mr. Phelps wants this report tomorrow, but I have to get some sleep. Goodnight, Maggie, I'm going home."

☆ "Eyes, stay open. Open, open, open. Oh, what's the use! I might as well go to bed."

☆ "Mom, I can't think of another sentence. Can I go play, now?"

☆ This arthritis cramps my hands so much, I'll have to stop writing now.

4.

☆ "Come on, you guys. Surely one of you can think of something worth saying."

☆ John stammered. Bill coughed. Susan started to say something. But they decided to just pick up the brooms and start to clean up the broken glass. Words seemed useless.

☆ Bob and Bill knew explaining wasn't their expertise, so they just sat there and stared.

5.

☆ "Get up, John. I've tried five times to wake you up."

☆ "John," his mother called. "Can't you at least pick up your dirty socks in the hallway?"

☆ "But, Mom, *Space Invaders from the Planet Gartara* is on, and then *Mutant Sock Raiders* is on next." ["Is" is appropriate in this dialogue because that is how a lazy boy would talk. But "is" would not be very effective in the narrative. We are showing that John is lazy, not stating it.]

☆ "Dear, what are we going to do about John? His supervisor at the center says he doesn't do half the workload of the other teen staff."

☆ "John, if you don't finish this task by the close of business Friday, I'll have to start paying you piece-meal and not hourly."

6.

☆ Bill and Gary planned to fish up at Kickakee Lake this morning.

☆ "I'll pick you up at 4 a.m. and we'll surprise all those fish up at the lake. Just think about it. We'll bring home so much fish, we'll have to buy new freezers for our wives. Back to the wild! It'll be great," Gary persuaded his brother-in-law.

☆ "We have to go buy some new life jackets. We've outgrown the ones we had last year. And you know Mom's rules about wearing jackets when we fish out in the boat," Bill mentioned. "Can you think of anything else?" Gary asked as he added life jackets to his list of things to do.

7.

☆ Rushing and dashing and packing and spending, we're never bored during the holidays.

☆ We love the holidays because we study about Jesus throughout the Advent.

☆ Polish the silver, vacuum the carpeting, clean the windows — Aunt Gladys is coming again this holiday.

8.

☆ Many horses weigh more than a ton.

☆ My dad can look Silver Lightning in the eye. After all, Silver is 15 hands tall.

☆ The horse strained. His owner urged him on. Captain Grant's muscles tensed as he started to pull. Just one foot, just one foot was all he had to drag the massive stump. Captain Grant wanted to please his owner and win the draft horse pulling contest.

☆ My horse, Razor Jack, loves me a whole bunch when I stretch up to give him an apple. I have to stand on a stepladder just to brush him down.

3) Less is More

✐ 1. Joyce announced.

✐ 2. Traditions

✐ 3. When you make up your mind, let us know.

✐ 4. If it rains, close your windows.

✐ 5. Ladies will shop at the stores with the best prices.

✐ 6. Heather was thrilled with the idea. [Bonus: reword it without the borebee: Heather jumped for joy when she heard the idea.]

✐ 7. Jimmy Stewart played the part of a man who had a six-foot-tall imaginary rabbit for a friend.

✐ 8. Patton was a general in the army.

✐ 9. Ronald Reagan was the oldest president of the USA.

✐ 10. I helped my mother last night by setting the table.

5) Time Travel

1.

Captain Kirk walked on the bridge and said to Lt. Data, "Marty McFly will arrive on the locomotive DeLorean at high noon. Prepare an Away Team to greet him." Doug looked over and said, "H.G., we're going to have fun meeting other time travelers here on the spaceship Intraprize."

Doc Brown sat down and patted his dog, Einstein. "Oh, yes. It'll be grand to see Marty again."

Whit asked if anyone would like a banana split.

The tractor beam locked onto the DeLorean and pulled the tired traveler on board. "It was worth the trip," Marty said when he saw the Doc. "When did you arrive?"

Doc Brown looked at his chronometer and said, "Tomorrow."

2.

Captain Kirk will walk on the bridge and say to Lt. Data, "Marty McFly will arrive on the locomotive DeLorean at high noon. Prepare an Away Team to greet him." Doug will look over and say, "H.G., we're going to have fun meeting other time travelers here on the spaceship Intraprize."

Doc Brown will sit down and pat his dog, Einstein. "Oh, yes. It'll be grand to see Marty again."

Whit will ask if anyone would like a banana split.

The tractor beam will lock onto the DeLorean and will pull the tired traveler on board. "It was worth the trip," Marty will say when he sees the Doc. "When did you arrive?"

Doc Brown will look at his chronometer and say, "Tomorrow."

3.

Captain Kirk walks on the bridge and says to Lt. Data, "Marty McFly will arrive on the locomotive DeLorean at high noon. Prepare an away team to greet him." Doug looks over and says, "H.G., we're going to have fun meeting other time travelers here on the spaceship Intraprize."

Doc Brown sits down and pats his dog, Einstein. "Oh, yes. It'll be grand to see Marty again."

Whit asks if anyone would like a banana split.

The tractor beam locks onto the DeLorean and pulls the tired traveler on board. "It was worth the trip," Marty says when he sees the Doc. "When did you arrive?"

Doc Brown looks at his chronometer and says, "Tomorrow."

4.

Captain Kirk had walked on the bridge and had said to Lt. Data, "Marty McFly will arrive on the locomotive DeLorean at high noon. Prepare an Away Team to greet him." Doug had looked over and had said, "H.G., we're going to have fun meeting other time travelers here on the spaceship Intraprize."

Doc Brown had sat down and had patted his dog, Einstein. "Oh, yes. It'll be grand to see Marty again."

Whit had asked if anyone would like a banana split.

The tractor beam had locked onto the DeLorean and had pulled the tired traveler on board. "It was worth the trip," Marty had said when he had seen the Doc. "When did you arrive?"

Doc Brown had looked at his chronometer and had said, "Tomorrow." [Isn't that horrible!]

10) Alkaline Adjectives

1.

✎ Bill told a lie that grew and grew and grew.

✎ Without a blink of an eye, Bill boasted about the twenty-pound fish he caught — without a rod.

2.

✎ Her beauty shone in the morning sun.

✎ She had sparkling eyes — brighter than gold — and a very kind smile — sweeter than honey.

3.

✎ As the sun set, it looked like Saturn placed in a pastel painting.

✎ Scarlet and purple, orange and blue, the sunset had magnificent color.

4.

✎ When Abe found out his friend had stolen a tape, he told his Mom and Dad and asked them for advice.

✎ Abe had done something wrong; but he said it was my fault.

5.

✎ Bill struggled and strained as he moved the box. He would need help.

✎ Bill lifted the forty-five pound box containing a door.

6.

✎ The rosy glow of her cheeks brightened her mother's day.

✎ Katie had bright eyes and a song on her lips.

11) Ponderosa Participles

1) Mother drew a graph showing the history of the kings of Judah.
2) After finishing all the homework, the children turned the television set on.
3) Running at full speed, we saw the man win the race.
4) Calculating her bank balance, she discovered the deposit was for the wrong amount.
5) Wanting to drink her blood, the mosquito bit Bethany.
6) By salting food at the table, people consume less salt.
7) After kissing her son, the mother saw him wipe it off.
8) Checking the temperature of the candy, the chef turned the burner down.

14) Moreover

1) Tex helped Lonny load and haul more than twenty logs.
2) Yesterday, Pa shot more than ten quail.
3) During the last decade, my children have grown ten years older. [I prefer "during" rather than "over" though both are technically correct.]
4) My truck gets more than 21 miles to the gallon.
5) Mom has asked that we memorize more than two Bible verses a week.

Sentences:
☆ My farm has more than twenty cows.
☆ Dad spends more than $20 on his favorite ice cream.
☆ My brother mows grass more than fourteen hours each week.
☆ The clerk pointed over to where the milk was.
☆ Tomorrow we will walk over to the rock.

17) Who's That

1) Mrs. Peddleton, who lives across the street, backed into our garbage cans again this morning.

20) Racing to the Finish Line

1) Witnessing to someone is like opening a present at Christmas.
2) Bob really was confident in the Lord when he started to tell his testimony.
3) He was calm, but he did feel his pulse racing.
4) The roar of the race was louder than he had imagined it would be.
5) They waved at Mr. Gareth. He smiled and kept walking quickly back and forth wearing the sandwich billboard covered with words.
6-10) The "negative" is effective as it is to contrast with "It did tell of a loving Saviour."

27) Love is Lovely

1) I enjoy fresh-from-the-garden green beans.
2) I love my dog. (Yes, we do *love* our pets.)
3) I like the new mall.
4) I love my father very much. (To distinguish from the love of a pet.)
5) I think his haircut is very handsome.
6) I savor ice cream.
7) I enjoy my bike.
8) I listen to that new music album dozens of times daily.
9) I love Jesus with all my heart.

Writing to God's Glory

Indexes

Index

Jill Bond and The Bonding Place:

A Family Ministry Serving Families

Public Speaking:

Are you planning your next ladies' retreat, book fair, or special events schedule for your church, support group, or organization? Jill Bond might just be the answer.

Jill has traveled around the country encouraging families through Biblical presentations. Jill's style is friendly, humorous, practical, and professional.

When Jill started her ministry, she saw it as equipping the saints. God's vision is so much more clear and broad. God has also used these presentations for evangelism. While a lady might not feel comfortable visiting a Bible study with you, she may be open to a cooking or a creative writing class.

Jill has spoken to small Bible study groups and to thousands at conventions and retreats. Her main prerequisite is prayer. She tries to be faithful to God's direction.

Jill has a range of pre-prepared presentations, or she can develop custom presentations for special groups. Some of her current topics include:

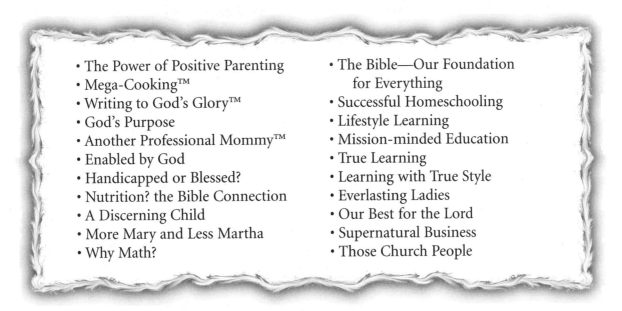

- The Power of Positive Parenting
- Mega-Cooking™
- Writing to God's Glory™
- God's Purpose
- Another Professional Mommy™
- Enabled by God
- Handicapped or Blessed?
- Nutrition? the Bible Connection
- A Discerning Child
- More Mary and Less Martha
- Why Math?
- The Bible—Our Foundation for Everything
- Successful Homeschooling
- Lifestyle Learning
- Mission-minded Education
- True Learning
- Learning with True Style
- Everlasting Ladies
- Our Best for the Lord
- Supernatural Business
- Those Church People

Jill also has a selection of professionally produced audio and video tapes available. Her six-hour *Dinner's in the Freezer!*™ seminar is available as a complete set of video tapes for personal rental, purchase, or for video seminars. A professional studio was hired to tape one of her *Writing to God's Glory*™ workshops for adult writers and teachers of writers. That video tape is also available for rental, purchase, or for video seminars.

Ministry Minded:

The Bond's ministry, The Bonding Place, not only includes speaking services and products, but also two sub-ministries: PREACCH (Parents Rearing and Educating Autistic Children in Christian Homes), and His Writers (A Christian Writers Fellowship). These ministries offer one-on-one counseling and prayer support. They coordinate as much hands-on ministry with Jill's speaking schedule as time allows. She currently writes a regular column for the magazine, "Home School Digest", and numerous other articles for national magazines and newsletters.

Though Jill has been on dozens of radio and television shows (local and national), if you haven't seen or heard her on your favorite broadcast, contact that show's producer and let them know you'd like them to bring Jill in as a guest.

For More Information:

Brochures are available for Jill's services and products. You can contact Jill for more information by sending a SASE #10 envelope along with your specific request (or personal letter) to:

Jill Bond
c/o GCB Publishing Group
229 S. Bridge Street
P.O. Box 254
Elkton, MD 21922-0254

Or you can reach Jill via e-mail or the Internet. Her e-mail address is BondingPl@aol.com, and her web site address is www.bondingplace.com.

Please note: Jill can only answer those who do include a self-addressed, stamped envelope. Please allow ample time for a response. Thank you.